Rise and Fall of a Racketeer

Based on a True Story
Steeltown U.S.A

By Ron Chicone

Rise and Fall of a Racketeer by Ron Chicone
Copyright ©2013
ISBN: 978-0-9885902-4-3
Library of Congress Control Number: 2013912379

La Maison Publishing, Inc.

Acknowledgements

Over two years of toil, highs and lows, many sleepless nights, questioning my ability's, boring my friends and relatives, and searching, beseeching for opinions, knowing they will not be truthful because after- all, they are my friends. When it comes right down to it, what the hell do they know about writing a book? Of course, this being my first attempt writing the great American novel, what the hell do I know about writing a book? Without these advocates, I would have truly been lost. So without further ado here they are:

Joan Lyons: My companion of over twenty years, who refused to pamper me. Ron Chicone Jr.: Whose knowledge of grammar-trumped mine. His suggestions were valid and added to the flow of this book. Holly Ballante: Graciously allowed me to use her former profession as a main platform for the diversity exhibited in this manuscript. Fred Yane: The inspiration. Marie Elena Holmes: Patiently listened to my paucity ramblings. Jerry Pallante: Along with Ms. Holmes, gave me a connection to my Italian heritage. Chuck and Liza Kitzmiller: Stroked my ego and gave me the stimulation and encouragement to continue my quest. Linda Nicolls Ottoson and the Melody Lane Writers group: They listened and gave help and education to my errant ways. Donna Greene: Authored two best-selling books and said, "Yes you can." Kevin Lyons: Gave me the impetus for the design of the book cover. Janet Sierzant: Who led me down the bumpy road of publishing, and finally put it all together. To all the ladies' of the Aquanique, that I leaned on for their knowledge of the English language, I give my heartfelt thanks. To these, and others that I may have overlooked, you have my sincerest thanks.

Ron Chicone

Prologue

Racketeer! What makes a racketeer? What drives men to operate outside the confines of a society that pretends to abhor racketeers yet pays homage to the individuals who flaunt society's conventions?

In this book, I attempt to answer the question, what makes a racketeer? This missive soars above the mundane and not only lets you peek inside the persona of one individual, but a multitude of other interesting men and women who make up the world of gangsterism. You will hear the banter among men who are intimately involved in the nether world. It takes the reader backstage to the way things really work, how power is used, and why. Not only successes, but also failures along the way.

In this book, I will carry you on a stirring rampage of travel to cities that are steeped in romanticism and raucous nights, Miami, Bermuda, Las Vegas, Palm Beach, Myrtle Beach, and other places that inspired stirrings of culture and history, such as Charleston, and stoic, no nonsense cities such as Cleveland, Pittsburgh, and Los Angeles. The further you reach into this novel the more intriguing it becomes.

Can anybody be a whole person without love, devotion, loyalty, and the ability to turn inward and analyze his feelings? My characterization of one such person gives you the depth of his emotions concerning all the ramifications of life itself.

My main character had ambitions that carried him to the fringes of immense wealth, yet suffered a dearth of that special thing that made life worth living. It was "love," but in his case, he never really found it. The closest he came was unrequited love. Therefore, you see, it was not only money, nor power, but in any lifetime, it must include "love."

I believe my book to be a true-to-life chronicle of the life and times of the Mafia in Youngstown, Ohio. My interest in writing with authenticity has been paramount in the creation of this work.

As an author, it is not only incumbent on me to create a manuscript that produces a feeling of satisfaction in our ultimate customer, the reader, but a longing for more. The timeline of this novel stretches from my early years of the nineteen forties into the nineteen eighties. This era was truly the impetus and the face of the Youngstown notoriety which occurred in the ensuing years. My tenure in Youngstown ended in 1950 when I entered service and never returned to reside there.

This novel came about, as I was involved in the creation of my first writing attempt, an uncompleted manuscript tentatively titled "Winners and Losers." While engrossed in the Chapter on racetracks my mind returned to the time I was growing up and to a friend of mine that followed in his father's footsteps and became a somewhat popular bookmaker. I was kept informed of his progress through an uncle, on the Youngstown police force. I eventually found a published phone number on this individual and contacted him. The conversation went something like this, after not having contact for some sixty years:

Nick: "Yeah"

Ron: "Hey, Nick, How you doing."

Nick: "Who the fuck is this."

Ron: "Ron Chicone"

Nick: "So who the fuck are you."

Ron: "We were friends back in Briarhill and grew up together."

Nick: "Jesus Christ, you mean the fuckin' kid that lived around the coroner on Dearborn Street, The Lattanzi kid. (My mother's maiden name.)

Ron: "That's the one."

This started the dialogue that led to this Book.

Ron Chicone

Chapters and Synopsis

Chapter 1-Youngstown Steel Town

Here is the background of this- one- of -a kind city. Immigrants, steel industry, organizational structure of the Mafia, and the game called the Bug, fought over by Cleveland and Pittsburgh mobs.

Chapter 2-Murder Town

Murders were rampant in Youngstown. One that stands out in my mind was of a Capo called Cadillac Charlie Cavalaro, a neighbor of mine. His car was wired with explosives; when he turned the ignition, it set off the charge. Everything went as planned except for one thing, the morning he entered his car he unexpectedly was taking his two children to school. One son survived but with permanent injuries; Charlie's body was found in two pieces. This incident was the facilitator that brought two warring factions of the Cosa Nostra together. This was after seventy-five car bombings and 11 murders. Car bombings were called Youngstown tune-ups.

Chapter 3-Mafia and the odyssey of Nick Lasko

The start of Nicks career, his nose broken and bloody revenge.
Nick took careful aim and smashed the bat across his face with all the gusto he could muster—given the limited space, he had between the cars. Blood spurted in all directions, some of it reaching Nick's face. This was very satisfying to him and he would have liked to have taken another shot with the bat, but

was afraid he would kill the bastard and that was not his intention.

Chapter 4-Vegas days

Fabulous Vegas and love enters the picture. There was a profound shyness about Jenny. It made Nick come to the realization that the more he pushed to make out, would only push her further away. As he perused the situation, he realized that everything about her was soft and understated. Her skin was slightly bronzed and her clothes were expensive and exhibited exquisite taste. The form fitting dress was white with heavy gold chains around the waist and formed a V-shape in front and matched the delicate gold necklace she was wearing. The dangling and swaying gold earrings which could barely be seen went willingly with her shoulder length hair that hung in curls and swirls illuminating the angelic structure of her face.

Chapter 5 -High school Hi Jinx's

This small city did not have golden arches, but it dam-well had gold in the form of those belching steel mills, that filled the coffers, bank accounts, and pockets of its denizens. The ruthless fixing of high school football games.

Chapter 6-Organizing the Congress of Concerned Citizens

This organization would form the basis of Nick's power and future wealth. Nick was too successful and the Wolves were gathering, they wanted their piece of the left over entrails they somehow felt entitled to.

fuckin' information? which I hope is a figment of someone's imagination, or are you getting' fuckin' senile?"

Chapter 13- The Commission

Appearance before the New York Racing Commission. A fixed race?

Chapter 14-Casino

Toying with the possibility of opening a casino much like the former Jungle Inn. A ribald idea, not palatable to either mafia faction.

Chapter 15-The Grand Opening

Planning and executing the grand opening of his estate. The pathway to becoming a lobbyist.

Chapter 16-Winning with Holly Not only on the track.

This was the first time he felt the fire and intensity of her nature, the red hair cascading down her back indicated. Now all of a sudden she was responding with arms wrapped around him so tightly, he could feel her vibrating. The tightness of her arms was promising greater delights to come.

Chapter 17-The family man with conscience

This year was heavy with snow and he enjoyed shopping downtown at Strouss and McKelvey's, Trudging through the snow in his boots with the clasps open so he jingled a bit when he walked, excitedly looking at display windows where animated figures of Santa Claus and the elves along with images of reindeer flying through the snow filled night, filled him with an ecstasy never again to be experienced in his lifetime. He pressed his face against the window, completely enthralled with this rich scene of overflowing huge moon and brightly twinkling stars, and if he did not have visions of sugarplums dancing in his head, he did have deja vu of the time many moons ago when his parents took him Christmas shopping.

Chapter 18-Gulf Stream Attaining satisfaction

The brutal killing of prized racehorses.

Chapter 19-Star struck

This chapter contains an episode of Sinatra and Dean Martin, In Miami.

Chapter 20-Catastrophe— dead horses

When Holly heard about the fire and four horses that were destroyed, she was leaning against a stall, as the news washed over her she felt all the strength leave her body and slowly slid down until she was sitting on the cement floor. Tears started flowing down her cheeks; the sadness that overcame her was all encompassing.

Chapter 21-Miami and the Nightlife

Nick looked at Judy and said "darn it, I don't have a date would you like to go with me? It's this Saturday."
Her eyes lit-up. Are we talking about Frank Sinatra?"
"We sure are!"

Chapter 22-Home and the big bang.

The end of a romance. The grand opening of his estate. Bringing the influential together.

Chapter 23-For Sale

Selling the legislators.
Gaining prestige and influence.

Chapter 24-High School Football

Unbelievable fixing of local high school games.
"Well, let me give you a clue, I care very much and you sonofabitches are going to pay, you're not fuckin' around with the local authorities when you're fuckin' around with me, just looking at you makes me sick, so getting rid of you permanently doesn't make me sad."

Chapter 25-Palm Beach

The capital of "chic." The very epitome of class, haughtiness, and snobbery. Vast wealth and huge estates.

Chapter 26-Back home in Youngstown

The beginning of the great money wash. The entry ticket to a gusher of wealth.

Chapter 27-The Myrtle Beach Time

Rushing for golf course assets.

Chapter 28-Bringing the C.C.C. to heel. Problems and more problems.

Many times he asked himself, if he could do it all over again, would he take the same path, his answer was always the same, yes. If he was able to fast forward to a time in his life when the old man with the scythe was standing beside him, would his answer be the same, probably not, but the old man with the scythe may be standing next to him now.

Chapter 29-The Beauty of Bermuda

Establishing overseas bank accounts. Years later as thoughts of his second visit to Bermuda haunted his reverie, visions of a dark haired, black eyed, brown skinned beauty floated in front of eyes that were now fading with age, but in his mind he was dining with her again in the spectacular reincarnation of the 1920's and 30's dining room.

Chapter 30-The Ghostly Charleston experience

The sailboats on the bay were nothing short of spectacular with the moonlight playing its glow, brightening and darkening as the clouds scuddered past on their heavenly journey.

Chapter 31-Myrtle Beach

Obtaining cash generating golf courses. Muscle never hurts.

Chapter 32-The beginning of the end.

Your egalitarianism has failed you at this crucial time in your life.

Chapter 33-Decline and decay.
A new beginning.

"Let me say this, Nick: just knowing you was worth it. It's true that all things must end, even life itself.

RISE AND FALL OF A RACKETEER

Murder Town U.S.A.
Youngstown, Ohio

By Ron Chicone

A twisted mass of bodies, auto wreckage and building material litters the backyard of 164 Roslyn Drive, where a car exploded Nov. 23, 1962, killing long-time racketeer Charles "Cadillac Charlie" Cavallaro, 60, and his 11-year-old son. Cavallaro's 12-year-old son was badly injured.

Revisiting Youngstown's explosive past

By PETER H. MILLIKEN
milliken@vindy.com

YOUNGSTOWN

Fifty years ago, a long-time local racketeer, Charles "Cadillac Charlie" Cavallaro, and his 11-year-old son, Tommy, were killed, and another son, Charles Jr., 12, was critically injured in a North Side car bombing.

It is one of 82 unsolved local underworld bombings spanning a decade that would result in the creation of the phrase "Youngstown Tuneups." In a 1963 cover story, the *Saturday Evening Post* dubbed the city "Crime Town USA."

But what was different about the Nov. 23, 1962, Cavallaro bombing was that it was the first time children became victims of such violence.

"The Cavallaro bombing crossed the line because innocent life was lost," possibly that of a child, and a ser-

Charles Cavallaro

"This just shocks the sensibilities of the community, especially a community that's very family-oriented," said Fred Viehe, a Youngstown State University history professor, who teaches a course on the history of organized crime.

So overwhelming was the outrage, U.S. Attorney General Robert F. Kennedy ordered a full-scale FBI investigation.

"You couldn't turn away

Chapter One
Youngstown Steel Town

Have you ever been to Youngstown? I'm talking about Youngstown, Ohio. If you have, you know enough not to return. If you haven't, don't go. If you're passing through, don't stop, keep on going. If you live there, I'm sorry.

This was a "Three M City" noted for Mayhem, Murder, and Mafia, and became the most notorious small metropolis in the country, hence the moniker, Murder town USA.

Car bombings were so rampant the term Youngstown tune up was synonymous with this small town.

Harsh words, I am sure. But this was Youngstown before and after the lifeblood of this place closed.

Steel mills were the alpha and omega for this small town, and it is struggling to return to what was formally a green, verdant valley, and is succeeding.

Having been born and raised in this former steel town, the call to return is ever present. You can never forget the blast furnaces, Bessemer converters, coal chutes, railroads, railroad cars, and the way the night would have a fiery glow that burns in my memory all these many years later. And who can forget Idora Park, Mill Creek Park, and the many other things that were the infrastructure of this once bustling and busy valley.

Things that were needed for steel mills were roads for transportation, water to cool the red-hot ingots, a place to put what we term as slag—the crap that was the waste from the furnaces—and along with these things, men that were as tough as the ingots of steel they produced.

The Mahoning River flows through the center of this once beautiful valley. But beauty is what you deem it to be.

Beautiful trees, flowing rivers, soft breezes and clean air are what you may think of when you think of something beautiful, or is it smoke, soot, belching train engines and fat wallets that gives your family a better way of life, maybe that's what you think of as beautiful.

Many of these men, when in what they termed the old country, never knew prosperity, never knew what proper health care was, and never knew if their children would get enough to eat at their next meal. They made their way to America in the toughest way possible by scraping their pennies together, begging and borrowing from friends and relatives, and booking passage on tramp steamers, or steerage class on passenger ships. Many left their families behind, hoping that when they made enough money in America they could send for them. These men did not have dreams of vast wealth, nor did they believe that the streets of America were paved with gold. All they wanted were the Four Freedoms that President Roosevelt so eloquently talked about; Freedom of Worship, Freedom of speech, Freedom from fear, and Freedom from want.

Countless men who came to America passed through Ellis Island, a hellhole for immigrants if there ever was one. This was where embarrassing and degrading events took place on these filthy, stinky people after they had just debarked from ships that barely had any sanitation facilities, or any privacy when they had to use the open latrines, and were herded together like pigs.

No matter, when they entered New York Harbor, lifted up their heads, and saw that awe-inspiring sight, The Statue of

Liberty, their hearts were lifted and filled with a renewed sense of hope.

If they were not rejected at Ellis Island for some imagined or real illness, they would try to find their way to a relative's home or anywhere they could lay their heads for a while until they found a job and were able to afford a hovel in the inner city. On top of all the problems they faced, one problem that evoked dread is when they were discriminated against or shaken down by corrupt police, or Irish mobs, or other ethnic gangs or wannabe Kid gangs. They needed somewhere, or something to turn to.

With the immigrants came a segment of the old country steeped in the rackets that festered in certain parts of their homeland, mostly Italian, particularly in the island of Sicily. This Island off the boot of the peninsula had suffered from various occupiers through the centuries, and necessity caused them to create an infrastructure that governed the island in a covert manner. They developed a secretive, well-concealed substructure of government consisting of cells that were not omnipotent as was generally supposed. The tentacles of their influence were confined to an area much like a ward or precinct in our country. They controlled their area with the help of other cells with which they had intercourse. The organization was structured as follows:

Boss of Bosses – Capo di Tutti Capi, controlled several Families.

Boss – Patrone or Capo, the head of the cell, who made all the final decisions with the advice of a Consigliore.

Consigliore—a lawyer figure that settled disputes involving other cells. Not necessarily a lawyer, but a person whose advice was highly esteemed.

Sub Boss – Capo Regime, saw to it that the orders of the Patrone were carried out and acted as go- between.

Soldiers – Soldati, the level that carried the most risk. They were in intimate contact with the people. Discipline that had to be carried out was their responsibility.

There were other informal levels that depended upon the cooperation received from members of the Famiglia.

This was the loose structure that was carried to the shores of America. Mafia is described as a criminal organization in Italy, but it wasn't that at all. It was a group of citizens that got together to try to protect themselves from a corrupt government that governed until the next corrupt government took over. The people wanted this protection. It was the reason the government of the moment could not break the Mafia. It was known as Cosa Nostra which translated to "our thing" or Cosa Stessa "the same thing." One of these two phrases was used when introducing one member to another.

When these immigrants arrived in this country, conditions for them were not much different from the old country. Most of the police were of a different nationality, and discrimination was common. This had the immediate effect of establishing a Mafia-type organization that protected the people from unscrupulous politicians, and others who tried to shake them down for the few pennies they had. This is where Mafia stepped in— or as it was known in those days— "The Black Hand." The moniker came about because whenever there was a problem in the Family, a note was sent to the wrong-doer with a warning to correct this situation. The bottom of the note was signed with the emblem of a black hand.

Many times, this had the desired effect and would send chills up and down the wrongdoer's spine. In most cases, he would comply with the request. Anyone who did not comply could expect damage to his business, or bodily injury, or both.

Youngstown, Ohio, had a heavy ethnic population. Because of the steel mills, jobs were readily obtained by anyone seeking work. Certainly, wealth was abundant because of well-paid jobs in the unionized mills.

I grew up in two different sections of the town; one was called Smokey Hollow, and the other Briarhill. The former is where I lived with my parents and the latter where I lived with my grandparents. It seems to me I spent as much time with my grandparents as I did at home with my parents.

I was born in 1933 and did not leave Youngstown until I enlisted in the Air Force in December of 1950 at seventeen years of age. My childhood consisted of the usual hijinks for which boys were famous. We were not poor, but we had to watch our expenditures.

The real difference in the way I grew up as opposed to children in better neighborhoods; my area was mostly Italian and predominantly immigrant.

The Mafia, or the Cosa Nostra, was a fact of life, and many of my neighbors were involved in gambling. The most popular was what we commonly called the Bug, known in other parts of the country as the policy numbers racket. It consisted of betting on numbers from 100 to 999 bet in a set of three such as 244 or 876 or 666. If one of your numbers hit, the payoff was about 700 to one. Numbers could be boxed, and if the numbers came out in any combination, there would be a payoff of about three hundred to one. Compare that to the lottery that is now ubiquitous with a payoff of about 50%. The Mafia was paying 70% or better.

The numbers and money wagered were collected by people called runners, and were turned into clearing houses where money was deposited, and payoffs were made. Each runner had a book and each page had a carbon copy; the bettor received the carbon and the runner kept the original. Any amount could be wagered. Most bets, as I recall, were in the range of twenty five to seventy five cents. Doesn't sound like much, but it was a huge business. To find the winning number, all that was required was looking in the newspaper and finding the final three numbers of the amount of stocks traded on the stock exchange that day, or possibly, the amount bet at a designated racetrack, commonly called the "Handle." The runners would also double as bookies taking bets on almost anything. They were on the bettor's side, because if someone won, it would usually mean a comfortable tip and the customer would bet more on the numbers or the horses and just like a modern day casino, the bettors always eventually lose.

Turf wars invariably broke out if your runners were infringing on another territory. Territories were assigned through various get-togethers generally held in the back rooms of favorite Italian restaurants. Here is where agreements were hammered out.

Problems occurred when greed or a misunderstanding of an agreement was apparent, and then all hell broke out.

Chapter Two
Murder Town

Murders were rampant in Youngstown. And car bombings were especially prolific. One that stands out in my mind was a Capo called Cadillac Charlie Cavalaro. His car was wired with explosives; when he turned the ignition, it set off the charge. Everything went as planned except for one thing, that faithful morning he entered his car he unexpectedly was taking his two children to school. One son survived but with permanent injuries. Charlie's body was found in two pieces. This incident was the facilitator that brought two warring factions of the Cosa Nostra together.

The Cleveland and the Pittsburgh factions had differences concerning the various aspects of gambling in this high betting town, where many times more money was wagered on high school football games than on major college games. It was never intended that innocent bystanders were to be harmed.

The populous of this city were extremely protective of their families. Violence happened with regularity and was quickly dealt with when it did happen.

One warm summer afternoon when I was about 11 years old, I was sitting on my front porch. The driveway was in front of the house and ended at the front porch steps. At the time, I had my leg in a cast. I had broken it playing sandlot football with my friends. Suddenly, hurrying down the driveway, walking quickly, was my godfather. He was carrying a small handgun and looking left and right. I called out to him, "Teenie, what's wrong?"

Not actually looking at me, he said, "Some black bastard has Marion." (Marion was his daughter; she was about seven years old). Teenie was not tall but though short in stature—he had a personality that was large in its own way. Fiery would be one way to describe it. He had a strong loyalty to his family and friends.

Excitedly, I hauled myself up on my crutches and hobbled into the house hollering for my father. I shouted, "Dad, Teenie's in the driveway with a gun!" My father, a rather large man with the ability to take adversity in stride—formerly an old time bootlegger— quickly went outside and talked to Teenie, who in earlier times was my father's best man at his wedding.

From the waving of hands, I believed that Teenie described to my father what was going on. From my vantage point, which was cowering in the open doorway, I was not privileged to hear the conversation. They proceeded to the back of our home where they were joined by another man whose voice I recognized as my godfather's brother, Jay Castor.

My mother, who was extremely apprehensive, and me, whose heart was about to jump out of my chest rushed to the window on the East side of the home that gave us a view of our neighbor's back yard and across Carlton Street, where other homes and garages were located.

We could not see what was going on behind the house, but we eventually heard a voice yell out, "Come on out of there you black bastard." I later found out the black man was cringing under our back porch where another door was located that led to our cellar. Promptly, he ascended from under the back porch and commenced running as hard as he could.

He was dressed in loose clothing, a tall, slim, figure taking giant strides. As he was crossing our neighbor's yard, I heard the unmistakable loud bark of a shotgun. With that, I observed the loose clothing on the black man flutter as the buckshot penetrated his shirt. It never slowed him down; at this point I saw Jay, Teenie, and my father, Larry, emerge from the rear of the house. I watched Jay take aim. He fired. Once again, I saw the flutter of the man's shirt and this time his gait had a hitch in it, but he never stopped.

They all crossed Carlton Street where they faded out of my view as they went behind houses and garages. I again heard the sharp report of the shotgun. This time when the black man emerged from the rear of a garage, he was staggering, but his resolve to keep going was unimpaired. As he tried to climb a fence, he arrived at the top of it; Jay once again took aim and squeezed off another round. This time the man tumbled backwards off the fence and lay still.

I raced from the house as fast as I could hobble on crutches, down North Walnut Street, across Carlton Street.

Unbeknownst to me, the Youngstown Police had already arrived and were tending to a clutch of people that were rubber-necking the action. The police were trying to keep them out of the way of the gunshots.

It appeared to me that the Police had no desire to become involved in saving this black man, or to make a determination of guilt.

Youngstown Police were no strangers to shootings in neighborhoods like Smokey Hollow. Their primary mission was to keep as many people from injury as possible and to see they returned unharmed to their family when their shift ended. I managed to work my way to where the black man was lying, and got there in time to see him take his last breath as a death rattle. (This occurs when blood wells up into his throat and as he takes a breath, he emits a rattling sound.)

25

Eventually, a Grand Jury was impaneled and the participants were found not guilty. The court went on to say, 'They acted as any reasonable person would have acted given the same set of circumstances.'

The facts surrounding this event were never entirely clear. Let me give you the story as I pieced it together.

Teenie's daughter was playing in front of her grandparent's house that was taking care of her on that particular day on North Walnut Street. This would have been normal. Her parents did not live far down the street, so she was accustomed to traveling between each home.

Apparently, on this particular day, a black man passed by and something happened between them that frightened the little girl who was seven or eight years old at the time. She ran into her grandparents' house hysterically crying.

Her grandfather Phil ran into the street and gave chase to the individual while the grandmother, Pauline, telephoned Marion's mom Bella, and the message was apparently misinterpreted by Bella. What she heard or thought she heard was, "Marion was kidnapped or assaulted by a black man." She relayed this misinformation to her husband who immediately grabbed a pistol and started running toward Phil's home. In the process, he passed his brother's home on Emerald Street, relaying the information that something had happened to Marion.

Teenie's brother Jay now joined the chase.

Someone gave them the location of where the perpetrator was seen which was in the immediate area of my home. The black man may well have been a customer of our landlady whose home was next to mine. She was engaged from time to time in the selling of a little bootleg hooch.

This unfortunate event made a lasting impression on me. If there was a lesson in this incident, it was that a human life should not be taken so casually. People will take extreme measures when their families are threatened, especially given the background of these immigrants who, in the past, bore the responsibility for the safety of their families. There was not a local militia or any organization that cared enough to give them a helping hand.

It so happened that a few months before this event, about two blocks down on North Walnut Street, a woman arose and went about making breakfast for her husband. Sometime after he went to work, she heard a noise in the cellar, and proceeded down the steps to see what was going on, and must have happened upon an intruder.

When her husband returned that evening, he found his wife brutally murdered.

The intruder was never apprehended. In today's world, the husband would have been the first person considered as a "person of interest." In those days, it was something never given any consideration. We just never heard of a killing involving a husband and wife. Families were too close for that to happen— at least that's what we thought.

Every time I passed by that place, I shuddered to think of what happened in that home. All these many years later, in my mind's eye, that home stands out in all of its dark, stark detail.

All of the foregoing is meant to give the reader an understanding of how this city became Murder Town U.S.A., and to correct many false impressions of what constituted the Cosa Nostra.

Most Italians viewed the Mafia as an entity that was in many ways benevolent. In my neighborhood, Briarhill on West Federal Street, a club called The Todd Civics was located. It was a fraternal organization (ha, ha, they'll get a kick out of reading that) with a Bocce court in the rear that was under lights for evening play. If there was a problem in the area—maybe a political issue or possibly trying to locate a job, or other things that came up—many times it could be solved at this club.

If there was a future pay-off involved, it was more in the nature of an obligation that was felt for the good things that may have been of help to you. To highlight this type of situation, my own grandmother was involved in circumstances that appeared on the surface to be ludicrous, and we took it lightly at the time. Of course, this particular incident strikes at the very core of our Democracy.

I was probably about 13 when this occurred. Being an avid reader, I was looking over the Sunday Youngstown Vindicator, our local well respected newspaper when, as I opened to the front page, the headlines jumped out at me; "Poll workers Indicted by the Grand Jury." Forgive me if that was not the exact reading of the headline, but the passage of time may have dulled my memory a slight bit. Underneath the headline appeared the pictures of my grandmother and two of my aunts, along with a neighbor or two.

I was taken aback at this revelation and immediately showed it to my grandmother. She just as immediately grabbed it from my hand, threw it away, and refused to talk about it at all. Of course, I eventually did get to read the entire article. It chronicled the fact, as poll workers, they were all involved in forging votes at our local precinct for the Democratic Party. One of our neighbors was on the ballot and was running for something or other, which now escapes me.

I believe that consultations were held between my grandmother and the Democratic Party. It was decided that she would plead guilty to all of the vote fraud, absolving the others involved. From that point on, I never heard anything more about the case and it became a nonissue in our neighborhood and our household. My grandmother, who was the most fascinating person I have ever known, never served a day incarcerated.

She was a remarkable individual. I recall she almost singlehandedly held our family together during the most trying times of the great depression. Everybody lived at her house; nobody, but my grandfather had a job. Bless her soul, she would hit the streets knocking on doors in the better neighborhoods, asking if there was anything she could do for them, cleaning, painting, hanging wallpaper, or most anything that she could do to earn a few bucks. We made it through the depression, and I never recall ever missing a meal or going to school without nice clothes.

The closeness of our family was almost entirely due to that magnificent woman, and I know if I make it to the hereafter she will be waiting for me.

The point I'm trying to make is that we as immigrants, and descendants of immigrants tried to do the right thing as we saw the right thing to do.

The foregoing I included to give a background picture and allow you to take the measure of how a Youngstown, a Pittsburgh, or Cleveland underworld was created. I especially wanted to bring you, the reader, into the world of a real racketeer.

James Anthony Traficant, Jr. (born May 8, 1941) is a former Democratic politician and member of the United States House of Representatives from Ohio. He represented the 17th Congressional District, which centered on his hometown of Youngstown and included parts of three counties in northeast Ohio's Mahoning Valley. He was expelled after being convicted of taking bribes, filing false tax returns, racketeering, and forcing his aides to perform chores at his farm in Ohio and houseboat in Washington, D.C. He was sentenced to prison and released on September 2, 2009, after serving a seven-year sentence. He ran for office again but not re-elected. He had strong connections to both Cleveland and Pittsburgh gangs.

Sandy Naples the patriarch of the Naples Brothers, Billy and Joey

Sandy Naple's girlfriend, Maryanne Veranzic, who was shot-gunned to death along with Sandy while sitting on a porch swing.

Sandy Naples' short-lived successor and brother Billy Naples.

Joey Naples: Killed in a mob hit in 1991 while inspecting the construction of his new home in Youngstown.
The author attended high school with Joey.

A gathering of gangsters at a restaurant in Cleveland's Little Italy.

Vince DeNiro, gambling boss and bombing victim.

Dominic Mayo, a suspect in the bombings of Naples, Cavallaro and DeNiro.

Billy Naple's death car.

The notorious Jungle Inn, operated for many years as a flurishing casino, with the knowledge of local officials.

One of the gun turrets, located inside the casino.

James Traficant

Charles Cavallaro

Larry and Helen Chicone Father of the author
Well known bootlegger— circa 1931

The halcyon days of bootlegging 1931

Running between Cuba and Miami

Chapter Three
Mafia and The odyssey of Nick Lasko

Nick and I grew up together and did all the things normal kids do. As I recall, the worst things were knocking out a few streetlights. I remember the time, around Halloween, we pelted the passing buses on West Federal Street with rotten tomatoes we pilfered from gardens in the neighborhood. We thought it was great fun to see the tomatoes splatter on the side of the buses.

On one particular night, the bus driver's window was open, and we inadvertently slung a ripe missile through the opening and hit the driver with a rather satisfying splat. The bus driver did not take kindly to this act and proceeded to stop the bus and try to chase us down. With our little sinful hearts beating rapidly, we managed to escape the wrath of the injured party. Of course, it was our neighborhood, and we knew all the hiding places. It did place enough fear in our little souls that this was a shenanigan we never tried again.

Nick is not a big man. He is about 5'10"inches tall and weighs 200 pounds. Blue eyes and light brown thick curly hair gave him the look of a male model and woman found him attractive. In his business, he was always aware of the problems a liaison with the opposite sex could entail; consequences he was not ready to accept. His view of the fairer gender did not include a home and family. His fulminations centered primarily on sex and fulfilling his needs.

Toughness was a part of Nick's persona and came naturally to him—an inborn trait. Not that he used it as an inducement to accept his way of doing things since he came across as mild mannered and exceedingly enthusiastic on whatever subject he was elucidating. This individual characteristic won him many friends. Along with this was the ability to induce other people to accept and believe the various stories and imaginations he was willing to sell at the time. Compassion was something Nick came upon easily, but he never let it intrude on business. After all, business was business.

Graduating from High School in 1952, he decided to go to work for one of the local businesses. He accepted a highly satisfying job and was rather contented. But in his formative years, he had developed a love for horseracing.

His father was much involved with gambling as a Bookie and a bettor, so Nick learned to decipher a racing form at a remarkably young age. He loved horses, and whenever he had the money or could cadger a free ride, you would find him at Old Charlie's horse riding stable. Horseracing was a calling he became abundantly familiar with and knew well. He followed this vocation and the various aspects of gambling for the rest of his life.

The big betting was on football, and that is where the money was to be had. At the time, there was a type of one-page football parlay card called a football pool. All the major college teams were listed on the face of the card along with the points, or in football parlance, "the spread". On the back of the card was the payoff. As I recall, if you bet 3 teams and they won, the payoff was 5 to 1; the real odds should have been 9 to 1. You can readily see how much money was made by the purveyors.

Nick was employed in a facility that had a contingent of employees who enjoyed betting these cards. Naturally, Nick was there to take advantage of the instincts of the average guy.

The take from these Parlay Cards became larger as time went by. Eventually, Nick was making more money from the cards than from his salary.

A brisk, late-autumn November day was a day that for Nick would stand out in his mind as a game changer.

As he was leaving work at 5:30 p.m, a large black Cadillac pulled up in front of his place of employment with two men in the front seat and two men in back. Nick remembered they were impeccably dressed in hats pulled down low over the eyes. The guy on the passenger side motioned to Nick who approached the vehicle rather puzzled, but not showing any hesitation. The two guys in back got out of the car, and as he neared, grabbed him and between them steered him into the rear seat. Nick, who could be rather combative when provoked, was too surprised to be able to react in a manner that would hinder his passage into the rear seat. Nick immediately hollered in a loud voice, "What the fuck is going on? Get your fuckin' hands off me!" This outbreak got a response from one of the gentlemen who struck Nick's face with a heavy object. Blood spurted from his nose and mouth. Stunned, he was not capable of returning any meaningful aggression.

As things calmed down, the man in the front passenger seat spoke in a calm, non-threatening voice, "Nick we mean you no harm. Your activities have started to dig into the pocket of a much respected man in this area, and I am suggesting to you that you meet this gentleman and come to some kind of understanding."

"What the fuck kind of understanding is it with this gash across my nose!" Nick was talking in a muffled voice; he had his handkerchief out and was trying to stem the flow of blood.

The speaker slowly turned and fully faced Nick, the features of his face now clearly evident. Later, Nick vaguely remembered this face, especially the prominent nose and protruding chin. "Let me remind you that if you do not meet with this certain gentleman, you'll remember that blow as a gentle love tap. Now get out of here, you'll be hearing from the man."

41

As they shoved him out of the car, Nick became his usual belligerent self. Trying to reassert himself, he yelled, "Fuck all you ass-holes. Don't call me because I ain't goin' to meet nobody!" He said this with at least some apprehension, realizing that these men were connected, and were not there to merely pass the time of day.

Reflecting on this encounter, he realized that the man with the prominent chin was a Soldato called Billy Barbone, who was primarily used as an enforcer but was not a hit man nor was he a so-called "Made" member of the organization. "Made" referred to someone who had carried out a hit on orders from a Capo Regime, who would in turn receive his instructions from a Patrone, who may have received his mandate from a Capo di Tutti Capi.

A Capo di Tutti was generally a partially retired member of the Organization who was held in high esteem by all members.

Nick went directly to his doctor. As he entered the office, the receptionist could plainly see the blood streaming down the front of his shirt and dripping from his face and through his hankie. The doctor saw him immediately, and asked what had happened. Nick made up a cock-and-bull story about having fallen.

The doctor had to place several stitches in his nose and found that it was broken. Thank God Nick did not lose any teeth although a couple were loosened.

On the way to his modest home, a typical bachelor's pad—he felt the anger rising inside and knew he would have to meet this cocksucker, but did not want to make it easy for him. Nick was already formulating plans for whomever this bastard was who wanted to talk to him. In fact, he was eager to meet him.

His phone was ringing when he entered his apartment. One of his best friends from work was calling and apparently had seen what happened.

Nick explained that his aggressor was just a guy who had lost money with him and was rather upset, but it was nothing to get excited about since they had already settled their differences.

His friend asked him about his nose and whether there was anything, he could do to help.

"Yeah, he broke my nose," Nick said, "and I've got it bandaged, but I don't need help. I'll see you tomorrow, and if I need anything, I'll let you know."

When he hung up, Nick was fuming. God, I hate to go out of here with my face looking like this. I know I'll meet everybody in the world and will be asked a ton of questions I don't want to answer, but I've got to do it. I want to act as normal as possible. The less people know the better. But I know one thing, that bastard responsible for this is going to pay a big price!

Things more or less returned to normal and Nick kept distributing the football parlay cards. Weeks went by without the call that he was expecting, so using his idle time, he kept calling around to make sure of the identity of the Prick who had smacked him.

As his nose healed and the wrapping was removed from his proboscis, he started to get around a little more. One of his favorite places was a club called The Capri Lounge and Restaurant. As he entered for the first time since the incident with Barbone, his friends gave him their version of the Bronx cheer and wanted to know for the umpteenth time how his nose had been broken. Nick stuck to his story of a disgruntled bettor.

The owner of the club, Rinaldo "Rennie" Servino, came over and quietly said, "Nick, before you go, I need to have a private conversation with you."

"No problem Rennie, I'll pop into your office sometime tonight."

As the evening wore on, Nick was taking the usual barbs and playful insults that came along with having close friends, and the conviviality was being enjoyed by all. Little did he know that this evening would propel him into the higher echelons of bookmaking, and put him on the road to abundant riches that would see him enjoying large homes, fast cars, and faster women, not to mention encounters with the Cosa Nostra.

Nick, being only half-Italian, could never be accepted into the organization as a full active member. Although he eventually did become a close associate, it was not without some bumps along the way.

A fault that kept Nick from being accepted as more than a friend of the organization was something that plagued him most of his life. The fault was his bull-headedness. He did things his way or no way, but he eventually learned to accept certain things or have his nose broken again, house destroyed, cars vandalized, and various other monstrous actions that were not pleasant to contemplate.

As Nick was getting ready to wrap it up for the night, he almost left without seeing Servino, the owner. A little lit-up from partying, he suddenly remembered and bounced his way into Servino's office.

"Have a seat, Nick, I've got a proposition for you." Servino's countenance was dead serious, and his words were being squeezed out of thin, tight lips. "How would you like to be the sole bookie for this club?"

Nick knew him to be a highly astute businessman. "What are you talking about, Rennie?"

"I need someone who's honest, dependable, and can keep his Goddamn mouth shut. If it gets out that there's bookmaking going on here, bam, they take my license—,and then I'm really fucked."

"You mean they could put you out of business?"

"No, but then I would have to hire lawyers and fight it out in court. If the mob finds out I'm allowing someone else to take the action, it might go hard on me because I believe they have their fingers in those Black and Whites (Youngstown police) and the court system that has all those fuckin' nigger judges who are all on the take."

"So why not let those assholes take the action and the vig and leave me out of it?"

"Nick, once you let those button men hang out here, they'll all try to be tough guys, and will chase away your regular customers. Besides, they are all trying to scam each other, and then you got trouble, not to mention the drugs that come along with these dirt bags. The reason I have approached you is your reputation for honesty and always paying off. I want to do my customers a service. They don't have to get involved with the scum bags and will not be placing their bets in the club. All they do is call you and place the bets over the phone. That way, no bets are placed here at the club. Money will be exchanged privately between you and the bettor, but again, no money will be exchanged at this club. Capisce?"

"Listen, Rennie, I appreciate the confidence you have in me, but I have some concerns. Number one, I'm small potatoes. I don't have money to back the play that many of your customers will want to give me. It would mean that I would have to contact a lay-off man and bring the assholes back in."

"No, no, we don't want that and I have anticipated your problem. Nick, I'm willing to back your play until you are on your own and established."

"Second problem, I'll have to quit my job."

"I can't advise you on that. It's between you and whatever confidence level you have—and depends on how big are your cohunes."

Nick just smiled.

"Now Nick, I'm going to present you with a further clarification. I'm taking most of the risk, and you will be taking all of the vigorish and providing the personality and work. However, I will from time to time be asking for some of the vig. Do you have a problem with that?"

45

"Well, it depends on how much and what the time to time means."

"Nick, you will have to trust me on that."

"Let me think it over Rennie, and I'll let you know. There's a small problem I have to solve right now."

On his way home, Nick was thinking about this fuckin' Barbone character. He could feel his temperature rising and face flushing and knew there was only one way he could feel normal again—he had to wreck Billy Barbone. He would have to do the job himself because that's the only way he could get any satisfaction. He wanted to see this man bleed, and he wanted to feel the thud when he smashed the bastard's nose. That action would also be his calling card, so the sonofabitch would know who did it.

One thing led to another, and he found out that Billy's favorite watering hole was a place called the Ali Baba, located downtown on West Federal Street.

Ali Baba became a place that Nick frequented very quietly and unobtrusively. After long observation, he found that Billy's preferred parking spot was in the rear of the building, and he generally would use the rear door when entering or exiting.

A problem became apparent when Nick parked in this parking lot and found it was too well lit. He would have preferred to wreck this asshole in Bill's own yard, but his instinct told him there would be too much security, so he knew the job would have to be done in the rear parking lot of the watering hole.

Another problem put pressure on Nick. This was the beginning of August and the exhibition football games were getting underway. If he was to throw-in with Rennie Servino, it had to be now or never, and he was inclined to go with the offer.

His difficulty stemmed from the fact that in this business, you never knew how far the ties with the Cosa Nostra went. Nick was well aware he was not of full Italian heritage, and would forever be on the fringes of the organization.

When Rennie talked about Vig from time to time, and given that an explanation was not forthcoming with this utterance, gave Nick reason to pause. It could very well mean that Rennie was working with the organization, and it may mean that when the time was ripe, and they needed a scapegoat, Nick would be it. He always remembered a guy telling him that when he sat down at a poker game and looked around the table for a sucker and didn't see one, then he knew he was it.

Nick's naturally suspicious nature has stood him in good stead throughout his life. It's probably the main reason he is alive as I write this.

Nick understood that time was short. One evening in late November, he returned home and went directly to the garage where he secured a baseball bat he had used many times in high school and sandlot pick-up games. He had always been a talented athlete and was familiar with swinging baseball bats. He placed it in the seat next to him in the car, and as evening arrived, he commenced to travel to the Ali Baba club.

Just down a-ways from the Club was a very old but beautiful theater called the Warner Theater. There was parking behind this old structure that was no longer in use, however, a garbage and junk strewn, never used alley-way existed that led to the parking lot behind the Ali Baba. The power box for the parking lights at the lot was at the end of the alley. Nick knew that the lights could not be turned off for any length of time because somebody was sure to come searching for the power box.

Nick had to station himself near the rear entrance and try to stay concealed while at the same time able to see through the rear door. He was able to successfully perform this act, but he also knew that Barbone was a creature of habit, and he was able to predict the approximate time Barbone would leave the premises.

As Barbone prepared to leave and walked toward the rear door, Nick raced for the power box carrying a heavy bat and at the same time trying not to stumble into any of the parked cars. Just before, Barbone came out of the door, Nick pulled the handle on the box, and most of the lights went out—but not all of them. This is not what Nick had counted on, but it was too late to abort the mission. He crouched down and raced low between cars, finally reaching a spot that this asshole had to pass.

When the proper time arrived, Nick jumped out and quickly swung at Barbone's knees, the idea being to render him unable to pursue on foot. Nick heard the bones crack, and Barbone yelled and fell to the ground. Then Nick took careful aim and smashed the bat across his face with all the gusto he could muster—given the limited space he had between the cars. Blood spurted in all directions, some of it reaching Nick's face. This was intensely satisfying to him, and he would have liked to have taken another shot with the bat, but was afraid he would kill the bastard and that was not his intention. He did not want Barbone dead—that was too easy—but wanted him to live with that broken face for a while, as he had done.

His problem solved, at this point Nick accepted the offer from Servino. He was now in the business that would make him the most sought after Bookmaker in Youngstown. Once the word got out that Nick was taking action, his phone kept ringing. Nick's business continued to expand, word of mouth was a tremendously powerful way of eliciting new customers, but he also had a decidedly easygoing way of doing business, and would generally give dead-beats some leeway in paying their debts. Many times, if a guy was having a particularly hard time, Nick would say "Forgetaboutit" and maybe slip him a couple of bucks to see him past the hard times.

He would absolutely not revert to muscle. When he ran into a situation where a client was beyond redemption, Nick would just eliminate that individual from his action book. Overall, he was very easy to do business with.

As a result of his policies, the amount of "take" kept expanding and you can bet that the organization had an eye on him.

As time went by, he hired another guy to take calls, and rented a vacant place on Davis Lane in Briarhill. The rented edifice was formerly a Clearinghouse for the numbers racket, a.k.a. The Bug. Nick was not unfamiliar with this place; his home whence he grew up was next door. At one time when Nick was a youngster and the bug was in full swing, he would break in at night and could usually find some coins that had been overlooked during the counting operation—generally about 75 cents to a dollar.

Finally, the call he had eagerly awaited arrived. Since he had wrecked Barbone, however, there was a part of him that was feeling some trepidation. They had to know that he was the culprit who had smashed the goofball's nose. Revenge was a hallmark of the mob.

Nick took the call and recognized the name Vinnie Solerno.

"Nick, I'm calling to arrange a meeting between you and a guy who respects you very much."

"If he respects me so much, tell him to call me himself. In the meantime don't call me."

"Hey, wait a minute for Chris sake, don't hang up! Hold on a fuckin' minute, I'm Vinnie Solerno. You probably know me."

"You mean the guy that got his ass kicked out as a lawyer and was disbarred?"

"Yeah that be me. What the hell, I'm still employed, and I represent certain people that don't want too much recognition. Capisce? The guy I'm calling for is Tommy Trado—they call him Briarhill Tommy. Look, you name the time and place; I'll see if I can arrange it."

Nick said, "Hell, I do not want to be an asshole, but everyone in this town knows what I did to Barbone. I figure that somebody put a contract to whack me, so I have to be careful that I will not be in a position to make it easy for the bastards to take me out, and then throw my body in the Mahoning River."

"Listen to me Nick, nobody wants you whacked. After all, we want to make money and not step on the other guy's toes. Tommy knows that you are extremely popular, and you're doing a decent business, so Goddammit, don't be such a fuckin' stubborn Prick and listen to the proposition. Besides, you're from the neighborhood and that counts for something. If you put aside your belligerence, it will be to your benefit."

Nick remembered Solerno as a standup guy that was dumped on by the organization for money laundering. Solerno was a short balding guy with a personality that was honest and engaging.

"Okay," Nick said, "here's the deal. The meeting will have to be in a highly public place, and somewhere that's a neutral location. That way, we're not as likely to have any muscle present. Remember, Tommy comes by himself, and I will be unattended. My suggestion is Randall Mall in Cleveland, the food mart. By the way, that's not a suggestion, that's a requirement."

"Jesus Christ Nick, that's in other people's territory. If Tommy is seen there, they gonna think something's going on that they are not in on. That's where the Babe is operating, and you know he's the muscle for Scales The Fish. If they find out, then Pittsburgh won't be far behind and then we are all fucked."

"Come on Vinnie, Pittsburgh already knows what's goin' on."

"Yeah, but they'll wonder what the hell is this about. There's no reason we should be there in the first place."

"Look, Vinnie, arrange it. Then call me and give me the time. Okay?"

Nick knew there was no way in hell that Briarhill Tommy was going to show up by himself. It was a foregone conclusion that he would have muscle along for the ride, maybe more than one, and Nick would arrange for his own muscle to tag along.

It was not that long ago that Nick played football for his High School, and in fact, was good enough to be named all-city center. Not bad for a kid who weighed 160 pounds soaking wet. He was the lightest lineman on the team, but his guts and determination made him an excellent player.

Nick had a close friend who played line on that same team, Joey Russell, and he now hung out at the Capri. He was bigger now than he was in school, going about 6'3 and 250 pounds and possessed a disposition that was really sweet and had no intention of ever hurting anybody. The thing that made Joey formidable was his imposing massiveness. Nick knew he could use some money, especially the way things were with the steel mills not presently hiring, so he contacted Joey about being his bodyguard for just one afternoon. Nick offered him a rather nice stipend, and Joey readily accepted and asked if he would be getting in any trouble.

Nick said, "Don't worry about it, Joey. All I want is for you to be noticed. You're only going to be there as a prop." Nick just wanted the guy he was meeting to think he brought muscle to the meeting, because he was damn sure Trado would have plenty of goons with him. "Nothing's going to happen; there will be too many people around. And I will work it so that one of the security guards will be watching. If anything does happen, just get the hell out."

Finally, after a long period of time—about three or four months—the call from Vinnie came.

"Let me guess," Nick said, "he does not want to use my suggested meeting place."

Vinnie continued in a low voice. "Tommy wants nothing more than to accommodate you Nick, but he can't understand why in the fuck it has to be in Cleveland when you grew up in the Briarhill neighborhood."

"Because I have an aversion to swimming in the river with my feet in cement."

"C'mon Nick, for Chris sake, you know that's not going to happen."

"Oh yeah! Tell that to the couple of guys they fished out last year who were so badly decomposed they still don't know who they are.

"Okay, here's the date and time. Make it next Monday, 8:00 a.m. And don't be late."

"Wrong. Make it Monday at 1:00 p.m. When it will be crowded—the way I like it."

"No problem. Consider it done, but remember, come alone."

Nick smiled. Yeah sure, fuck you.

Upon reflection, Nick decided that maybe a backup should be in the cards. A kid he knew from childhood he thought could fill the bill, a kid who had no compunction about acting with his fists if, God forbid something should go wrong. Nick knew him well. His name was Dominic Lavelle. The reason he did not pick him in the first place was because he was Italian and you could never be sure how far up the relationships would go until you hit somebody that was connected—like uncles or cousins. The other thing that worried him; the more people that know or have an indication of what's going on, the more at risk you become.

When you are successful, Nick mused, rats tend to come out of their holes to get a raggedy ass piece of the gruel.

Monday came, and Nick organized his little crew. They would drive themselves, each in his own car, to Randall Mall, arrive about fifteen minutes early, and if at all possible, sit at each end of the food court. Nick would choose a conspicuous location and let Briarhill Tommy join him.

When he arrived at the food court about 10 minutes later than he had planned, Nick feigned obliviousness to Tommy and went directly to one of the security guards to ask him a couple of innocuous questions that had nothing to do with what was currently going on. He wanted to be sure that Tommy had preceded him and would be aware of the interaction between the security guard and Nick. Of course, this little by play did not go unnoticed.

He then worked his way between the tables—still not looking at Tommy—and finally selected a table pretty much in the middle of the action and settled down to await the next move.

Tommy took no time pushing his way to Nick's table—a shrinking violet he was not. He loudly scraped a chair across the floor and sat down with a thump. Tommy was not born in this country, having emigrated from Sicily, and was a true Sicilian, bedrock of the Mafia. Every Capo di Tutti Capi was of Sicilian decent. In his broken English, he said to Nick, "Whatsa matter for you, non si come dire al tempo?" (You don't know how to tell time?)

Tommy Trado was the epitome of a well-dressed mobster, with slicked back hair, long aquiline nose, and a personality that made him comfortable to be around. You could tell he was conscious of his weight. Many Italians love their pasta and pizza and generally have a problem with extra pounds,

53

but not Tommy. He looked like he had just stepped out of Gentleman's Quarterly.

"Hey, Tommy, fu a lungo guidare," (It was a long drive) Nick said. "I did the best I could. Now, let's get right to it."

"I know, I know, buta first let me aska you howsa you Famiglia? Everything okay? You know ifa you need anything, youa justa aska an' I makea sure you have what you need."

"Famiglia okay. I'm here to listen"

"Nick, the reason I'ma want thisa meeting is because you and me justa try to make a living, an' you know things are tough every time a new couple of guys get elected they talk about howa they goin' to clean upa the rackets, and then you know they got to throw a few people in the can. Look, I spend lotsa money gettin' the righta people in the righta positions. I know you have been doing a good job on the things you do, but Nick, we have all got to kicka in with the grease or else trouble will come our way and neither one of us wants that."

"Tommy, I know there's one thing we got to clear up between you, me, and other people."

"Okay, Nick, whatsa that?"

"This little thing between me and Barbone. I'm worried there are some people who won't let go of this thing."

"Nick, take it froma me, every buddy knows thatsa whata you did to Barbone isa only something he hada coming becausea it wasn't in the cards that he breaka your nose like he did an' by retaliating likea you did, only gained you respect, so forgetaboutit, it's over."

"Okay, Tommy. What do you want me to do?"

"Nick, do yourself a favor, and give a little of the jack you're taking in to the guys thatsa in your corner trying to do what'sa best for our little piece of the pie."

"Tommy, how much are we talking about? You know I'm not a rich guy, I'm just small potatoes, and I do not have an organization. But, all of this smacks of bigger stuff than me."

"Listen, Nick, gimme a break, you're an up and comer anda your future isa unlimited. Let's start at $500.00 a month and go from there."

"Are you fuckin' crazy? I can't afford that kind of money. This meeting is over. I'm outta here." With that Nick imprudently got up and started to make his way to the exit.

Immediately, a big ugly guy with a lopsided out of proportion body blocked his way, and now big Dominic became involved in the confrontation. At this point, Tommy rushed up and defused the situation by asking his man to step down, and he said, "Hey letsa not makea any waves."

"I'm not making waves, Tommy. Like I said, I'm outta here."

"Nick, you know you not showa respect and I'ma gonna not hold it against you thisa time, but ina future, I may not be as nice. Froma now on, you calla me, I'ma no calla you."

Nick was followed out by his entourage, and when they reached their cars, he said, "Boys, head on over to the Capri and we'll have a drink and get something to eat. It's on me."

As he drove, Nick sensed a deep satisfaction that he hadn't let some Prick push him around. He realized that at some point in the future, he would have to pony up some cash, but he did not want them to think he was a push-over.

He walked into the Capri and was greeted much like a conquering hero. His boys were already there and had been running their mouths. Nick was extremely angry, and said, "Why can't you Mother Fuckers keep your mouths shut? Jesus Christ, you're going to get me killed. I got some fuckin' news for you, you think Trado didn't notice you two assholes, if you have any brains at all, you'll keep your traps shut and try to be inconspicuous."

Rennie came by about this time, and said, "Nick, get down to my office now."

Nick's natural inclination was to resent orders, but he knew what Rennie wanted to talk to him about, and business was business. As he walked down to the office, he threw one more blistering look at his two idiot cohorts.

"Nick, what the hell is going on? You got two knot heads upstairs claiming you told Briarhill Tommy, in essence, to go to hell."

"Rennie, that's not what happened. Tommy wants me to pay protection, and I know that I'm probably gonna have to come up with some amount of grease. I'm just playing the game, basically saying to Tommy that what he wants is too much—it's not what I can afford. Eventually, Tommy and I will come to an understanding, and everybody will be happy."

About this time, a commotion is taking place in the bar, and one of the guys comes down and says, "Jesus, there's cops all over the goddamn place and they are looking for Nick."

Nick immediately left for the bar and confronted one of the cops, "Hey, what the hell's the problem?"

The cop said, "Are you Nick Lasko?"

"Yeah, I am. So what's the beef"?

"I've got a warrant for your arrest."

"What's the charge?"

"Illegally accepting wagers on the outcome of sporting events, which is illegal not only under the laws of the State of Ohio but also under Federal laws. Nick Lasko, you are under arrest. At this time, I don't believe handcuffs are necessary, so I will attempt not to embarrass you further. Please go with me to the first cruiser at the curb."

"I know its useless telling you, but you have no right to arrest me without any evidence."

"Nick, I'm sorry, but I have a warrant for your arrest and it's my job to take you downtown and book you. After that, it's up to you and the judge and your lawyer."

Nick kept loudly protesting while he was being booked and was roundly ignored. He was placed in a cell without another word being said, and there he sat for the rest of the night, cogitating on his next move. He knew he had just been checkmated by Briarhill Tommy Trado.

In the morning he asked the head fuckup, this was an inmate who won some privileges because of good behavior—they call them trustees—to make a phone call. He was told that phone calls were not allowed until six p.m. that night.

He said to the trustee, "Listen, would you get word to Mr. Trado that Nick Lasko would like to talk to him?"

"I'll see what I can do."

In a few minutes, they took Nick down to the booking office where Trado was waiting on the phone. Nick picked up the phone and said, "Look, Tommy, I think we have had a misunderstanding. Things are clearer now."

"Nick, I knew thata you figure things out when you hada chance to thinka things over. Froma nowa on, me and you gonna be good friends. I already pay your bail, everything okay, Ima talk to you later."

As the Sargent processed Nick's release, he told Nick that he would have to appear before Judge Gorman next Wednesday at 10 a.m., and to have $1,000 cash with him.

Nick headed out into the sunshine and knew he would do anything he could in the future to stay out of the slammer. If he had to cooperate with the boys that count, he would!

The following Wednesday at 10 a.m. sharp, Nick was in court. He was surprised to find that there was only one person in the courtroom; a black Judge who asked him a few innocuous questions and told him the fine was $1,000 and to place the money on the desk. Goddammit, Nick thought, that black sonofabitch is gonna rip off that Goddamn money. For Chris sake, is everybody on the take?

It was easy to answer that ubiquitous question.

Nick knew that gambling was a fairly benign crime, usually incorporating a sentence of maybe a fine, or thirty days to six months in the slammer.

He instinctively knew to never get fucked up with drugs, or robbery, or things that could carry a potential for long prison terms. He also knew that if he became too close to the Cosa Nostra and had to ask for a favor, he would be putting himself in a position where he would have to return the favor, and may involve more than gambling situations.

Now was the time to concentrate on his business; he tried to get around the North side of Youngstown as much as possible, letting people know what business he was in. He was not interested in stepping on any toes, so if someone wanted to place a bet, and it was a long way out of his jurisdiction, he would refer that person to another bookmaker. In that way, he kept peace with everybody and the other bookmaker appreciated the business and would return the favor.

Chapter Four
Vegas Days

The next night Nick stopped at the Capri and Rennie handed him a note and said, "It's all set, write the day and time, Caesars will take care of everything including the plane, room, and all the girls and food you can eat."

"Goddamit Rennie I do not want any favors."

"Look my man, when you get favors like this you do not turn them down, because some people may become insulted and think you don't want their friendship. I'm sure that's not your intention, is it?"

Nick decided to take about $5,000 with him, but he did not intend to use it all. Even though his business was gambling, he really was not a gambler, and that $5,000 was pretty hefty for him at this stage of his career. He always needed back up funds in the event he would have a losing period. It was never possible to predict a heavily losing week. You might do a weekend taking in $50,000 and paying out $70,000. It was not probable, but it was always possible.

Boarding at the Youngstown airport, the plane was an excursion flight direct to Vegas. This meant it was a private flight paid for by Caesar's, and only for high rollers that were being comp'd by the casino. Of course, everything to make these gamblers happy and comfortable was being done for them, up to and including a Concierge.

Each high roller was informed of the limit that Caesar's would go on the hook for, and that depended what the book was on that particular gambler. Caesar's took into consideration such things as credit rating, the history of previous visits, the amount of time spent at the tables, and the amount of capital wagered. Who sponsored the player was also important in setting the limit of credit approved for him. In this instance, Nick was approved for $50,000, far more than his credit rating would have supported under normal circumstances. Of course, this was because of his sponsor. Nick was not certain who it was, but suspected it was Tommy Trado.

Introductions were made all around, Remembering the names of people introduced to him was not important to Nick. But most of them remembered him. He really did act like a gangster. It was the way he dressed, and the way he talked, and the deference shown him by the Concierge, and he was the only passenger picked up in the notorious Youngstown. The thing that added to his aura was his adeptness at maintaining a mysterious depth to his personality by not talking too much and keeping his own council.

In about five hours the plane touched down at McCarran International Airport in Vegas. The passengers were escorted to a limo and taken to Caesar's, only about a mile away. This was the first time Nick had been in Las Vegas and he was in awe of the fabulous garishness, but also the extreme beauty that impressed him right down to the pit of his stomach.

The limo pulled into the round drive in the front entrance where they arrived and were escorted directly to their rooms. Nick could hardly wait to explore the casino and it was not long before he was perched on a chair at one of the numerous lounges, savoring a Youngstown favorite, whiskey, and beer.

All around him whirled a world he never knew before. Slot machines, flashing with expressive lighting, bells ringing, saluting the winners, the craps tables that were crowded with the ever nascent players, Blackjack tables were lined in a row and placed in a quieter part of the premises, and oh yes, the people— all sizes and shapes— but the ones that attracted our man were beautiful woman, elegantly coiffed, and fitted in fashionable ensembles not purchased at J.C. Penny's.

As his eyes hungrily devoured these visions, Nick could not help but notice the many baubles that hung around their necks, and the opulent rings that adorned their manicured fingers, and the flash and glitter that matched the pure ambiance and flickering lights of their surroundings.

Almost too much for one normal man with a libido that was now at its zenith. The cocktail waitresses filled out their much-abbreviated costumes to a point where he started wondering where in the hell did they find these girls.

His next move was to the five-buck Blackjack tables that were crowded. He had to vie for a seat. It was not too unpleasant, however, when a cocktail waitress approached asking what he was drinking, and giving him an up-close of the two magnificent features that were the hallmark of these hostesses.

Nick, with the luck reserved for the newly arrived, made winning a very welcomed archival event. The amount he was winning reached a prodigious sum and would be filed away for future pleasant memories.

The other prodigious amount that would be remembered in the morning was the alcohol that he had consumed.

He eventually staggered over to the Crap tables that were a complete conversion from the sedate Blackjack tables to a boisterous, raucous, enervating environment.

The Pit boss, observing the play of Nick, and realizing he was in his cups, approached him and said as gently as he could, "Sir, I'm going to have your chips counted and you will receive a receipt for the amount of your winnings, and I will have you escorted to your room. I want you to get a good night's sleep so you will be bright and full of pep tomorrow and you can resume your place here. I'll be looking forward to seeing you tomorrow night." Nick offered no resistance. At this moment, he knew the party was over for this day and if someone would show him where his room was, he was more than happy to exit the fabulous and exciting casino and completely collapse into oblivion. Hopefully, he would live to return to the action at a later time.

As he returned to the edge of reality in the morning, he felt like someone was dropping bricks on his head. Opening his eyes was no small task; they seemed to be adhered together, and he had to use his fingers to help open them. His mouth was in a firmament that was all but useless to him, with taste buds that were inactive. However, hope springs eternal and he gathered himself as best he could and somehow found the bathroom where he perused himself in the mirror. With a scathing glance, he resolved that drinking of the kind he did last night would not happen tonight and, in fact, he would consider never drinking again— a resolve that lasted until about six pm that evening.

He gingerly walked to the extravagant breakfast buffet, where a layout of food that truly approached emperor's expectations awaited, but alas our good time Charlie could not get his stomach on the same page as his eyes.

As he was picking at his food, he remembered that he may have had some money parked at the cashier's desk. Feeling somewhat better now that his stomach had settled into a quieter part of his body, he hurried to the money desk. The cashier asked if he had the voucher they had given him last night, and for the life of him he could not remember any voucher. After telling her his name and producing identification, the cashier proceeded to count a little over $20,000 and recommended that Nick keep it at the Cashiers Desk until he had need for it. This was unbelievable, he had no recollection of having won that much money, and all of a sudden his overall outlook on life took a radical turn. His head and stomach became synonymous with the rest of his body and what a joyous day it had become. *Time to* stroll *outside and see what Vegas really looked like.*

The middle of July in Sin City was generally sweltering and this day was no exception. As he stepped on the sidewalk, the oppressive heat struck him with the force of a punch to the gut. He easily avoided this uncomfortable situation by stepping into the next casino.

Anxiously trying his luck again, and hoping the winning streak would continue. Still feeling the effects of last evening, he sat at a sedate blackjack table, but unfortunately the cards were not coming his way. He lost in a very short time about $1,000 and decided to go back to Caesar's Palace where dame fortune had smiled on him.

When he entered the casino, he felt more at home and decided to visit the card room where that old gamblers' seven-card stud was being played. He felt that this game was more up his alley; he had played many hours of stud with his pals back home. The problem with this game, he was not playing with his old pals. This was a new genre of player. These were experienced and sharp gamblers. Many of the players seemed to be disinterested in the game. Some were reading newspapers, others were playing Keno at the same time. He noticed that he was calling more pots than most of the other players. He lost another substantial portion of his chips before he figured out that the sucker at this game was Nick Lasko. He very badly wanted to win at this table because it was the one game he was familiar with.

The problem; he was now playing with players who in most cases were well versed in the intricacies of poker. If not professionals, then most were dam close and Nick was used to playing with amateurs.

As much as he wanted to stay at this game, he decided to return to the area of past conquests.

As he passed one of the cocktail lounges, contemplating whether or not to indulge, his eyes happen to alight upon a rather fragile but well-constructed brunette. She was definitely not the girl next door type, sitting by herself looking rather lost.

Nick was not altogether ignorant of the ways of the world, knowing that Vegas was filled with women on the make— either working girls or Hollywood types looking for the next meal ticket— he decided to approach her and find out what game she might be up to, or if he could at least type cast her.

"Excuse me, miss, but were you looking for me?" While smiling broadly at the same time, he used a line that had just occurred to him.

She slowly lifted her eye's, drinking in his figure and then languidly letting those large, soft, deep brown eye's meet his still bloodshot blue eyes. Her voice was as soft as a fluttering leaf in the fall, "I'm sorry, you're not who I was looking for."

"I'm sorry too because I was undeniably looking for you. Are you new to Vegas?"

"No, I live close to here. Los Angeles is my home, and I assume your next question would be if I'm unattached? It looks like the answer is yes, at least he hasn't shown up yet, and I'm starting to feel like I have been stood up."

"No, you haven't. Let me introduce myself, I'm Nick Lasko, I'm here from the other side of the states and will only be here for a few days. With that in mind, I will have a very abbreviated period of time to get to know you. From here on I'll change my name to Fast Nick."

"Slow down Fast Nick, I don't know you and with the impetuosity you have exhibited, I'm not sure I want to know you."

"Okay, now that you have decided to be my friend, what is your name?"

"Dam, not only are you fast and impetuous, but you're hard of hearing to."

"C'mon, it's only a name. Lie to me, but give me something to call you rather than hey you."

In a voice so soft, Nick had to lean in close to hear, she said, "Try Jenny." As Nick leaned closer, she chose to lean away.

There was a profound shyness about Jenny. It made Nick come to the realization that the more he pushed to make out, would only drive her further away. As he perused the situation, he realized that everything about her was soft and understated. Her skin was slightly bronzed and her clothes were expensive and exhibited exquisite taste. The form fitting dress was white with heavy gold chains around the waist and formed a V-shape in front and matched the delicate gold necklace she was wearing. The dangling and swaying gold earrings which could barely be seen, went willingly with her shoulder length hair that hung in curls and swirls illuminating the angelic structure of her face.

Nick's heart was pounding in a fashion he was not familiar with. He said, "May I offer you a drink?" Her answer was negative and not encouraging.

Nick was now desperately searching for the words that would magically entice her to have a "get to know" conversation with him, but the words were not there and he could feel her growing coolness toward him.

She quietly and gracefully rose from the table and started walking away. If there was such a thing as love at first sight, Nick was feeling it. He animatedly walked after her and lightly caught her arm, she seemed rather surprised. He said, "Please, would you at least meet me for dinner or breakfast or lunch or coffee or anything? I promise I will be the complete gentleman."

She said, "Please Fast Nick, I believe you can see I'm not interested, but maybe we will see each other around these premises before you leave, you never know." With that, she quickly walked off.

Nick's first instinct was to run after her. However, he knew it would just turn her off. He watched her get on an elevator and by the indicator could tell the floor or floors the elevator stopped.

Nick knew he would turn heaven and hell to see her again— after all, he was not without connections— immediately went to the manager's office.

The secretary politely asked him. "How can I be of help?"

Nick said, "May I speak to the manager?"

She replied, "What is the problem? It might be something I can solve."

"Ma'am, this is a matter of considerable personal urgency. It will truly be a matter between me and the manager. What did you say his name was?"

"I did not say, but his name is Mr. Greene, and what did you say your name was?"

"I didn't say, but you can tell Mr. Greene that Mr. Lasko wants to discuss a matter of considerable importance".

"Please have a seat Mr. Lasko and I'll see if Mr. Greene can see you now."

In a short time, she returned and said, "Mr. Greene will be available in about an hour."

Nick lurched from his seat, "NO, he will see me now!" and walked past a protesting secretary into Mr. Greene's office.

Greene stood up and did not take kindly to the interruption. "Hold on, wait a minute. To what do I owe this unwelcome visit?"

"Mr. Greene, this will take just a bit of your time. My name is Nick Lasko, from Youngstown, and I am a comp'd guest of this Casino, sponsored by people who are personal friends of mine in Youngstown and Pittsburgh. If you don't know of them, then we can cut this meeting short and I will explain to some of my people that we are not as well known at Caesar's as we should be."

"Nick, how can I be of help to you?"

"Let me be as frank as I can. I want you to know I'm not a masher or a stalker, but I happened to have met a woman I would like to see again. I don't know her name for sure, but I know her room is on the 10th floor. Her first name may be Jennifer. She comes from Los Angeles. I will appreciate any information you can supply me about this young mystery woman, and speaking of appreciation, my gratitude will know no bounds if you could also arrange for one of your floor men to contact her and ask if she will meet me in the lounge for a cocktail."

"Mr. Lasko, please understand that my mission is to make sure that our guests have a pleasant and refreshing stay while here at Caesars, and this would include not being bothered with unwanted meetings and requests from strangers. However, because we have mutual friends, I will attempt to have you notified when and if she decides to visit one of our restaurants without an escort. I will do this just once, and I hope this will be satisfactory to you."

"Believe me; I'm very appreciative of your efforts on my behalf."

Nick was more than a little annoyed by the answer he received; he wanted a more accommodating response, but for now it would have to do. With this irritation still on his mind, he decided to rejoin the crap tables and hopefully regain his winning ways.

He was warmly received at the table he chose, the pit bosses must have been briefed about Nick, and they tried to make him feel welcomed.

The table was cold this evening and the money was leaving his hands as fast as it had been coming in the previous night. Nick was still a neophyte gambler, not the experienced, hardnosed gamester he would become. Any pro would tell you when it's not your night, pick up your chips and walk away and live to play another day.

But now the fast play of the Dice, the two croupiers, the urging on of the other players, the chips sliding over the green felt surface of the craps table, the feel of the two Dies in his hand as he threw them against the backstop at the other end of the table, betting the field numbers and having one of them hit and paying 25 to one— actually the worst bet in craps is the field numbers—would not take Nick long to figure out that almost everything he did while gambling at Caesar's was wrong. He attended one of the most expensive universities in the world, some people never learn from it, but Nick was a fast learner. One thing he learned, the casino always wins. So he knew that the name of the university he was attending had the most famous name of all; Fuck You University at Las Vegas, sponsored by many famous names.

He kept plunging thinking that his luck would change any moment. Soon all the money he had won plus the capital he had brought with him was gone. Finally, he decided to pack it in and reassess his situation at the nearest bar. All his good feelings about Caesar's seemed to have disappeared, and now he realized the amount of money he lost was not something he could afford.

Worry about money pushed Jenny to the back of his mind. This left him with two decidedly different problems. How would he meet and impress Jennifer, especially with limited funds? And how to win back the money he lost. Solve one problem and he solves them both.

Nick's future will make these two problems look like mosquito bites on an elephant's ass. He continues gambling using his $50,000 line of credit. Eventually, he realizes he is not going to be able to win back the money he has lost. He feels emptiness in the pit of his stomach and for the first time in his life, he is helpless in the face of adversity. Right now, desolation surrounds him.

The hour is late and Nick decides to return to his room, this time he is perfectly sober; he wants a clear mind so he can think about the money he has lost and what to do about it. In other words, what action he can take to make him *whole* again.

Early morning arrives and he receives the clarion call he so anxiously wanted yesterday but not so much today.

A runner bangs on his door and tells Nick the girl he wanted to meet has just entered Caesar's breakfast room by herself.

Nick entered Caesar's Emperor Room and tried to act as casual as possible, slowly strolling in and around the tables as he neared her table she softly called out to him; "good morning Fast Nick, what brings you out at this ungodly hour"?

Nick's gaze swept over her and once again, his heart nearly jumped out of his chest. She was dressed in softer hues of blue and seemed to be in a pale blue haze. The only word Nick could think of that would describe this vision was "ethereal." To Nick she was created through poetic imagination, not of this world, celestial in nature.

He said, "May I ask what you are doing up at this ungodly hour?"

"Yes, I have an early morning flight home."

His heart sank.

As this was going on, a waiter delivered a message to Nick; it said "call home, extremely urgent." He knew this had to be something related to business and business came first.

Nick turned to Jenifer and in a tortured voice said, "Jen I must cut this fabulous time with you short, but before I go, I absolutely need your phone number."

"I'll go you one better than that Fast Nick, here's my card with all the information you will need to contact me in the future". Nick was not expecting this, his spirits brightened, but he knew he had problems at home.

As he made his good byes, Jennifer said as a parting shot, "by the way Fast Nick I like your eyes the color blue they are now, not the red they were when we first met."

He smiled to himself and thought, "I must have looked awful at that first fateful meeting. He still knew nothing about this girl, and looked at the card. It was for a high-end clothing boutique, with only her first name. He surmised she was either the owner or manager, it did contain a phone number, and this is all Nick needed. With this lead, he could hire a private detective to get all the other information he would want.

Chapter Five
High School Hi Jinx's

Nick went to his room and immediately contacted Tony, one of his employees of which he had two. Neither was Italian, and that's the way he wanted it because most Italians in Youngstown had relatives that in some way were connected and he was trying to keep his distance as much as possible, he was already in deeper than he intended to be.

"Tony, what the fuck is the problem".

"Nick you won't believe this but there's a high school football game tonight and somehow we took $30,000 on one team and only $10,000 on the other team".

"How in the shit did you let this get so far out of hand?" Nick was yelling now because he instinctively knew that the fix was in. Youngstown was unique in that more money was often bet on high school football games than on college games.

"Okay Tony listen to me, shut that game down and give me the names of the people that bet on it." Nick knew he had to contact all of the bettors and cancel the wagers on the team that was getting all the action, but when he looked at the names he realized that most of the heavy bets were made by connected individuals. This meant that he would be unable to unravel what had already taken place; He now knew that he was in trouble and had to contact his backer, Rennie at the Capri and let him know what was going on. Nick's world was now spinning out of control, and he had to get a handle on it.

When Rennie answered the phone, Nick felt relieved, *"Thank God!"*

"Rennie this is Nick, I'm still in Vegas and will be on my way home this evening. Look, Rennie I have some very bad news on the big game tonight between the city rivals. Apparently the fix is in on the old school and my guys have informed me that they have taken $30,000 plus on the old school and only $10,000 the other way. The thing I wanted to do, is cancel the bets on the old school, but when I looked at the names, these are all connected guys."

Where do we go from here."

"Nick are you up to date on your payments to Trado"?

"Hell yes".

Okay, Rennie said, "Give me the names of the bettors, and I'll get back to you".

Nick did as Rennie wanted but he still had a sinking feeling in the pit of his stomach. *He knew that Rennie would call Trado and if Briarhill Tommy fixes it, he knows that he will be further up Tommy's ass and the hook is now firmly set in his mouth. Now whenever they ask anything of him, he will have to comply. But he was desperate. How in the shit did all of this happen?*

As he thought about it, he realized what kind of Goddamn fool he was.

He lost not only all the money he had arrived with, but was in hock to Caesar's Palace for the marker they had extended him.

And now for Chris sake because he was off in Vegas making a fool of himself, his business was getting all fucked up back home.

Rennie called back with the news that all the bets were canceled on the old team, which meant Nick would end up making about $20,000 on the game, assuming the fix went as planned, this would be a great help to what he owes Caesars.

He kept asking himself, How in the fuck did he get in this situation?

Now, he was not only in hock to Caesars but also Trado and Rennie.

Nick was grateful to board the plane that evening and get back to a more normal existence. He only wished that it was true that what you did in Vegas stayed in Vegas.

Chapter Six
Organizing the Congress of Concerned Citizens

On our street, Dearborn Street, in Briarhill, resided some of the best handicappers in the sport of horseracing. Nick associated with these people, but he could see they were not living in mansions, and was smart enough to realize the people making money were the people taking the bets. He knew you had to be an absolute idiot to bet on horse racing.

Not to bore you with numbers but the track normally takes 15% of the win pool and about 25% of the exotic pools that includes all other bets other than Win, Place, and Show. Now do you seriously think someone can make money betting the races? If you do, it behooves you to take a course in math that you obviously missed the first time around.

Betting the races comes under the heading entertainment, but a whole lot of people believe they can beat this sport. These are the same people buying lottery tickets.

Nick became the man about town. To get more business, you had to have a widening circle of friends that knew you, and knew your business. Nick always had a charming manner about him and made friends easily. The only thing he had to worry about was stepping on the wrong person's toes.

The more his business expanded, the more Nick became in the spotlight, and many of the wrong guys started thinking that Nick owed them something. In other words, they felt Nick did not own a franchise on the North side of Youngstown; nobody sold him the North side.

Nick heard these rumblings through Rennie at the Capri. They got together and discussed the ramifications of what was really happening.

The whole crux of the matter; Nick was too successful, and the Wolves were gathering, they wanted their piece of the left over entrails they somehow felt entitled to.

This should come as no surprise to anyone who has ever been in business. There's always someone out there who wants what belongs to you, the difference being, in normal business situations you aren't subjected to potential killers.

Killing Nick, to them, would be like swatting a gnat off your ass; after all they controlled the Mayor's office and the Police Department, not to mention a strangle hold on the prosecutor's office.

Who would miss him; no close relatives, no wife, and no children, only close friends and others who depended on him for a living.

They would put his body in that gigantic Briarhill Slag pile that has probably seen more than its share of bodies in its time. And that would be the end of Nick Lasko. In 30 days nobody would remember he ever existed.

His naturally suspicious nature took over about this time and he started wondering about his partner Rennie. Why was it he always seemed to have information before Nick had a handle on it? This gave him pause, but it was not something he wanted to ponder for any length of time.

Nick felt it was time he became more active in getting to know the people that mattered in his business, if this meant getting closer to Cosa Nostra then so be it!

He decided to have a meeting with Youngstown and other area Bookmakers. It might give him some insight into problems they may have been having similar to his own. He also knew that he would need a representative of the Mob present so as not to create the impression that he was trying to incite a small revolt.

With these thoughts in mind, Nick called Briarhill Tommy. When he finally got in touch with Trado, "he told him what was going on and how his suspicions were being aroused about members of the organization wanting to cut in on the action, without any authorization from a Capo."

"Nick" Tommy said, "you know I'ma take care of you because you my boy, buta you bring all these guys together and some of them not you friend. They backed by the Cleveland guys and thatsa who they paying. Buta you may be right, maybe itsa time to go toe to toe with these bastards anda finda out where we at."

"Yeah, but Goddammit Tommy I don't want to stir up a hornets nest."

"Nick, I wanta you to call Vinnie Solerno, he gonna put you Ina touch with somebody who's gonna be the guy you go to from now on. Nick, I'ma gettin' old, and I don't want to go through any more wars. Thisa new guy is a Made Man of Honor, and you show him the samea respect you show me."

"I will say, Tommy, I'm going to miss having you around. You were always honest and a pleasure to do business with. I always knew if there was a problem I could look to you to fix it. Goddamit, I hate we have to get old. Tommy, here is one guy that's going to miss the hell out of you."

When Nick hung up he was quite a bit shaken. If truth be told he was not ready for any wars and frankly the thought had never occurred to him. Maybe he was getting in way over his head, and there was only two options, go forward and become more involved, or get out of the business. With his current expenses the thought of *no money* nauseated him.

He decided to go ahead with the meeting even though it gave him a queasy feeling. If he made a good impression, then it could open many avenues, most of which were unforeseen at the moment. The one thing that stands out now is the need to increase his power and ability to influence not only the Pittsburgh faction, where he already has good relations— but with the Cleveland Men of Honor, it will behoove him to play both sides of the street.

Many of the rumblings that Nick heard— of the wolves wanting a piece of the action— he assumed were coming from the Cleveland guys. He felt at this meeting he would be able to solve the problem.

When Nick called Vinnie Solerno, a light went on in his brain. All of a sudden he realized that Vinnie was really the consigliore for the Pittsburgh guys, and was higher up than Nick had originally thought. So it would be is in his best interests to treat him with more respect than he had in the past.

Vinnie's secretary answered the phone and Nick thought *now he even has a secretary.*

She said "May I help you?"

"Yes you can. I'm Nick Lasko and I need to speak to Vinnie— It's urgent."

"I'll give Mr. Solerno the message and he will return your call."

Nick felt the anger rising and his blood heating up. He hated to be put off by some underling but his better sense took over and he replied, "Thank you for your understanding, I will look forward to Mr. Solerno's call."

Vinnie returned the call in a short time.

"Nick, I know what your call is about and I want you to know you're treading on dangerous ground. Unless you have a keynote speaker who can hold this conglomeration together, you will have chaos that could degenerate into things too terrible to talk about. I know you have a great personality but this is maybe a little out of your league."

"Vinnie, I have decided to go ahead with this meeting and give it all I have. What I need you to do is contact the Cleveland Honcho's and ask them to send a representative. I understand that you are to introduce me to my new Capo and I hope he's well informed about my idiosyncrasies."

"What Fucking idiosyncrasies are you talkin about? I thought we took care of them after the first meeting at the Randall Mall."

"Yeah you did, but I may have other ones you don't know about." Nick was laughing now thinking about the way Trado had him thrown in the slammer.

"I think the first thing we need to do is get you introduced to the new guy and have you two get comfortable with each other."

"Okay, but for chris sake I'm not going out on a date with this guy.

"Hey Nick, don't be a smart ass. Listen to me."

"There is an excellent Italian Restaurant called Chicone's on Wilson Avenue, where the service is impeccable and they know how to treat you. One of the owners is called Andy. Let's get this thing done now. How about tomorrow night at six? Andy will introduce you to Larry Ditullio. He comes here from New York by way of Pittsburgh. His loyalties lie with the Genovese family."

"Then what the hell is he doing with me?"

"Nick there's a lot you don't know about our organization. The Genovese family is like our Uncle and is interested in everything we do. You may not know this but the man who is the man in this area is someone you are well acquainted with— in fact, you went to school with him. I'm talkin' about Joey Naples and he's gaining a lot of power even in New York."

"Get the fuck out of here, I know Joey well— we were pretty good friends in school. In fact, he was about the only one who had a car, and many a cold winter morning he'd pick me up and get me up that fuckin' Craven St. hill. That hill was a real bastard on blustery snowy winter mornings. But Goddamn it was a joy to behold when we were kids and you were at the top of it, and you had your sled, and were going to have about a one mile ride downhill— avoiding any cars that were slipping and sliding all over the place."

"So you remember him."

"I remember Joey as a rather quiet serious type of kid that never had much to say; on the other hand my friends and I were pretty raucous. So look who turns out to be the tough guy. You never know?"

"Look Nick, after your meeting with Larry get back in touch with me and then we will have more to go on."

Chapter Seven
California Peach & Congress of Concerned Citizens
C.C.C.

In the meantime, Nick was working on that beautiful Honey on the West Coast. He had hired a private detective to find as much as he could about her personally and now had his report in his hands. Much of what the P. I. dug up Nick could have predicted. She lived in an upscale condo in Laguna Beach and devotes a considerable amount of her time in the style industries. She was considered one of the top designers in the business, planning and directing shows all over the West Coast that were engaged in the retail and wholesale end of the business.

The part of the report he did not like; she is married but apparently not living with anyone. She has a frequent visitor, currently an aspiring actor, who seems to be her current paramour.

Because of the type of business she is in, required her to attend many parties, and is escorted and courted by many erstwhile potential Beaus. He was astonished at her age; she was a few years older than he was.

Her past was no surprise. She held a B.A. in business from the prestigious University of California. She had entered and won many beauty contests both minor and major events such as Miss Peach, Miss Los Angeles, and Miss California.

She has a very full and eventful life. The one factor that disturbed Nick was the fact that she seems to be living way above her head according to the P.I.'s investigative report. To Nick this meant somebody had to be paying the bills and whoever that was had an inside Track to her heart. Ever heard of the Golden Rule? "Whoever has the Gold Rules."

Nick had only one option for the present and that was to call her on the phone and remind her that he was still thinking of her. On further contemplation, instead of calling her he called a florist and ordered the gaudiest ensemble the florist had, and had it sent to her. He would call her later when he had more of a chance to think about it.

At the appointed time, he arrived at Chicone's Italian Restaurant. He looked around and spotted a guy who was slightly stooped with bulging eyes. He introduced himself and asked if he was Andy. The reply was in the affirmative, Nick told Andy that he was there to meet a guy by the Name Larry Ditullio. Andy called one of the waitresses— a large woman with even larger bazumes— who led him to a private enclosure. As he entered, a large man with a luxuriant head of hair, a pockmarked face, with an unmistakable nose, rose to greet him. This guy towered over Nick and virtually— because of his appearance— could have a threatening demeanor, but after a few casual words, Nick found his personality interesting and conversational with a dry sense of humor.

They ordered large plates of Spaghetti with Meat Balls and all the trimmings and they ate with gusto—like it was their last meal before the Gallows.

Now they settled back with a warm glow and toyed with a glass of Chianti while they discussed the business at hand.

As Nick started laying out his plan of a meeting with all the bookmakers in the area, he could see Larry grow silent and his face become more serious and very intent on every word Nick was uttering.

After listening for quite a while to Nick's oratory, Larry finally spoke up. "I don't want to undercut your ambitious plan, but you are getting into a situation that if not handled with the utmost care could cause an individual or two to disappear. I can't tell you how that may happen, but I've seen it play out that way before."

"You are making yourself the central figure in this escapade and some guy out there says this motherfucker is getting too big; you may be the one that disappears."

"Larry somebody has to take the lead in settling these constant conflicts that are not good for business, not good for our clients, not good politically, not good for the organization, and not good for my pocketbook, not to mention, I'm always worried about my long-term health that some bastard might try to take it away from me."

"That's my job Nick, to see to it that your prospects for a long life are kept intact because the reason I'm here is because certain people high up have seen the job you have been doing and you may not know this, but you are a rising star in our organization and you are the reason I'm here."

"Larry, I'm truly flattered but I never wanted to be a rising star in any organization let alone Cosa Nostra. All I'm trying to do is make a living as best I can with the least amount of trouble possible."

"Let me say that's not possible. Your name is tossed around like Pizza dough, but it is handled with much respect. I'm going to be hanging around you rather closely so get accustomed to the idea."

Nick was now fully committed to the meeting. He went back to his place of operations that was now expanding to several operators manning the phones.

It was up to Nick to contact all the bookmakers individually, he did not think that anybody else could do it with as much élan as himself. Each of these guys was different and had to be handled differently. It was important that every one of the men knew this was to be a highly secret operation. If help was needed such as a secretary, or if they had a physical handicap, they could bring another person, but Nick would be notified at least two days before the actual event, and that person would be cleared by Nick himself before they would be allowed entrance to the meeting room.

He decided to hold the meeting at one of the past formally prominent hotels in downtown Youngstown which was now in a state of rapid decline. He felt that it would be one of the least expected places to host a convention of sporting- event bookmakers. He knew word would get out, but he would try to keep it to a minimum. Knowing reporters would be there, it was up to him to control the events taking place in the conference room. Reporters should be strictly excluded from the important areas where agreements would be hammered out. Besides, the local newspaper may have been compromised, and possibly a word from Pittsburgh or Cleveland may keep reporters at bay.

He booked the banquet room in the name of "Historical Society of Sports memorabilia", however in speaking to the various bookmakers, he learned they already heard of the meeting being referred to as the little Apalacin meeting. That was a meeting in the mountains of New York where the F.B.I. was able to round up some of the most important members of the Mafia.

Nick called Vinnie and informed him of what was going on.

Vinnie said, "He was already informed. "

"Vinnie who are you sending from the Cleveland faction?"

"I'm sending a very important guy from Cleveland called John Black Lacavoli, he agreed only because he wants to know what the fuck is going on over here."

"I will need him to be at the door before the meeting starts. If he will meet with me and Larry prior to the meeting getting underway I believe that I will be able to allay some of his fears."

"Just tell me the time and the place and I'll arrange things," Vinnie said.

Nick was having a problem with some of the prospective attendees, many were wary of possible police involvement and/or gang related retaliation for real or imagined past activities. Some had a predilection for keeping their business to themselves.

Nick's masterful charm and reasoning ability was eventually able to get commitments from the majority of the bookmakers.

This whole thing took place in the late summer of 1960 at a time when Youngstown was in full flower, and pockets overflowed with steel money. It seemed to Nick that it was imperative that these small businessmen organize to avoid conflicts of interest and any acts of violence that reflected badly on this area. "After all" he argued," we have had enough bad publicity. When we have an extension of criminal acts the citizenry tends to become restless, and before you know it they start electing officials that are reformers, and that is abhorrent to not only the small bookmaker but also to the Men of Honor.

Nick met with Larry and John Black one hour before the meeting started. This was the First time Nick had met John Black, who was accompanied and introduced to Nick by Vinnie Solerno. The thing that surprised Nick, Larry, and John Black knew each other and were very familiar even though they were on opposite sides of the fence.

John Black was surprisingly short— about five foot six— but had a loud, heavy voice that he used infrequently, his very nature and large features contributed to a menacing mood that seemed to surround him.

After becoming acquainted, Nick excused himself and with nervous energy started getting things in order for the soon-to- arrive attendees.

He wanted to be at the entrance to scrutinize all of the arrivals and make sure they had received the proper welcome. He knew everybody by their first name and tried to make each and everyone feel special.

After all were seated and comfortable Nick made his entrance and strode quickly to the podium.

In his opening remarks he wanted to stress the importance of this meeting and how all would make more money because of it.

Nick's gaze swept over the crowd and he felt very relaxed, knowing the speech he planned to make this morning would be very controversial. He began by saying, "I want to make everybody here Mafia— or in the vernacular of the Mafia— a man of honor. And here's why."

The rustling and whispering in the room ceased. He had their attention.

"If, by mafia, they mean having an exaggerated sense of honor. If, by Mafia they mean being furiously intolerant of bullying and injustice. If, by Mafia, they mean showing the generosity of spirit needed to stand up to the strong and understanding toward the weak. If, by Mafia, they mean having a loyalty to your friends that is stronger than anything, stronger even then death. If, by Mafia they mean feelings like these, attitudes like these—even though they may sometimes get exaggerated—then I say to you what they are talking about, are the distinguishing traits of the entrepreneur, that will stand head and shoulders above all others, and so I declare myself a man of honor and I am proud to be one. In this, I am asking one and all to join me."

The applause was a little stifled and a puzzled silence was evident.

And now the time had come to inform them of one of the principal reasons for this meeting. Nick knew it would cause the shit to hit the fan.

"Membership was mandatory, and dues would be paid on a monthly basis, and would be based on your income and your territory. This assessment to be determined by the board of directors."

Muttering, and a shuffling of feet told Nick he was about to lose them.

"Gentleman, I must inform you that membership in this club will carry some special privileges! First of all, your territories will be protected. That means no one else will operate in your province unless it is authorized by the board of directors."

"We will go to bat for you in any political action or other Inconvenience caused you by the police. That would include posting bail, and having an attorney present when needed."

There was one very important matter that Nick had to make them aware of, "it is incumbent on them not to become involved in the trafficking of drugs. This was just coming into vogue about this time. Cosa Nostra was violently opposed to anyone having anything to do with Drugs.

Nick informed them if they were brought up on charges of dealing, the consequences would be severe and they would jeopardize their entire lifestyle.

The uproar was disturbing and egregious; Nick was having a difficult time of it as the raucous behavior continued, finally he looked over to one of his own staff and said, "Please take down the names of the perpetrators of this demonstration." He said it loud enough to be heard all over the Hall, this attracted everyone's attention, and the hullabaloo came to an end.

After this, he got down to the business of creating an organization.

First order of business was to elect a board of Directors. The board would elect a president. All of this was done with input from the membership.

Nick declined the office of president and declared that he would rather be an advisor to the president and board of Directors. This would allow him to flow seamlessly between the mob and the new organization.

The follow up to this meeting was without precedent. There was yelling and crying, plus some very insightful arguments brought to the forefront by members that had to be addressed. Proposed assessments were the biggest problem.

Calls came from Cleveland and Pittsburgh factions to Nick expressing satisfaction, amusement, displeasure and a newfound awareness of Nick Lasko. He was not sure he wanted this recognition even though it appealed to his ego.

The name for this organization that was finally adopted "The Coalition of Concerned Citizens" or the CCC.

The one biggest concern of the mafia was the CCC eventually entertaining too much power and hold more leverage over the way things are conducted, thereby cutting into the power structure of the competing factions.

Nick's lifestyle was now beginning to change. The amount of money that he was earning was more than he ever dreamed of, and soon he was spending it as if it was coming out of a bottomless pit.

The home he had constructed was imperial in nature spread on 5 acres of land with imposing gates at the grand entrance. If we called it a home that would be a misnomer, let us substitute Estate for Home and that certainly is closer to a description that fits this residence. Included in this adobe was an Olympic-sized swimming pool, workout room with the most modern up to date equipment with an elaborate office, a master bedroom that was past grand with the bed resting on a raised platform, and gold plated fixtures in the marble bath. The rest of the home was equally grand. Nick spared no expense on this extravagance, with the money being borrowed from the Steel Union Pension fund through the auspices of the Pittsburgh Mafia.

Chapter Eight
Jenny, Jenny, Jenny And Tommy

Nick met and dated many of the local beauties in the area, but his thoughts kept returning to Jenny. He wanted to do something that would catch her fancy.

He called the P.I. that he had hired and asked him "How she was doing,"

He volunteered, "All was well, and things were going about the same way they were before, but he had heard that she was behind on some of her obligations."

This did not surprise Nick, "He asked the P.I. to do some investigating and try to pin point the area that seemed to be hurting her the most."

He came back to Nick and said, "The one thing that he could put his finger on; she was getting squeezed between the Chinese manufacturers and the clothing unions on the West Coast."

"The chinks kept raising their prices and the American manufacturers, under the boot of the blood sucking unions keep raising their prices to the smaller retailer cutting them out, and signing contracts with the big boys. The outlets that had been doing business with her were starting to change suppliers. Her fashions that had always been on the high end of the scale were now utterly ignored."

She communicated with Nick soon after the festoon of flowers he had sent her.

Her attitude was particularly encouraging, and "expressed interest in how he was getting along. She was especially pleased to hear from him."

Anxiously, Nick picked up the phone and placed call after call to Jenny but it was no easy matter tracing her down. The receptionist at Jen's office seemed to be confused and overworked. He left a message with her to have Jenny call him as soon as it was feasible, but Nick did not place a lot of confidence that the message would reach her. He thought, "What the hell am I paying a P.I. for, I'll let him find this girl."

Eventually, the P.I. found her in the City of Sacramento where she was apparently attending meetings with other small wholesalers getting together with the Governor and his staff to discuss the role the garment unions had in the demise of the small wholesaler and boutique retailer.

She was ensconced at the Grand Hotel of Sacramento. It seems she was one of the featured speakers and personages at these get togethers, and axillary meetings that were taking place at this Hotel and her room was crowded with attendees.

Nick called while she was busy speaking and holding court with significant dignitaries.

Graciously she came to the phone and immediately recognized the voice, and hollered out over the commotion that was surrounding her; "Oh, Fast Nick I'm so glad you called; however, this is not an optimum time, give me your phone number, and I'll call you back when things get a little quieter around here."

Nick was thrilled to hear the enthusiasm her voice held when she heard it was Fast Nick. He acquiesced in her request and held his breath in anticipation of her return call.

Her call never came that night to the chagrin of a seriously disappointed Nick. His anger was starting to grow. But it was a helpless anger. If he called her back that night, it would seem he was too anxious. At the same time, he felt that she was being uncaring and certainly arrogant.

Nick's angst did not have to be endured for long. The next morning Jenny called before he was barely out of the sack. She was truly apologetic, she said, "It was rather late when things cleared up, and she did not want to disturb him at that late hour."

"Please beautiful Lady, any time you call will always be the right time." Nick was unsure of how he should treat her. It was obvious she had a stunning beauty, fabulous in a soft way that was at the least astonishing the first time this vision comes into view.

In his circle of friends, it was the commonly asserted belief that you treat a queen like a Whore and a Whore like a queen.

He felt that it was highly unlikely that she would be unaffected by her beauty simply because beautiful girls are treated differently all through their lives. The statistics tell us that beauty gets those ladies better jobs, better pay, better grades, and better mates for marriage with mates that have more money. So how do you treat a woman that lived with these advantages and bring it around so that you can be first in her heart albeit with intense competition? Tell me, how can this come about?

In the case of Jennifer, she seemed unaffected. It seemed that her beauty was something that did not even occur to her, and she floated above the fray in a remarkably calm reserved manner.

They continued their conversation on various and sundry things for a rather lengthy time.

Nick finally got around to the aspect of her business involving the garment workers union. She informed him that is

91

the exact reason she was in Sacramento. She said, "They were not having any luck convincing the government that the union was trying to put them out of business unless they paid a tribute to the union bosses. The Governor and legislators were in the pocket of and owed their election to the Union types."

Nick said; "Jenny I had plans to go to California, and I was hoping that you would honor me with your presence at a dinner engagement, and I promise you that it will be to your benefit. I believe that at least in your case I will be able to entice the Union to be reasonable in their demands."

Fast Nick, "I have never known what you do for a living because up to now it was none of my business, but what you have just stated makes me think that your occupation may be less than honorable."

"Jenny, what you have just uttered is as far from the truth as you can get. Just this once I will tell you what I do, and you can take this to the bank. I help little people make money, maybe not in the way that governments would approve of because governments are not always on the side of the people as you are now finding out. They are generally on the side of the money interests that get them elected.

Jennifer if you will accept my help we may be able to come to some kind of understanding with these Union people."

"Jenny, because the nature of what I do is confidential I will ask you not to question my profession again because I will not be able to give you an answer. Do we have a deal or not?" Nick held his breath because depending on her answer, will determine whether this hoped for relationship can go forward. There was an excruciating pause before Jen answered. In these moments before she answered, Nick came to a stunning realization; that his loyalty and affection for his connections to the mafia took precedent even over his love for this girl. He knew that he had never been formally inducted into Cosa Nostra, but those that were in the know considered him one of them.

92

Jenny in a slow motion and drawn out answer ever so softly replied; "I can see that you have a deep and abiding respect for your profession, and I know that you have developing feelings for me and hereafter I will never ask what you do, but your feelings for me may disappear when you find out more about me."

"Jenny, because of what I do it is necessary to know all that I can about the people that surround me, so I may know more about you than you realize. Jenny tell me when you will be home, and I'll organize my trip, so it coincides with your schedule."

"Listen, Fast Nick, are you sure you want to see me? I'm afraid you may have feelings and intentions I may not share. It's not just you, it's any person that may be interested in me in a romantic way. At this time, other than friendship, I'm just not interested, I have a personal problem that I need to solve before I can become absorbed in my personal situation and start working on my private love life. But if you still want to see me? I will return home next week."

"Okay Jennifer, expect me next week. I'll call when I arrive."

The phone call with Jenifer was in some ways satisfying and in other ways vexing, but Nick knew what he wanted and was prepared to hurtle any obstacles and pursue his quarry until she became a part of his life.

Nick immediately started working on getting information on this West Coast Garment workers Union. He called their offices in L.A. and found out from the receptionist that the manager of that office was a guy called Sammy Garfolio, this was probably not the president, but it gave Nick some valuable info, the first and most noteworthy being that this guy was Italian. That did not mean that he was connected in any way with the mob. Because the Cosa Nostra was extremely weak on the West Coast due to the lack of Italian immigration to this area. He also knew that if the president was Jewish or Italian than they were probably connected.

The Jewish community had a large contingent because of their predilection for show business. The reason he did not bring in the P.I. in this investigation was his personal belief that when it came to Mob affairs, the less known by people that did not have a need to know, the better.

He eventually found the name of the president and he was neither Italian nor Jewish, and he realized that the negotiations would become more difficult than he had first thought.

He got in touch with Vinnie and asked him to get as much information as he could on this Union and the president that was named John Cuszach. Vinnie was not fond of interfering in anybody's love life because it usually ended up with unforeseen consequences. He told Nick this, but seeing it was one of their best guys he would get back to Nick with as much information that he could dig up.

When Nick received information on John Cuszach, he was staggered by the background on this man. He was clearly a man that lived a life on the edge. His rap Sheet showed he had spent more time behind bars than in front of them; he had a string of infractions including accusations of murder, armed robbery, resisting arrest, and various other appalling charges. He had worked in the garbage department for the city, was a professional boxer and a noted brawler and still hung around the gym where he occasionally put the gloves on with the active fighters training there, worked sometimes as a longshoreman and a truck driver many times driving trucks long distance with over the road big rigs. He was divorced three times and according to his rap sheet apparently a woman abuser. He had children that he rarely saw. All in all, he was an unsavory character.

Nick mulled over the fact that this bastard became the head of the Union, and he was pretty sure how he did it. He simply bulled, muscled, and murdered his way to the top if he had to. Murder is a strong accusation but according to this guy's past it was not out of the realm of possibilities.

"What the hell do I do from here?" Nick thought. If John had been a Man of Honor or in some way connected, then we would have some common ground and would have made an understanding possible. He knew that looking at the background of this Prick, there was nothing but trouble ahead.

Again, he calls Vinnie and asks for advice on how best to handle Cuszach; Vinnie said, "You must be a crazy son of a bitch to think that we would get involved because you got a Blue Veined Weiner in your pants. That guy means nothing to us; he puts no capital in our pockets in any way. So what the fuck do you suggest we do? Put the whole organization behind you so you can fuck your sweetie, are you nuts. Let me give you a piece of advice: chasing after a woman the way you are chasing this skirt is crazy and can only lead to no good. It's the world's oldest story."

What Vinnie was telling Nick he already inherently knew, but this is one time he would let the little Red Head control the big Red Head.

Nick knew that he was heading for a confrontation with Cuszach, and as he thought this out he was going to have to be smarter than him. He realized that to out muscle him on his home grounds would not work because Nick had virtually no backing from his own powerful group back home.

Nick had one more ace up his sleeve; there was a guy out there by the name of Tommy Satiano, formally connected with the Cleveland Mob and transferred to the Los Angeles group and was in line to become Capo di Tutti Capi, but Nick did not know him personally which would make it tough to talk to him without an introduction. Nick turned to the only guy that he knew with Cleveland connections. The guy that was an observer for the Cleveland faction when Nick was organizing the CCC group. Since that time, Nick found out that John Black was more than just a Soldato in Cleveland.

Nick was reluctant to contact this guy because of his menacing nature when Nick first met him, but his infatuation with Jenny took over his better sense, and he decided to call Mr. Black.

When calling John Black all he could get was a messaging service. "Nick reminded him who he was and asked him to return his call." When talking by phone, you had to be mindful of the fact, it was probably being recorded, especially in Cleveland.

John called Nick the next morning and said, "Yeah I remember you, what do you want."

"I'm sorry to disturb you Mr. Black, but I'm leaving for L.A. in a couple of days to solve a personal problem, and I thought that Mr. Satiano could be of some help, but I need an introduction to him and I thought you could be of help in this matter."

John said, "I remember that you were masterful in handling that meeting; I was quite impressed, so I'm not going to ask you what your personal matter is. Consider your request done." After making his gracious goodbye's Nick jubilantly hung up the phone. This was the first bright spot in this caper.

He was getting things into a clearer picture. He also wanted two men that knew how to conduct themselves in the event violence would break out. They would have to be conversant in the ways and protocol of the organization. This task was not difficult if the money was right. They would be tagging along with him wherever he went

Nick made reservations at the Park Plaza Hotel in downtown L.A. for himself and his two bodyguards. He loved grand hotels with a history and this hotel filled the bill, it was centrally located no matter which direction he had to go, it would be convenient.

Los Angeles International Airport was its usual busy and confusing self. Nick finally found the Avis counter and picked up his rental, a black Cadillac that fit the occasion.

He did not want to be looked at in such a manner that he would be considered a small town hick, but that's actually what he was, Youngstown was a city of only 130,000 people, of course its location gave it added importance, it was situated between Pittsburgh and Cleveland, this area was called the Rust Belt of the country because of the Steel Mills stretching along this corridor.

Nick was always in a little awe when traveling to large vibrant cities where building never stopped.

The three impressive looking men were wearing fashionable clothing that came from a certain look that Youngstown had all its own, to describe this look; it was casual in a structured and conservative manner.

At this time a look that was pure Youngstown was called a Jergans suit, The pants were cuffed with a 16 inch drape, the seams were double French seams, a vest that sported three tabs across the front, the belt loops had a drop of 1 ¼", the shirt was also tailored to match the suit, very sharp.

Nick was strict in the look that his employee's projected. Youngstown wise guys were able to take advantage of the Italian tailors that had emigrated from Italy, and they were fashion conscious and fastidious. As these three impressive men strolled through the lobby, they did attract attention. Nick wanted this attention. It might come in handy later.

As they approached the check in desk, introductions were made in a soft and dignified voice. They eventually were escorted to their rooms and all settled in except Nick, as soon as he could get to a phone he called Tommy Satiano.

Tracing Tommy down at one of his favorite watering holes was arduous but eventually accomplished.

"Mr. Satiano, My name is Nick Lasko I believe that Mr. Black of Cleveland called you about me and I am desirous of a meeting to discuss a problem that I have in the L.A. area. Would you have a moment anytime tomorrow?"

"Nick I'll be happy to meet with you. Whenever I'm able to do a favor for John I'm at your service."

"May I suggest breakfast or is that too early queried Nick?"

"As a matter of fact I'm an early riser and prefer to do business first thing in the morning."

"Tommy I do have two associates that are traveling with me, does that present a problem?"

"As a matter of fact it does, I would prefer they not be in attendance."

"Then they will not be there. Thank you Mr. Satiano for your indulgence in this matter. Do you have a preferred place for breakfast?"

"Actually your Hotel has a fine breakfast room. How about eight in the morning.

I'll be looking forward to meeting you?"

Nick knew that Tommy would talk to the front desk or have one of his minions do it, and find out all he could about the Nick Lasko party. Tommy had to be extremely careful, he had other irons in the fire, and he knew there were contracts out on him. Tommy was doing some cooperation with the F.B.I., so this was also a concern for him.

Tommy found out from the front desk how Nick and party were dressed and when he found out; he was assured they were from Youngstown, only Youngstown guys dressed like that.

With a bunch of trepidation Nick sat down with Satiano for breakfast, He was immediately put at ease by the natural and easy manner of Tommy, slim and well groomed, had features that were decidedly Italian, he was like the guy next store and you were having a conversation about fishing or cutting the grass or how to get rid of the weeds.

After the introductions and the preliminaries about the weather and such, Tommy said, "What is your problem Nick?" "Nick went on to explain about the Garment workers union. They were squeezing out the smaller shops and made deals with the larger Stores. This would benefit the bigger guys by eliminating competition, and Nick's close friend was getting immeasurably hurt by this setup. He intended to try to arrange a meeting with the head of the Union to see if they could work out some reasonable terms but because the president of the Union did not know Nick it would be difficult to get to see him."

Tommy said, "Nick I assume we are talking about that prick John Cuszach. You might as well be whistling in the wind. Talking to that cocksucker is an exercise in complete useless futility. That Union should be under our auspices paying homage to the guys who keep that bastard in business."

"I'll tell you what, I'll not only get you an appointment with that cocksucker, but I'll go with you. If he doesn't give us an appointment, I'll have his office fucked up. Whatever happens I know that the Bastard will insult us and who knows maybe that's just the excuse I need to obliterate this Prick once and for all."

"I know of his background, and he has been running roughshod over anybody that got in his way largely from his reputation. Well maybe you coming to me with your problem is just the impetus I need to get rid of this Prick."

Nick could see that Tommy was getting more and more worked up as he talked about Cuszach, he could tell there was utter hate spewing from Tommy's mouth.

Now Nick knew that this meeting was taking a turn that Nick wasn't ready for. He had envisioned a little sabotage to Cuszach personally, such as a broken leg or arm, maybe stitches in his face. But he never in a million years thought about, in the vernacular of Tommy, obliteration.

As Tommy was leaving he turned to Nick and said, "Wait for my call I'll arrange everything. With that, he was gone."

Nick thought; "yeah, what he is going to arrange is a hit that Nick very well may be a part of. The law has a way of indicting anyone who had anything to do with a murder. Just knowing and meeting with Tommy before Cuszach's demise could put Nick away for the rest of his life."

Now he's thinking, "Is this girl worth it, hell I haven't even fucked her yet, and I'm already putting my entire future in jeopardy, because of her, for Chris sake it's not like I haven't been warned over and over again. Who was it that told me this relationship may have unintended consequences; well Goddammit that's what's happening."

Tommy called Nick the next afternoon, after the usual preliminaries, Tommy said, "It's all set 10 a.m. tomorrow morning at Cuszach's office."

Nick arrived a little early hoping to catch Tommy so they could enter together. Nick was apprehensive and felt in some way there would be trouble.

This Satiano, as nice as he seemed, you could tell he was not the kind of person that you wanted to rub the wrong way.

As they entered the reception room there were several rough and tumble types sitting around, they all stood up, and one of them asked what we wanted, Tommy said, "We are here to see John. "

"Is he expecting you?"

Tommy said, "Your Goddamn right he's expecting me and you know it so quit fuckin` around and show us to his office. Goddamn I hate when somebody wants to fuck with you."

"Okay, Okay Tommy calm down it's the second door on the right." The two of them quickly went to the door and led by Tommy they almost exploded into Cuszach's office."

John Cuszach was momentarily taken aback by this entry, he said, "For Chris sake slow down, where the hell do you think you are".

"I think we are here in the mother fucker's office that for years has been ignoring what the shit you owe us, but right now we have another problem, I want to introduce you to Nick Lasko from Youngstown, he works with Scales the Fish and John Black, I'm going to let him explain the problem."

"I don't want to hear any problem you have, fuck you, I don't like your attitude. You lousy Dagos think you can run over anybody. So just take your Gombah asses out of here and go back to the sewers you slunk out of."

Unbeknownst to Cuszach and Nick, Tommy had arranged for a contingent of his associates to enter and secure the outer office. So the men that Cuszach had in the reception area were now impotent.

Tommy looked at Cuszach with a calm dead look in his eyes and said to John as he withdrew an automatic from his pocket, "You rotten sonofabitch. I want you to know that the boys you had in the reception area now have their balls tied in knots by my Dago Gombah people, and if things do not turn out so good in this office, they'll never again see what us dumb Gombah Dagos call a Famiglia, so you mother fuckin' bastard you better start beggin' for mercy because I'm eventually going to kill you and I really relish the thought of blowing the top of your fuckin` head off now. And in the vernacular of us Dagos, capisce."

Cuszach's face suddenly became ashen as he looked at the barrel of that gun, he knew that Tommy was a killer and would not hesitate to do exactly what he said.

"Okay, let's hear what your friend has to say."

"Well Mr. Cuszach I have a friend that's kind of the spokesman for the small clothing stores here in California. She happens to have a fashion-clothing boutique and between the rising prices from the Chinese and the tribute to your union, is

101

putting a lot of them out of business. I don't know if this is done on purpose to eliminate the small clothing stores in order to enhance the profit of the bigger merchandisers or not, but it's doing irreparable damage to my friend."

"Who is your friend?"

"Her name is Jennifer Lake."

"I've heard of her, she's that good looking thing that's been a kind of thorn in my side, but I'd sure like to fuck her."

"Take it easy John she's spoken for by me and if you make a move on her you'll have another guy gunning for you."

"Forgetaboutit I've already got enough bimbos that I'm running with."

"Mr. Lasko let me think about it."

Tommy immediately spoke up, he said, "There's no thinking about anything. You're going to lower that Goddamn take on these people, and for Jennifer Lake there will never again be a tribute to this fuckin' Union, now you sonofabitch, do you understand me? If you don't, just say it, and we will get this problem over with now."

"Okay Tommy I'll take care of this problem, but I don't want you trying to push me around in the future."

"Yeah, well don't depend on that. When you are paying your fair share to us, then maybe we'll be talking a different scenario."

Leaving this appointment was such a relief to Nick he felt completely drained. He was glad he did not get his two associates involved, this way, they don't know how close they came to being involved in a hit.

When he said his goodbyes to Tommy he said, "Tommy anytime you want to come to Youngstown just remember it's on me, anything you want because I honestly appreciate what you have done. Without you, this would have been impossible."

"Goddammit, today I have met and been in the company of a real man."

Tommy said, "Forgetaboutit someday you will return the favor."

Nick with a mountain of relief turned his attention to what he felt would be more pleasant aspects of this trip. He called Jenny as soon as he returned to the hotel. She was glad to hear from him and accepted an invitation for dinner the next day.

He was anxious to just chill out for the rest of the day going for a dip in the pool, having dinner with his associates, and talking about golf and sports in general over a few drinks would give him a chance to wind down and get his blood pressure under control.

That night he slept as if he was in a coma. In the morning, he had a hard time breaking that feeling of being drugged.

He eventually made it down for breakfast, where at long last, he was able to reflect on the events of yesterday, and what a close call it had become for him.

All of a sudden, he had a yearning and a hunger for good old Youngstown and getting back to the places he knew like the Capri and that beautiful new estate that he now possessed.

He was determined that when he got back he would have a party for the Grand Opening of his home that would be so large they would splash it all over the Vindicator, the Youngstown newspaper.

He met Jenny that night at the very best restaurant in the city he had some amount of nervousness telling Jenny that she was now exempt from paying tribute to the Union for as long as she remained in business. When he saw her it was always a thrill, but somehow the bloom was off the Rose. He gave her the news but instead of being thrilled, she was questioning Nick.

"How he had this thing done, and she wanted to know about the other small retailors."

Nick sat back, drank her in for a moment, and said, "Jenny many things can get done in this world because of having friends in the right places and this just happened to be one of them. Remember I said that what I did was not anyone's business but mine. Just be glad that it has turned out alright. However, I would council you do not go around tweaking someone's nose, and I'm specifically speaking of John Cuszach and the clothing union. You may want to picture yourself as a crusader for the rights of the little guy, but someone like Cuszach will trample you." "I'd like to leave you with this thought, Money makes right. That's what all the politicians hunger for, regardless of what you may think."

At this, Jenny started shrinking in her seat and became rather non-verbal. This disgusted Nick because if she only knew what he had gone through for her, it could have cost him a long penitentiary term or even his life, and she showed no appreciation.

At this juncture Nick decided to make his goodbyes, and if he never saw her again it would be her loss not his.

He called the airline as soon as he got back to the hotel and was able to book reservations for the next day, much to his relief.

Chapter Nine
Death of a Friend

His anxiety level was off the chart, and he just wanted to go home.

He got there late evening had his car parked at the airport and invited his two associates to stay with him, but they wanted to go home as bad as Nick did, so they declined the invitation.

He knew in this big house, even though it had state of the art security, with cameras all over the place, it was still lonesome and a little scary. He vowed that the next day he would start looking for trained security dogs that would also function as man's best friend, and hire a full time superintendent that would live on the property. But that was tomorrow, tonight he would just have to be lonesome and introspective, that's the way you become when there's no one to talk to. Oh what the hell, he would turn on all the TV's in the house.

Morning could not come too soon for Nick. When building this magnificent estate loneliness was something that never occurred to him.

He immediately set out after Breakfast to alleviate this situation. But this was not going to be as easy as he had thought, First of all, the dog trainers that he contacted told him what he wanted in a dog would be best if he raised them from pups. This created more bonding and in this way if he wanted a best friend as he said he did, that's what it would take. Nick pictured in his mind two magnificent German Sheppard's.

If this is what he wanted, he had to go to a professional breeder, and take a look at the Sire and the Dam. Dog's, just as humans, take after their gene pool, so look at the parents, and you just may get dogs that look like them.

Next was finding a Superintendent. It was not unlike searching for dogs.

He had special considerations; somebody that needed a good paying job, had to be reliable, a nice person, no criminal record, preferably not married, and no children, not to mention someone he could stand to see and talk to day after day.

How in the hell do you find someone like this. Suddenly a light went on. The kid that Nick knew from his old high school football team that he had hired to go with him when he met Trado, Joey Russell 6'3" 290 pounds and a sweet guy if there ever was one. He would absolutely fill the bill; all he had to do was find him. Off to the Capri he went that night looking for Joey.

Entering the pub he was met with an explosion of cheerful greetings, sort of like a long lost brother that had made it big and returned to celebrate his good fortune.

But that's not exactly the way it was, there was an undercurrent of watchful waiting to see if Nick had changed, and of course he had changed, he carried much more responsibility and there were aspects of his chosen profession that made laughter a much rarer occurrence. He was no longer the hale, hearty and well met, and the hell with it all, that he had been. He was a little more distant to his friends. The problem being that what they had in common was not the same anymore.

Nick asked around about Joey, and asked if he still came in. Someone volunteered that they hadn't seen Joey as much since he got married. Well what did Nick expect, that time would stand still just for him. They pointed out where Joey lived on Redondo Dr. near the Capri.

The one thing Nick had to do is see Rennie Servino, and he was nowhere to be seen, he hollered out where the hell is Rennie. Someone said, hey we thought you knew he's in the hospital, had a heart attack, and is not doing well.

Jesus Christ what the fuck hospital is he in. He was told Saint Elizabeths.

Nick raced to the hospital entered at Admitting and asked to see Rennie. The receptionist referred Nick to some of the family that was sitting in the reception area.

Rennie was in I.C.U. and could not have visitors at this time. Nick went directly to the family sitting in the reception area to express his concern and maybe to mention some encouraging utterances. He was informed that Rennie was not expected to live. He had a massive heart attack.

Nick was stricken by this news after all this was the guy if not for him Nick would not be where he was today. He not only got him started but backed him with his own resources and never asked for anything.

He thought as he was leaving that he owed Rennie big time. He would see to it that Rennie's grandchildren would have a decent start on their future education.

He would establish a well-funded trust in their names.

Even this thought did not alleviate his profound grief at the impending loss of a close friend and benefactor.

All things eventually come to an end, whether it's an endeavor or an era that you once encountered that no longer exists.

In our youth, we were full of energy, ideas, plans, hope, and we were out to grab life and shake it and dance on it and make it ours. But alas all of that falls by the wayside, and we are left with our aches, pains, and memories.

Continuing his search for Joey he heads for Redondo Rd., and goes to the address that he had been given. The door is answered by a comely looking woman whom Nick assumed was Joey's wife.

Using his powers of observation he noticed the toys strewn about, that could only mean one thing there was a child or children occupying this residence. He asked, is Joey home? She said Joey was still at work. Nick introduced himself and asked where Joey worked. He was presently employed at a paint and body shop on Belmont Ave. Nick knew of it and he was off, making that his next stop.

When he arrived at the facility, he spotted Joey and simultaneously Joey spotted him, they were happy to see each other and rushed to shake hands. After going through the preliminaries, Nick got to the reason he was here. He told Joey what he needed in a Super and asked, "If Joey would be interested?" Joey said, "You can bet I would." Nick asked "how many children it would involve," Joey said, "two, one that was both of theirs, and one that she had with her previous marriage."

Nick invited Joey and his wife over that night for dinner which Nick fully intended to be catered. This would give Joey a better perspective of the job. It would allow Nick to assess the qualifications of Joey's wife.

Nick's intention was to offer the position of housekeeper to her if he thought her qualified.

The dinner went well, and Nick found Joey's wife, Elizabeth, who he called Liz, was a lovely woman, and just what Nick ordered in a housekeeper. It was a forgone conclusion; they were hired, and prepared to take charge of this cavernous Estate.

Chapter Ten
Setting up the Kingdom

In the next couple of weeks, Nick was able to concentrate on his business. It was getting to that time of year when the playoffs were in full swing in baseball and the start of the exhibition season in football. He also had to be in contact with all of the members of the CCC (Congress of Concerned Citizens) and see that everybody was happy, hale and hearty; any that were not in good shape, either their health or their financial health, would become Nick's job to see that someone would be assigned to take care of the situation. If it was their general health, than he had to see that they were taken care of with the necessary health providers, if they were having financial problems, then Nick would assign a financial advisor to find out what the problem was and arrange for a solution, if it involved money, then loans were available.

If possible, he tried to talk to each member individually. Nick believed that personal contact was the one constant that everybody wanted.

He was frequently appearing in the news media and TV, donating to charitable causes and supporting projects for the betterment of the city. With Nick's rising profile in the media it made his job a little easier. Everybody felt privileged to speak to him.

The following year was an election year, and Nick intended to become a force in the local political machine, joining the Democratic party was a given, of course attending every meeting of the city council or any meeting that would be publicized on T. V. whether that was a water meeting, or streets and infrastructure meetings, would be necessary, and he wanted to meet all the candidates running for public office. Nick intended to contribute to the ones that had a realistic chance of winning.

The party he was planning for his new home was going to be opulent in structure with every VIP in the state attending. Possibly the Governor of the state could be enticed to attend if he was alerted to the fact that political donations may be in the offering.

Nobody was sure exactly what Nick did for a living other than a financial Shaman. It was suggested that he was a gambler but only in closed circles. Even though he had organized the CCC, he was only its advisor.

Nick's business was running smoothly with the three guys he had manning the phones and two more that handled the pay-offs. This enabled him to create a distance from his business. The folks doing transactions with the firm never knew with whom they were doing business.

Nick's persona took on more and more of a Great Gatsby look, and that's the way he wanted it.

The thirst for money however is and was never ending. He now was becoming a direct descendant of Tommy Trado. Everybody had to contribute to the pot, and if you want to call it protection money, then so be it.

It was imperative that he start branching out. There were communities all over Ohio that were in need of well-organized facilities to satisfy their need to gamble.

When he went into a new potential area, he had to find out who might be operating there. If he found they were a well-connected operation he would simply walk away. If it was a well-run operation but independent, Nick would than induce them to ally with him and receive certain benefits in the way of protection. Monthly tributes were expected. However if an organization that was well run did not exist, than Nick would set up his own operation.

His problems arose from the operators that had no intention of paying for protection.

Here are the steps that were followed:

1) Send emissaries to sit down and talk.

2) Send emissaries that were more menacing.

3) Take physical action; Smoke Bomb their businesses. This action did not hurt anyone but it sent a strong odiferous message.

4) A physical confrontation possibly resulting in a short hospital stay for the recalcitrant member.

If the individual was still being obstinate, the next step in his plan, threaten his patrons. This would give them pause if they continued to do business with him.

Generally, it never reached stage four.

Nick knew the importance of having tight audit controls and many times disciplinary action would have to be taken that generally involved actions one and two of the foregoing list and solve the problem.

With Nick expanding his influence, both Cleveland and Pittsburgh were taking an ever-increasing interest in his operations. Nick was candid with both of them. He did not want to run into any problems with either one. He explained that as "long as his gross take increased, the amount of grease they got each month was growing."

111

Nick was scrupulous in his bookkeeping and invited each of the contending factions to look over his operation at will.

Chapter Eleven
A Lifelong Love

Nick's ambition did not end at this point in his career. A thing that he had secretly harbored in his heart all his life was a love of horses and horseracing. He wanted to own a Racing Stable with a string of the most exquisite mounts that money could buy.

With his success came the Capital to facilitate this move into his fantasyland. He did have a penchant for planning his moves carefully, but there had been times in his life when he bit off more than he could chew.

The problem with racing; the money that is expended on this sport was and is enormous. The names that were in this thing were names like Phipps, Fairchild, Vanderbilt, and Bradley Hughes of Spendthrift Farms. These are not millionaires these are billionaires. Nick though well off was nowhere near the caliber of these farms. But knowing this did not discourage him.

Nick was a voracious reader of the Racing Form; he was not unfamiliar with the trainers, owners, and jockeys of his time.

As he thought about this endeavor, he decided to contact a skilled trainer before he purchased a colt.

He was in the habit of visiting Thistledown in Cleveland. The next time he went, he started paying close attention to the trainers that were running horses at this track.

The trainers that were running at this minor track were generally small owners and maybe had a little farm, and another job, and were just getting by. The reason they continued doing this was for the love of the sport. So it was a struggle for the owners, the trainers, the jockeys, and the track.

When Nick made an appearance there with his contingent of high rollers, they made quite a splash. They were loud and boisterous and flashed copious amounts of rolled up greenbacks.

They never stopped at the two-dollar windows but continued to the enclosed fifty-dollar window.

As they left the booth, there was always a group of people asking what you had bet on? The rationale being, if you were so successful that you could place bets at the $50 dollar window you must know something that was not generally known to the rest of the racing crowd.

Nick became a regular visitor to this track. On one particular day, a horse was running that seemed a little out of place at Thistledown. This horse had quite an outstanding pedigree and had been purchased by a group of investors.

The horse's name; "Magnificent One." This horse was impressive looking, appearing to be over 17 hands high. As he came out for the pre-race warm-up he was remarkably well mannered, and Nick's contingent decided to put a rather large wager on this animal.

The Race was one and 1/16 mile. At the start, the colt just bided his time running comfortably in the middle of the pack. At the top of the stretch, he exploded and won the race going away and getting stronger.

Nick's entire contingent rushed to cash their winning tickets. Redeeming these would not produce much in the way of a return on invested capital; the colt had gone off as a 6 to 5 favorite.

Nick just sat there, watching until the horse, the owner, and the trainer entered the winners circle.

He once more looked at the Racing Form and saw that the trainer was a female by the name of Holly Hutton, out of Clariden Farm. He wanted to get a closer look at the trainer and the syndicate that owned this horse.

When they gathered in the winner's circle, he was surprised to see a considerable consortium of what he took to be people associated with this horse. He managed to get a pretty good look at the trainer who was sporting a beautiful head of long, flaming-red hair.

Her face had a no nonsense air about it, but pretty nonetheless, and as he looked her over he thought to himself, "somebody had to help her into the Jeans she was wearing, they were that tight."

At this point, Nick decided that the horse would become his.

Nick and his group trouped into the backstretch where the barnes were located and found the Clariden Farm stable.

Magnificent One was still being hot walked and groomed. No one in particular seemed to be around.

The guys waited and talked among themselves.

One of them asked Nick "how much he knew or thought he knew about the Racing game?"

"Nick said zilch, Natta, zip, but if I want to know more I'll study it and then hire the best horse people I can find."

"Actually, I probably know more than you think I do because I have been a bettor all my life. My father was a top-notch bookie. I can remember hanging out at Randall Park Race Track when I was eight or nine years old. But much of what I absorbed about horses came from a horse riding stable called Charlie's. It was located just north of Belmont Avenue in Youngstown."

"When I was young, I would clean out stalls or anything I could do to cadger a free ride on one of the nags he had. So you see, I've had a lifelong love affair with horses."

Into the barn came Magnificent One, with his hot walker, who was actually the trainer with the red hair.

She did it all, trained, fed, cleaned the stalls, booked the races, hired the jockey's, and hauled the horses back and forth to the farm.

If the truck broke down, guess who the mechanic was? She was also the veterinarian on most minor problems that occurred, and some major ones, if the money was not available for the real thing.

She was also the organizer of the syndicate of 15 people that bought Magnificent One.

Nick tried to stop her as she was bringing the horse to the stall.

He said, "Just a minute Holly I want to have a word with you."

She brushed past him and muttered, "Goddammit I don't have the time right now, see me later." Holly figured it was just another bill collector being bolder than most.

He caught up with her, held her by the arm, and said "I want to buy this colt," she said, "are you fuckin crazy he's the best thing I've got in my barn, and if you don't let go of my arm I'll call the Goddamn Gendarmes and holler bloody murder that you are molesting me."

Nick was caught by surprise at the pure audacity of this bitch; he had a feeling of impotence. He decided to let it go at this point, do the smart thing, and think about it. He would not let her off easy; she would pay for this bit of impudence.

As they drove home that night, Nick became the butt of masterly teasing by his cohorts. Comments tended to be a little on the side of being emasculated, like, "hey Nick got any cohunes left, you shouldn't have tried to rape that Red Head, you're no match for her. The next time she may rape you," and other remarks that he took good naturedly, but it did burn a little.

Ever since he had Joey, Liz and their children move in, his home was bright and looked extremely inviting. He never thought he would enjoy having children around, but they have made his house a home.

The German Sheppard's are growing up and you could tell they were going to be handsome beasts, but he didn't think he could make legitimate watchdogs out of them, never the less they were going to be excellent pets. They had too much interaction with humans and were loved and petted too much. Maybe just the sight of these dogs would scare some strangers.

He told everybody in the house about the Racehorse he was going to buy. The whole household was upbeat about this turn of events.

The children were particularly excited and had a million questions, and wanted to know "when they could see and pet this horse."

"Nick promised that soon he would take them to the track and maybe they could even ride him."

Nick had his hands full planning the party for the opening of the house, and thinking about the problem of obtaining this horse, and his entry into the racing game.

About this time, he decided to have his party on February 14 Valentine's day. He thought it would be impressive to combine a Valentine Dance and the Grand opening of his Estate.

In his imagination, he could see the house all decorated for this party. Nick hoped he wasn't biting off more than he could chew. Hell he might even have to take dancing lessons, oooweee that may be taking things too far.

He searched for, and found the location of Clariden Farms in a suburb of Cleveland called Chardon, a small town composed mostly of farms and pastureland.

As soon as he could, He drove there to meet and see this Holly character hoping she would be there when he arrived. He drove up the long driveway unchallenged.

On to the porch, he strode and boldly banged on the door. There was an absence of a response from inside the home, so he decided to go to the barn where possibly someone may be working.

He found Holly and one of her hands busily tossing hay and cleaning stalls.

As he approached her, she looked up and spying Nick said "Jesus Christ what are you doing out here." She didn't know if she should be worried or not. She's thinking who the hell is this guy, some kind of stalker? Instead of laying down the pitchfork she held it tightly in her roughened hands.

"Don't come any closer; I can hear you plainly from where you are now."

"Holly you don't know me, but I can assure you that I mean you no harm. I was hoping you would have lunch with me and discuss business."

"If your business is trying to buy Big Mo—short for Magnificent One— than you are wasting my time and yours."

"Listen to me, I come in friendship, and the least you can do is accept a free lunch."

She thought about this offer with a modicum of resistance and finally decided this guy did not seem to present a danger to her, and accepted the offer.

She said, "down the road about 1/4 mile is a restaurant called Skeeters 19th hole. Meet me there in one hour."

At the appointed time, Nick arrived, and decided to take a table in the outdoor area where he felt that it would be more in keeping with the general character of the surroundings. A more beautiful day would be hard to find.

The ambience alone might sway her to his way of thinking. He doubted that, but it was worth a try.

She entered with a bold and feisty manner, spotted him, and trouped over.

"Let's order, I could eat a horse," and that she did, with a large hamburger and a heaping order of French fries.

Nick, ever conscious of his weight ate considerably less.

Now, he got down to business.

The first order of business was to introduce himself.

"Holly my name is Nick Lasko from Youngstown. I want you to know that I am a person that is well known and if you ask any of your friends from Youngstown they will be able to tell you of my reputation. I came today to make a proposal for Big Mo. I understand that you have not made this horse available, but it has been my experience that when the money on the table reaches a certain point, availability reaches another level. Now if you would, tell me where the availability point is on this colt."

Holly drank all this in, and responded, "I know you Mr. Lasko, you're a well know gangster from Youngstown, so I don't have to ask around, you're used to getting your way, but on this occasion that's not going to happen."

"Hold on a second, I strongly object to being called a gangster. You may not know this but I do a substantial amount of good, and donate to an excessive amount of charities. If I may ask, what charity do you support other than yourself, and by the way, my giving doesn't stop with the national charities but also on a personal level too."

"So get off your high and mighty ways or you may find yourself without a horse, without a farm, without a home, and other unpleasant things could happen. Carefully watch your attitude.

"Now let's get down to business and eradicate any bad blood there may be between us.

Remember you will never again call me a gangster."

Holly realized for the first time whom she was dealing with, and he was extremely dangerous indeed.

119

Holly said, "Give me a chance to think about it."

Nick said, "I will meet you the same time, same place tomorrow. Don't be late; here is my phone number, call me for any reason except to cancel our appointment."

Nick did not want to fuck around anymore; from here on out it would be hardball. But when thinking about Holly, she seemed to be a hard ass broad, maybe just the kind of trainer he would need.

Tomorrow was another excellent day, and they got down to business without the usual preliminaries.

Nick said, "Give me a number." Holly was more pliable now after doing her homework and asking around about Nick, and finding out that he was more formidable than she had imagined. She now knows that the horse would be sold, so she put a number on the table after she explained that she would get a cut, and then 15 other investors are standing in line to get their share.

Because this is a syndicate, she would need to have the other owners sign off on any sale of Big Mo, However, if the money is right, I believe the acquisition will go smoothly. The figure on the table, $200,000.

"For some reason that figure is not reasonable, what was the thinking behind this figure?"

"Well the syndicate paid $100,000, and because this horse is a winner with an exceptional pedigree, he is worth $200,000."

"Let me point out, Big Mo has been running at a cheap track. What the hell is going to happen when we bring him to Gulf Stream, or Belmont? Shit we may have to drop him into claimers? I'll tell you what, take $150,000 and don't be greedy."

"That's the only offer you will get from me. If this one is not accepted, then the other offers may not be in the form of cash. There is one other stipulation. You will be employed by me as my trainer, at a remarkably handsome yearly income plus expenses, it will be worth your while."

"My God you're pushy. You may steal my horse, but you will not steal my life.

"Listen to me, you can spend your life farting around on little two bit tracks or you can be racing at Belmont, Churchill downs, Aqueduct or Gulf Stream, and having horse flesh that can run with that company. Your choice. Think about it."

"You have until dark tomorrow to reply to my offer. After that I'll forget about you."

The next day the meeting took place and Holly acquiesced to Nick's offer, but she wanted some clarification. "She wanted to know if she would be in complete charge of the operation?"

Nick said, "Holly, I expect you to run this in an entirely independent manner. If I have questions or concerns, I will directly contact you. If your performance is not up to my standards, I will replace you.

"Excuse me, but I would have never accepted your offer if I did not think that I was unable to give 110%."

"Even though you still own the farm I will expect it to be properly staffed, clean, and spotless in every way. Have I made myself clear? One other thing, I will expect you to accompany me to the auctions in Kentucky and New York and assist in the selection of additions to our stable."

Holly replied, "I don't intend to train any horses I personally did not have a say in their selection. That's an area of expertise that I excel in."

"If I may be so bold, I would like to know if there are any problems in your personal life that would infringe on you doing a yeomen's job for me."

"If you mean a love life, rest assured none exists, and no intentions for future relationships at this time."

"Please keep me informed as to the condition of Big Mo and when he will be racing."

With that, the meeting was over, and Nick could get back to the other problems back home.

Chapter Twelve
The Eternal Problem Money

As soon as Nick reached home he was informed that Larry Ditullio wanted to speak to him.

Larry speaking slowly and deliberately, said, "Nick, what the hell is this shit that you are going into the horse racing business, is this true or have I been given the right fuckin' information? which I hope is a figment of someone's imagination, or are you getting' fuckin' senile?"

Nick admitted, "Yes it's true."

"Then we are requesting that you give up some of your other operations. Nick, this horseracing is a losing proposition and frankly you can't afford to take on any more debt. Do you realize how much you owe to the pension fund?"

"Larry, I need to have the guys give me a chance. A little breathing room is all I need."

"Nick, you have a hefty payment coming due in thirty nine days. If you don't make it, you have big problems. I don't care how popular or important you think you are, when it comes due, they will want their money."

Nick worried, but knew he couldn't show it. "Don't worry about it Larry."

"How are you going to take care of all the pies you have your fingers in?"

"It's not a problem, you guys know I run a tight operation, and so far everyone is getting their share of the vig."

"Okay, you got the silver tongue right now, but let's hope nobody puts any acid on it."

Nick realized that he probably was a little over his head and it was a tossup if he could meet the payment on his debt to the pension fund. He knew he could always borrow from the CCC, but that was something he was loath to do. The other option— the one he was depending on— Big Mo was running a large money race in two weeks at Belmont that would involve quite a bit of wampum.

He needed to find out who the trainers were of the favored horses and approach them with a proposition that would be hard to ignore, and painful if they did.

They only had to hold their entries back and make sure they allow other horses to progress ahead of their horse, and Nick would cut up the purse in equal shares. Of course the other part of the equation was the amount of money they could win betting on the horse they, or Nick's associates would make known just before the race, as long as they place their bets through a bookie and not at the track where they would affect the odds.

There were two trainers who had horses entered that had the speed to beat Big Mo. Nick sent two emissaries to carry on conversations with them and to relay the propositions.

One of the trainers was very amenable to the action and one was not, and he— who forever more would be known as the Prick—made a full report to the racing commission. In neither case was the name of the horse that was supposed to be the winner mentioned.

After the emissaries assured the amenable trainer the deal would be consummated, a substantial amount of money-changed hands, and the emissaries disappeared.

As the appointed day of the race approached an awful thing took place. The recalcitrant trainer who had balked at the offer withdrew his horse because of a mysterious lameness that appeared the morning of the race. But that's racing for you, the strangest things seem to happen when you least expect them.

Big Mo won, but Nick sweated out a close call with another horse that was not expected to contend. If Mo had not won, Nick would have been in much hot water.

Following the race, Nick was faced with the problem of what type of retribution he had to inflict on the offending trainer.

The intractable one was even now hollering to high heaven about the damage done to his highly regarded horse and demanding an investigation.

Nick intended to make sure this trainer never again gave him a problem. In fact, he would try to put him out of the game if at all possible.

It wasn't long before the New York Racing Commission and the Attorney General's office issued subpoenas to anyone who may have been involved in fixing the race, and of course, the winning horse's owner and trainer were issued Subpoenas. That meant Holly and Nick's presence would be required at the hearing.

Of course the news splashed all over the Youngstown newspapers almost before Nick received his subpoena. He immediately contacted Vinnie Solerno asking him to recommend a top notch New York Attorney; Vinnie gave him the name of a prominent lawyer that had participated in much work for the Genovese Family who was the real Capo DiTutti Capi of the Pittsburgh organization. This information was not generally known even among members of the Famiglia. His name was Gerald Hamm, and he had many connections in the political structure of New York State.

When Holly received the subpoena, her anger reached a boiling point. She did not stop to phone Nick but got in her car and raced to Nick's office in Youngstown.

Holly arrived with her anger reaching unreasonable levels, got out of her car slamming doors on her way to confront Nick and bolted into his office hollering at the top of her voice, "You dirty sonofabitch, you rotten cockroach, you are one of the most real low-life bastards that I have ever run across. You take over my life, cheat me out of one of finest pieces of horseflesh I have ever owned and the very first race with Big Mo, you conspire to fix it. What the hell is wrong with you, Nick? Are you just an inherent cheat who can't do anything that's clean and good and ruin all those around you?"

"Calm down Holly." Nick said

Holly could not be placated and went on to say "For the first time in my life I'm being called up to be questioned about a race that was apparently fixed. You know it will be in the Cleveland Newspapers, and Clariden Farms will forever after have its reputation besmirched, whether its true or not, and the tentacles of this creature you have created will reach out to enfold me and devour all that I have tried to build."

"Holly you have not given me a chance to respond and defend myself," Nick said in a quiet reasonable tone.

" Don't give me that shit; I've heard enough about you that tells me you had something to do with the fix being in."

"Holly I'm trying very hard not become angry and upset, because the absolute truth is that I am innocent of these charges. Let's start by you telling me what you have heard that has given you such a negative image of what I do."

"Well one thing, you are a bookmaker and have control over most of the bookmakers in this state, I have heard you are associated with the mob wise guys, and that you shake people down for protection money."

"Have you also been informed that I lie, cheat, and steal?"

"After what has just happened, I do not think I need to be informed."

"I'm sorry, have you and your friends been disappointed with the $150,000 I paid for their colt? Have you been disappointed with the salary, and commissions plus generous expenses you have been receiving?"

"I want to say this…"

"For God sake Holly keep your dam mouth shut. Frankly I'm tired of the vilification and scorn that you have directed my way. If you will return home and inform all the investors in Big Mo that I will be happy to return the horse to its previous status if they will return my $150,000."

"I believe it's too late for that."

"No, it's not too late, I'm sure you would like to think that way."

"So I did not steal your horse, its more than likely you felt that it was a steal from me on the price you got for that colt. Let me further inform you that the number of charities that I contribute to is far greater than anything you have done, and I would include all your friends in that statement."

"Look Nick, don't try to make yourself look like a saint."

"Goddamit Holly, I know that you do not want to hear this, but many of the things I have done was for the betterment of families whose only interest in this life is to make a living as best they can."

"Did you know that all the small bookmakers who have been complaining that they are being shook down now have a union called the CCC that provides them protection against competition, and they now have free health insurance for their entire family? Including interest free loans if they run into hard times, not to mention the CCC will be by their side in good times and bad. Now can you guess whose idea this was and who organized it? Now can you guess who contributes large amounts of money to political candidates and is active in getting the best people into office? Have you done any of this stuff or even thought about being involved in your community. Have you thought and contributed to the children who have exceptional problems such as M. S.? Have you volunteered to help at the shelter for the homeless. As for those Mob Wise guys, yes they do engage in gambling, prostitution, loan sharking and other things that only exist because people want them."

"Since you're sounding off, tell me about all the car bombings in Youngstown. These are taken so lightly that they have a acquired a name all their own, they are referred to as—car tune ups."

"Murders happen because of conflicts among themselves and never involves their families. It happens in the course of doing business. It's not like our legal system where if a guy is condemned to death it takes ten years or more to carry out the sentence. In the Mob, if a sentence of death is declared it's carried out immediately."

"I did not need a fuckin' speech"

"Oh, you absolutely needed to hear this speech."

"Nick, I am angry, and for that I am sorry, but Goddamit you did not have to insult my intelligence with your choir boy act."

Ignoring her last utterings he went on to say, "Now you have vented on me and me on you, and I am giving you my guarantee that I had nothing to do with what occurred at Belmont.

"I will try to put this behind me and not let it fester like an open sore."

"When you are in a high profile position as I have become, then you can expect things like this to come along." "Why in the world would I try to fix a race when I had the best horse in that field? Does that make sense to you? If it does, then you are not as smart as I thought you were."

"Nick, I want to believe you, but all of the signs are pointing the other way."

127

"Holly, look at me, I am at this moment working on a meeting with the commission. After I tell them the real story, I do not believe you will have to appear before them. So rest easy and we will straighten out this matter in a very amicable manner."

A meeting was established for the following week with the New York Commission. Nick vowed to not get involved in anything like this again. However the matter of the reluctant trainer has to be taken care of. But all in good time, no hurry.

Chapter Thirteen
The Commission

The more Nick thought about the grand opening of his house, the more he realized he needed a professional to plan, and organize, and decorate the Estate.

As he was pondering this conundrum, a faint flicker presented itself in his mind which he immediately dismissed, but it kept coming back, the name that was firing wildly in his brain, *Jennifer Lake*, the more he thought about it the more he realized she would make a perfect host, but that was something he would work on later, right now his thoughts had to stay on the meeting with the commission.

Nick called Gerald Hamm and invited Gerald for dinner Wednesday evening the night before the commission meeting, this way they could plan what would be said there.

After getting an agreement from Gerald, Nick said, "I'll meet you at your office and we will go from there."

Nick flew to New York Tuesday morning and checked into The Plaza. He, freshened up, dressed, and arrived at Mr. Hamm's office at five.

His offices were impressive to the eye, the furnishings were luxurious, but not in an overstated way, in other words it was not ostentatious.

His secretary, who was still there, was businesslike and had a long leggy appearance, wore glasses and a no-nonsense demeanor.

She ushered Nick into the inner sanctum. Gerald or Jerry as he preferred to be called was an extremely affable person, Had an imposing height probably 6'2" with a face that exuded good nature and a structure that inherently made you want to smile back.

Jerry said, "Nick I am so glad to meet you. Vinnie has told me so much about you that it made me anticipate this meeting much more than the usual clients. Don't get me wrong they are all interesting to me but it is tiresome hearing about the marital woes that so many people seem to have. Even though I am happily married with two beautiful children I believe that I would advise anybody thinking about getting married; don't! Of course I'm being facetious and I only wish that everybody could be as happily married as I am."

"Well Jerry, I'm not married yet, even though I've had some very close calls. In my business it requires that I'm away from home many evenings and things happen unexpectedly which requires my absence from my domicile, such as this commission thing which is completely bogus."

Nick, erase any thoughts of this thing from your mind, we will take care of it tomorrow, but for this evening let's enjoy ourselves."

"Jerry do you have a restaurant in mind."

"As a matter of fact I do, Jack Dempsey's comes to mind and if you have never been there you will be pleasantly pleased. Maybe Jack himself will be there to greet us."

Nick was thinking this is a first class guy, no wonder he is a very successful attorney, he looks like a person that could sway any jury and sweet talk the birds out of the trees.

When they arrived at Dempsey's Jack Dempsey was not there to greet them but they were certainly treated with respect and dignity and it seemed that Jerry received a warm welcome.

When the Wine steward came to our table, Jerry said "Nick don't let me influence you please order what you want. I personally do not drink so I will not be ordering." This impressed Nick, he asked Jerry, "Why he did not drink,"

"I find that it impairs the mental process, and for me to be the best I can be I need to be sharp and brilliant in every way. A good lawyer must be thinking of his next case with all of his senses as finely tuned as a winning race car, for instance tonight I will be watching you to see what your personality is like. Do you have a temper, or are you rather laid back, are you a good actor, or do you come across as a person that has an ego problem. All of this will determine how much I want your input tomorrow in front of the commissioners."

"Much of what happens and the kind of decision we receive is many times based on how the defendant is perceived not what the truth is. It should not be that way but unfortunately that is the reality and we must deal in realities."

The banter continued in a light vein and as the evening wore on it couldn't have been more delightful but perhaps the cuisine had something to do with that.

Nick gave him a synopsis of his background but of course he would not tell him everything, Nick found out through bitter experience that the less people know about you the better it was.

Jerry asked some rather pointed questions about the related murders that Youngstown was noted for, in response Nick replied, "That he didn't know any more then he read in the papers" and directed the conversation away from anything having to do with the Cosa Nostra. Jerry persisted in questioning what Nick did for a living, "He replied I made quite a bit of money in some very lucky investments, and I parlayed that

131

money into other avenues that in most cases have turned out to be like gold."

Jerry said, "What would you consider your most successful venture.

"Jerry, without bragging there were many of them, you see I have all of my life tried to help the little guy in whatever his endeavor was. A particular one that comes to mind was an organization that I created called the Congress of Concerned Citizens composed of small entrepreneurs that were being snuffed out by larger competitors. By organizing we were able to give them a modicum of protection from unfair competition, health insurance for themselves, their families and their employee's also a bank that they can tap if for any reason they run into money problems, not to mention a forum for them to elucidate and receive support for any perceived problems they may have, and seek remedies for them. So you see my one mission in life is to better humanity."

"Well Nick you have impressed me, not what you have accomplished but the way you say it. Tomorrow you will have a bigger role to play, and I will take the smaller subjugated role. I will be there to help if needed, but I like the way you emote."

Jerry obviously felt that a heartfelt statement from Nick would carry more of an impact then a statement from an attorney. His instincts were generally right on.

Jerry and Nick arrived a bit early at the office of the Commission. The place was nondescript and a little threadbare but this did not alleviate the anxiety that was felt by Nick, as a matter of fact his juices were now flowing and he felt rather put upon, and reflecting on the fact that he was singled out because he won a horse race.

As they entered the chambers of the commission, seated behind a long table were 3 men with a very serious and stern look on their faces.

Everybody was introduced and at least one of the Commissioners knew Jerry and they were familiar with each other, judging from the salutations that took place.

Jerry and Nick sat in two chairs placed in front of the long table.

The Commissioner, that seemed to be in the forefront of this inquisition— that's what Nick felt it would be— shuffled a sheaf of papers in front of him and seemingly reading from them said "Nick Lasko, you have been brought before this commission to explain and defend yourself from certain allegations that have been made that a particular horse race you participated in may have been compromised in a manner that may have some indication of a criminal act."

"If I may, you are talking about a criminal act, what if you please, would that be?"

"It is a criminal act to fix a race, and a prized race horse has been permanently injured at an irreplaceable cost to the owner of that horse."

"Again, if I may, please indicate to me the evidence that has been presented to this Commission, that what has been alleged is of a true nature?"

"We have an affidavit from the horse owner. He that he had been approached by two men who requested that his horse be restrained during that particular race."

"And how about the injury to the horse, what is the evidence that the injury did not occur during the normal course of training that happens frequently to active race horses, and was not just accidental?"

"Well Mr. Lasko, there is no explicit evidence on this, other than coincidental with those men having approached that trainer."

"And of course the word of a disappointed trainer will be taken as the gospel truth."

"I think you can understand that all allegations must be investigated. That is our job."

"Are any other trainers or owners being brought up before this commission?"

"Not at this time."

"If I may present to you what my concerns are; First and foremost I am not guilty of these heinous acts as you seem to want to put on my shoulders alone. Given the fact that I am the only owner called before this body, not to mention the matter of the missed time from my business and the cost of the plane, the cost of the hotel, and the cost of hiring an attorney to represent me in this matter.

My trainer is highly upset and has threatened to quit.

My reputation for philanthropy in my state is unequalled.

I am a contributor to practically every known cause that has anything to do with the little guy or the segment of our population that is unable to help themselves, because of mental illness or a job loss that may have caused them to lose their home and threaten their families with improper nutrition."

"Because of this Commission, my name has been bantered about in the newspapers causing my good name to be muddied, and this has happened on unsubstantiated charges connected to *horse race fixing,* and I'm the only one being investigated. Well how would that look to you if you were reading the papers? It makes me look like I'm guilty even before the facts are presented."

If it is possible, I will confer with my attorney to see if there are any civil actions that can be contemplated against this Commission.

However the least I would expect is a statement completely exonerating me and my trainer of any charges connected to this incident and is disseminated to the proper news organizations."

"Mr. Lasko we are sorry for any inconvenience that this issue has caused you, understand we are only doing our job."

"To have only called on me is not doing your job. The fix, if there was one, could have been done by anybody, whether or not they owned or trained horses, but to have zeroed in on me was a definite miscarriage of your duties that has caused irreparable damage to both myself and my trainer, and by inference anyone that is associated with me. I am at this time requesting that you have the decency to cancel the subpoena you have served on my trainer. Also, please notify the papers, in her, or any area, where this erroneous news has been disseminated, and tell them this commission has completely exonerated myself and my staff, and explaining she, Holly Hutton and Clariden Farms has been completely absolved of any wrongdoing."

"Mr. Lasko, be assured we will do all in our power to clear up any misconceptions that this investigation has caused. We certainly had no intention of this very private incident getting into the media, and for that we are sorry."

You have made a very interesting presentation of how this has affected you and maybe we have stampeded, and alluded to innuendo that we should have treated as such before coming to any conclusions."

"Of course your trainer will not have to appear. Tell her she can disregard the subpoena and please do not leave your employ."

"This meeting is now at an end and this investigation will now be concluded. You are free to leave and we were delighted to hear your presentation which helped immensely in the termination of this incident. Thank you and God speed."

Jerry and Nick did not say a word until they got into the car and then Jerry started laughing so hard that tears were running down his cheeks, he said, "Nick where the hell did you get your oratory skills. It was beautiful you put them in such a position that they were ashamed of themselves."

"I myself wanted to cry when you talked about feeding the homeless. I did not have to say a thing and I'll tell you what, this ones on me. To keep a lawyer quiet is the eighth wonder of the world."

"Let me tell you something mister know it all, I had a secret and that secret is the reason I had them cowed."

"Well pray tell what was the secret?"

"The secret was I had a gun pointed at them."

"What the fuck are you talking about?"

"The gun was you, you were the gun, you and your reputation was the deciding thing in that room."

"They were not afraid of me, or taken in by my oratory, they know that the gun I had sitting next to me could have caused them unprecedented amounts of problems. That's the reason I wanted you in there even if all you had to do was look pretty. So go ahead and charge me you were worth it."

As soon as Nick returned to his office, he called Holly and gave her the news that she would not have to appear before the Commission and the newspapers would be informed.

Retractions of the original story would take place.

Holly seemed to be mollified.

Nick wanted to know, and asked somewhat pointedly, "Was she still employed by him or should he begin looking for another trainer."

Holly said, "She was still the trainer and has realized that she jumped to assumptions that were not justified. From now on she would try, as hard as it will be, to keep her mouth shut."

Nick for his part, felt it was a tremendous relief to have the onus of the race fixing charge lifted.

He had so many things to attend to that he would not need any more diversions. Except for one that kept tormenting him and the name was Jenny, should he or shouldn't he, what a conundrum; it was turning into a sore that would not heal.

He knew instinctively that he needed someone to do the job, even if he offered the position to her he did not think she would take it.

The other problem that was weighing on his mind was the forever search for more capital.

The estate that he had built was now a chain around his neck. He knew that he would have to take action and reduce his expenditures in this area or increase his income.

Fixing the race and getting the payoff had not been the answer he had envisioned. By the time he got through with all the expenses associated with that caper, he would have been better off if he had just let the horse run, and if he finished second he would have been further ahead.

A second place payoff would not have had to suffer the anxiety attacks Oh well, the profession that he had chosen inherently had a lot of fear and angst that came with it.

Chapter Fourteen
Casino

Thinking about the money problems finally led Nick to solutions that were not palatable to him:

 1. Put the estate on the market.

 2. Cancel any plans for an opening party for the estate.

 3. Forget about Jenny.

 4. Eliminate donations to various political parties and individuals.

 5. Let Joey and his family go, but he would find other work for them.

 Nick decided that these solutions were not agreeable to him. So the second solution came into play. He could try to expand his bookmaking operations to other states, but he felt that the opposition he would receive from other Famiglia may prove disconcerting.

 There was one conception that in Nick's fertile mind was outlandish and at the same time conceivable. A gambling casino, if he opened in the City of Youngstown, even though it was a huge risk— the mayor was already beholden to the Pittsburgh Family— It should prove to be a feasible operation.

He called Vinnie his contact between him and the Pittsburgh faction and told him what he was thinking. Vinnie said "Not a chance."

"Nick asked, why do you think this proposal would be a problem?"

Vinnie responded, "Use your head Nick; we have a nice relationship with the powers that be in Youngstown. If we stick this gambling stuff up their nose's there will probably be an uproar from the citizenry that would put too much pressure on everybody in the hierarchy of the town, the next thing you know, the citizens will want to change the powers that be.

Nick if you want to do a casino, pick a small burg that no one knows, with its own Sheriff, and a small population, and you can employ most of them in the casino, that way it lessens any protests that may develop."

"Vinnie, I know that sounds reasonable, but I'm thinking about the number of customers that I can attract way out in the boondocks, I may be sitting with my finger up my ass just like Bugsy Siegel did when he opened the Flamingo in Vegas. It didn't draw flies because it was too far away from anything. I want and need profits right now not tomorrow."

"Use that bright mind of yours and figure out how to attract a crowd."

"All right Vinnie here's the other problem, money! I would like the Pittsburgh and the Cleveland guys to come in with me and do most of the funding."

"Nick the one thing I can say, is you've got big cohunes. I'll tell you what, find the burg, and get together the plans and how you intend to operate, submit everything to us, and Cleveland, and then you may find collaboration with your plans. But it's going to have to be a very attractive situation to acquire any interest."

In the meantime while the foregoing febrile cerebral, and largely an iconoclastic endeavor that will never come to fruition,

139

was going on, Holly called, "I'm taking Big Mo up to Saratoga for two large races.

Nick said, "I understand they have a large auction at Saratoga. If you can, attend the auction, and if there's anything worthwhile bid on it up to $30,000 and let me know."

Nick hung up smiling, The Travers stakes is where Big Mo is entered and will be a highlight event with $750,000 purse, and he will also be entered in the Whitney with a $500,000 purse, each could be a great payoff and sorely needed.

Nick knew that spending money at the auction was a necessary situation, he had to start establishing a stable with horse's that will give a return on investment. He had to depend on Holly and if his assessment of her was correct, he would eventually have an enterprise that would greatly enrich his net worth.

When Holly was traveling to far off tracks it made sense to have more than one horse that you were trailering. Going with just one is very expensive. There was not only the cost of the van and trailer, but also the cost of stabling your horse, you had to pick up the cost of your trainers nourishment and lodging for her, and other incidentals that could amount to a pretty penny.

Now Nick was entering on another escapade that would require time and money. His first problem was finding the burgs that were potential sites for a Casino; they had to be places easily accessible with good transportation entries and exits. The trip had to be reasonable in cost and not prolonged in time. Of course, there was the problem of finding local officials who were obeisant and not so steeped in morality that making money for their region through the sin of gambling was not objectionable to them.

The first thing he did is get out a map, and start looking for the small townships close to population centers. He identified several with potential. Many of the small towns did

not have, their own constabulary, instead they were patrolled by
the state police, and that situation could present a problem.

The next problem was to see how many of these small
town mayors were amenable to going on the take.

He found a great place that was located extremely well,
very near vacation attractions, Sandusky and Cedar pointe, both
areas were growing very quickly. But a bright red light was
flashing in Nick's mind, how do you bring the two mob factions
together when the county was clearly in the Cleveland mob's
jurisdiction.

Nick felt with everybody getting a piece of the action, all
should be on board, In other words, just like buying stock in a
new business, you could bring the fathers of the county and the
cities, into this fantastic enterprise, and he, Nick, using his
powers of oratory could incubate dreams of untold amounts of
money being made from this escapade. Of course, Nick could
foresee that he would end up not advancing any capital of his
own, and why should he? After all, the whole undertaking was
Nick's baby, he alone was responsible for the outcome of this
endeavor.

Costing the mob money could lead to consequences not
pleasant to contemplate.

In Nick's mind the thought of Bugsy Sigel sprawled out
on his girlfriend's couch with many bullet holes through his
body and one directly in his eye, did give him pause. This was
the price Bugsy paid for costing the mob money.

Nick decided that he should talk to the people that
needed to be convinced.

First, the mayor of the city that was the most likely
prospect.

It was difficult to arrange a meeting until Nick was able
to heighten the mayors interest when he talked about the new
infusion of money and jobs that would be generated with this
new type of club that would provide top notch entertainment in
an exclusive venue, and would increase the tax base to the

entities involved, not to mention a little something for his retirement, so when he steps down from public office it will make the transition less painful.

The Mayor responded saying, "that he certainly could not condone any form of gambling in his jurisdiction. His hands would always remain clean, and he would listen to the elders and citizens that may have religious or moral objections to any form of gambling that would tear apart the community. Of course, if this business was operated in such a way that it benefited the entire community with jobs and additional capital, then he would certainly not interfere in the operation of such a fine enterprise."

When the meeting concluded Nick knew that this city official was in his pocket.

Next was the Chief of Police, He made an appointment with the head of this department and his assistant. He approached this confab with the same story that he gave the mayor, with a few minor exceptions.

After explaining to the two men what a wonderful type of enterprise he envisioned and making sure they understood the value that would accrue to them personally, he said, "of course he would want and welcome police protection that in any undertaking of this magnitude would require an increase in the number of men, patrol cars and extraneous amounts of equipment that my group will willingly underwrite." The two men realized that this would be an extension of their department, increasing their power, and potentially increasing their compensation.

The big problem still remained, the matter of bringing the warring factions within the organizations together, and make them realize the cash benefits this enterprise could generate.

The heads of the Cosa Nostra in both Cleveland and Pittsburgh were partially retired, so he had to project his proposal to Capo's that may not have the full authority to authorize such an ambitious project. He thought to himself, the hell with it, let Vinnie and Larry carry the ball.

One of the problems was the impossibility of putting something like this down in writing. The agreement has to all be verbal and he did not think that in the case of Larry he was a good enough salesman to carry it off. He had more confidence in Vinnie, a former lawyer.

Nick decided the best way was to get the two guys that were the most representative of each faction and pitch them in person.

Calls were made to Vinnie and Larry and they expressed their extreme pessimism in the project. Nick told both of them to get the best representative from each faction and arrange a meeting and have a dialogue with them.

A meeting was set for November and all felt Nick's estate would be the safest place to hold the get together. The Pittsburgh rep would be Stephano Guliano and Cleveland's rep would be Anthony Vilanotti.

Nick was not familiar with either one of them, but he was assured by Vinnie that they were very important, so be on his best behavior and don't become too overbearing.

Chapter Fifteen
The Grand Opening

In the meantime he had to do something about the grand opening of his home in February. This party would be of particular importance.

If he pulls this grand opening off as planned, it would increase his influence with the legislators, and he would become the go to guy for anyone seeking state or municipality contracts for anything of importance which would be the building of all infrastructures, roads, bridges, rights of way that would be required by railroads etc. Evan large entities, utility, water, gas, telephone, electric, garbage, and he would be able to provide this service on a fee basis with kickbacks or should I say a fee arrangement for the legislators that would be involved in the negotiations, to the charity of their choice. I think we can guess what charity that would be.

He called Jenifer in L.A. and found her extremely busy. He said Jenny, "Have you had any further troubles with the Union?"

"Not one iota of a problem, and I have you to thank for it. Fast Nick, I want you to know how much I appreciate all that you have done for me, and I would like to see you again."

"Jenny at the moment I am in the throes of planning the Grand opening party for my new estate. Everybody that is of importance in this state will be here, and I desperately need a hostess during that evening and I cannot think of anyone more charming and beautiful than you. Besides you owe me one."

Jennifer thought about it for a long moment, "When is this event to take place,"

"February 14 Valentine's Day, I intend to have the place festooned with hearts to compliment your heart shaped face and adorned with roses which will harmonize with your beautiful eyes."

"Fast Nick, I will do it, but handling such a festivity and celebration of the opening of your estate, I'm sure will take me a while to become acclimated to the various personalities and their station in life. I will need to arrive about a week or two ahead of time."

"I don't mean to be forward or suggest anything, but I want you to stay in my place while working things out. My superintendent, his wife, and children reside in one wing of my home. I will have a special part of the home where you can ensconce yourself."

"My, that sounds like a large place."

"It is very large; I may have gone a little overboard when building it. I hope you will be pleased with it when you arrive."

After this conversation was completed, Nick was elated; he had solved the problem of a hostess and especially overjoyed the one he had found had the social graces and great experiences dealing with various types of people. Jenny previously had competed in beauty pageants and had a special type of beauty. She still had that eminence of freshness in her personality that gave her a down to earth quality that everybody could appreciate. Not only that, but she would be staying for an extended period of time. Which gave him a feeling of great satisfaction?

Now the real problems begin, getting the invitations properly worded to convey the message that he wanted invitee's to absorb, and making certain the honored guests would attend.

The invitations were a special inspirational piece of work, primarily designed by Nick.

The cover of the invitation was a large picture of the estate, gaily decorated with all the Christmas decorations, and a setting from Currier & Ives of fresh falling snow glistening like white diamonds. At the bottom was the embossed name of the recipient, it opened like a heart shaped book.

As they opened this invitation Nick inserted a statement of purpose, the reason that this event is being held.

"If I may, I would like to offer you all the courtesies of my home in recognition of the many favors and blessings you have bestowed on me over the months and years of our friendship, that I might in some way repay your great participation in the betterment of the people of this state."

"For my own part, I know many things that we are hoping for, and many things we aspire to bring about in this state can only be done through the proper funding of our aspirations, and God willing I will be standing by with the help you may require."

"May God bless you and give you the strength and foresight to carry out the many accomplishments that you foresee for the future."

The invitation was R.S.V.P. and requested that an answer be returned within a short period of time. Nick was looking for 100 percent attendance, and if an answer was not forthcoming within a reasonable period, he would personally call and make them aware that his funds were not without some limitations and they would be jeopardizing future funding.

Nick enlisted the help of Liz and Joey, his superintendent and wife, for the difficult job of decorating the house and grounds. He knew it would require an extraordinary effort on their part.

Chapter Sixteen
Winning with Holly

Thank God Big Mo was earning gobs of money by running first and second in the two events that he entered. Holly was doing an exceptional job.

She acquired two new thoroughbreds to install in her menagerie. An unraced two-year-old colt of nondescript pedigree but wonderful conformation and sleekness of form had caught her eye at the auction. The other, she acquired through watching for promising horses that were running in claiming races, and though this horse was performing poorly on the track and nobody wanted her, Holly was able to discern a great amount of potential promise. To put the icing on the cake, so to speak, the owners were getting ready to pull this mare from the track. Holly knew by looking at her history that she had been over raced, so she contacted the owner and for a few dollars she was able to bring this mare under her wing. Holly liked her pedigree, and felt that even if she was unable to rehabilitate her, she might make a great mare for breeding purposes.

As soon as Holly returned home to Clariden Farms, Nick made it a point to travel there with an appropriate gift to celebrate her triumphant return. He had flowers delivered and presented her with a stunning jeweled timepiece.

When he arrived, he went directly to the barns where he knew he would find her. She was in the first barn he entered; working so diligently that at first she did not notice him.

Nick upon seeing Holly for the first time in a long time, was overjoyed, gratitude for the way she was handling the horses welled up in him, he grabbed her and kissed this bundle of fire hard on the mouth. Resistance from Holly did not exist, instead this was the first time he felt the intensity of this woman's nature, the red hair cascading down her back indicated.

Now all of a sudden, she was responding with arms wrapped around him so tightly he could feel the vibration and the tightness of her arms, promising greater delights to come.

Never in his life had he run across a woman so very earthy and strong. The need for her was welling up in him to a point he thought he would explode.

They fell to floor that was covered with straw, and Holly wiggled out of her jeans with an urgency that was beyond anything she had ever felt before. This sexual encounter was not only about sex but also admiration and an element of love. Nick did not have time to pull down his trousers he just unzipped his pants and with great urgency entered hotly squirming Holly. They climaxed within a short period of time and continued until they both fell away completely exhausted.

Neither one of them wanted this to happen. They both believed that you should never have a close relationship with somebody in a position to help or hurt in your career, in other words never mix business with pleasure.

They understood that the money they received from this horse racing operation was dependent on the other participant; they wanted nothing to interfere in this setup.

After the loving, a long period of silence took place while they composed themselves and got their clothes in some semblance of order, finally Nick said "I'm starving lets run down to Skeeters place and grab something." Holly being eternally hungry, was very amenable to this suggestion.

Once they arrived at Skeeters 19th Hole the conversation happily turned to horses and the next move that Holly would make in relation to Clariden Farms.

Holly, being a formerly practical and down to earth person now had dreams of expanding the farm and racing operation to heights never dreamed of before. Nick's aspirations seemed to be rubbing off on her.

"Nick there is a thing that I must tell you. You know the Prick who made the claim we had fixed that race and ruined one of the best pieces of horseflesh he had ever trained, well he was still running his mouth, and giving us a bad reputation?" 'Many people approached me and gave me this information. I personally took a hike over to his barn to ask him to tone it down a bit.'

"His verbiage to me was at the very least, obnoxious, loathsome, and abominable to name just a few of the adjectives that I'm familiar with."

"Can you repeat some of the words and statements he used?"

"Okay I'll try, Mother Fucking Bitch, Your fuckin' stable, you, and your boss are an absolute blight on this great institution of thoroughbred racing. You and your boss are abhorrent, inherently unable to do anything that's clean and aboveboard, is that enough or should I go on?"

"Holly I get the general drift of the repartee. Listen to me carefully, I will guarantee that the next time your paths cross— if they ever do— in the future, you will not be subjected to this type of objectionable speech. I'm glad you told me about it, remember the steps I have to take may be objectionable to you but there are many things in life that have to be stamped out, before a hideous organism can spread its filth all over an area that may directly or maybe even indirectly affect your life and possibly even your future."

After this nasty part of the conversation they went on to more pleasurable things to talk about. Nick and Holly knew to make Clariden Farms a really profitable commercial enterprise, it had to mature and eventually move into the horse breeding side of the business. This brought up the subject of retiring Magnificent One and letting him stand at stud.

His limited record, would not command the type of fee you could expect to get if he had a more extensive background, on the other hand if you allow him to keep racing he may improve his record, and stud fees would increase substantially, the downside to this scenario, if the devil comes a-calling and something untoward happens that ends his racing career or possibly breaks a bone and causes him to be put down, now that would cause a huge loss to Clariden Farms and Nick Lasko.

Upon reflection they both decided to retire Big Mo to stud and take the purely conservative road. Not another word was spoken about their hasty and badly considered sexual liaison.

Nick decided to handle the big mouth himself. If he could possibly avoid violence he would, but if it required a stronger statement he was not above putting a little forcefulness behind his words.

He sent one of his emissaries to locate and get all the information on this idiot that he could.

In the meantime Nick had to attend the meeting at his home with the Capos from Cleveland and Pittsburgh, the purpose of the meeting was Nick's proposal to open a casino near Sandusky.

At the appointed day in November, at ten in the morning, they arrived like visiting heads of state; all black Lincoln's, four of them.

Their arrival came two at a time one limousine in each entourage, bringing with them their second in command plus bodyguards. Well so much for being unobserved.

Nick watched from the front portico of his home with mounting concern. Eyes were everywhere and may not be friendly.

You would have thought it was a parade down Main Street. This was unexpected by Nick and his superintendent. Where in the hell do we put the entourage and entertain them for the hours we may be in conference?

As they arrived at the columned portico front entrance, Nick greeted each with his limited Italian, "buongiorno." (Good morning) They were impressed with his home.

Vilanotti said "Li placere e tutto mio" (the pleasure is all mine.) As Guliano came up the steps the first thing he commented on was the estate, "La Residenza magnifico" (Your home is beautiful.)

Nick led the way to the grand salon with its magnificent furnishings and saw to it his guests were comfortably seated.

"Signori cominciamo." (Gentlemen, let us begin).

At a nod from both men, the proceedings began.

"I have arranged to have Liz place a table with coffee and other calorific entrée's for your pleasure. She would gladly serve you individually but I did not want anyone going in and out the room while we would be discussing various things that should not leave this room, capisci."

Stephano voiced the question Guliano was thinking. "Why did you build such a large home?"

"Signore, I have always realized that political connections are the lifeblood of powerful people all around the world. As much as people like to denigrate large mansions, they are still in awe of those that own them, for instance on February 14—Valentine's day, I will be hosting the grand opening celebration of my estate, and in attendance will be every noted politician that holds power in this government including the Governor, so you see the investment I have made will not go for naught."

Guliano interrupted, "don't give me the bullshit, *for naught,* talk English or Italian, but cut out the crap *for naught.* For Chris sake."

Nick said," I did not intend to speak above your head. I'll try to do better."

Vilanotti interjected, "fuck that bullshit, talk the way you want to. Let's get on with this."

Nick went on to say "I intend to reap many rewards in the future, and if we cooperate with each other, and I'm talking about the Cleveland group, and the Pittsburgh organization, then there is no stopping us on the way to lining our pockets with impressive amounts of coin of the realm."

His guests did not look happy and in fact had a disdainful look.

"I realize I am not a made member or even a Soldati in either faction nor do I want to be, it's better that I remain in a neutral position and be the one that will bring hope, peace, and many dollars to all of us. In the years we have worked together I think the things I bring to the table, my honesty, integrity, and ability to manage the various enterprises that reward us all-- are irreplaceable."

Guliano said,"hell yes, let's give the devil his due."

Vilanotti shook his head in agreement.

"Yes, I know that I personally started the businesses that are now making all of us better off but I realize that without the cooperation of either of you I could not be operating today. You have the ability to take over my operations anytime you want to, but that would result in infighting and would leave many people "morto" (dead). That's not something we would want to happen, in another words "tu sei pazzo", (crazy) and you have to replace me and lose my management ability that would hit you where it hurts, in the pocketbook."

Anthony took it from here; "The thing we came for was to discuss this casino that you have proposed. Why do you think this would be uno buono cosa?" (A good thing).

"It would fit what we do and I am able to put the important people in Sandusky on our side."

Anthony said, "How do you know this to be true"?

I had individual meetings with them and they indicated in a meandering way that they were "a'minabel" (amenable) to my proposal."

Anthony continued with some amount of distain, "Did they say hell yes we'll do it and provide various favors for your protection? And did they say when a new administration comes in we will guarantee their cooperation in the future? Did they say these things?"

"Well no, they did not say that, not directly."

Anthony continued, "Then what the fuck are we talking about? You know Nick you have not been around like I have. Thirty years I have been in this business. You are still growing up and you are sucking up what people you think are of substance tell you— or are indicating that they are telling you in a roundabout way— and they have no intention of helping you except to extract as many dollars as they can before they fuck you. If I killed as many people that have fucked me in the past their bodies would fill The Cuyahoga River. But let's assume that we go ahead and build this Casino of yours and these people that you think are your friends "afrigetta" (stick a Prick up your ass), this after we have spent a million maybe more. We would be obligated in some way to get back at them, now let's see how many are there? Five, ten, twenty, maybe more! Jesus Christ, we'd be spending all our time working over people that aren't putting any grease in our pockets. No Nick this does not comprendere (comprehend). I speak for Cleveland when I say we will not be involved in any way in this project, and furthermore we will not allow you to become involved. It matters not what the Pittsburgh people say because what you are talking about is clearly in Cleveland's jurisdiction. So let me make this clear to you, I appreciate your hospitality and I have enjoyed your Magnifico home, plus we in Cleveland think a lot of you, but this project will not become a reality. What say you Stephano?"

"My feelings have been expressed by you Anthony and we would reiterare, (reiterate), your estimation of Nick, we hold him in the piu alta stima, (highest esteem), he has brought a hell of a lot of youth and unbridled enthusiasm to an organization that was becoming moribund and Nick was just the spark we needed. We certainly wish we could approve of this venture, but it does not have a redeeming value and can only bring us much grief. So Nick we also are of the opinion that we cannot allow this to become a reality."

"Signore Gentiluomo I have appreciated your input and I believe that you have made me see another side to the equation. I realize now what a potential fool I may have become. I believe I was blinded thinking of the enormous profits that would accrue from this endeavor. I now feel foolish having brought you a considerable distance to hear a proposal that was not given enough thought and would have depended on people that may have just been stringing me along."

"You know, we had a good example of that some years back when a very successful Casino was operating just outside of Youngstown's jurisdiction called the Jungle Inn. They had everyone in the small burg they were operating in, on the take and things went along just peachy until the state fire marshalls got involved and closed them down once and for all in 1949. As I recall, all of the owners and employees were able to wiggle out of lengthy prison terms."

Our business is over, "I want you to enjoy yourself; I made plans for an expansive luncheon."

So if you would like to bring your associates into this ballroom and mangia with us, than please, I'll invite them in."

The social continued unabated until early evening.

When they decided to leave, Nick said, "arrivederci e Buon viaggio and wished them a safe trip home."

There would be no casino and Nick felt a little relief. He may have secretly been harboring uneasy feelings to this undertaking and was glad that he had this powwow with wiser heads then he. Another secret of life had been learned. Never rush in like an elephant without getting a map to guide you around the fragile things creating a roadblock. In other words, the best advice available.

Nick realized he was by his very nature impetuous and many times like a bull in a china shop. There are times he liked to throw shit on a wall and see what sticks. In the foregoing case nothing stuck and considering the many hours he fucked away on this scheme, he should have been more cognizant of what the outcome would be, and worked this out in his mind before jumping to deficient solutions.

Nick poured a drink and walked back to the grand salon. He crossed to the tall windows and looked out over his domain.

Well the world will not come to an end and there are other ways he could make an ass of himself. One way was to confront the asshole that turned him in to the commission in New York, and gave Holly a bad time. I have refrained from mentioning his name because of his great reputation as one of the foremost trainers in the country. I truly do respect him for that, but his vitriolic mutterings that gave way to vicious attacks on Holly and myself, are untenable to me. I probably deserved them, but not Holly. However, he should have more intelligence and check out with whom he is becoming rancorous.

He probably feels secure because of his friendship with a few connected guys, and I believe he trained horses for a couple of them. The connections would be with the New York mobs.

Nick's connection was so tight with the people he worked with, that this guy was no threat to him. Nick knew he could do anything he wanted to this guy, and there would not be a peep out of the New York outfits.

The guy that Nick had given the job of getting information on this loudmouth prick, reported where he could be found. It was best to wait until Gulf Stream near Miami when it opened in January.

The Prick would have a string of very expensive horses running at this meet. If Nick wanted to, or needed to damage this guy's life, this was the place to do it.

Chapter Seventeen
The family man with conscience

Everything went well for the Christmas season. The estate was decorated beautifully and guests were flowing in and out of his home with regularity. This was the way Nick liked it.

This year was heavy with snow and he enjoyed shopping downtown at Strouss and McKelvey's, Trudging through the snow in his boots with the clasps open so he jingled a bit when he walked, excitedly looking at display windows where animated figures of Santa Claus and the elves along with images of reindeer flying through the snow filled night, filled him with an ecstasy never again to be experienced in his lifetime. He pressed his face against the window, completely enthralled with this rich scene of overflowing huge moon and brightly twinkling stars, and if he did not have visions of sugarplums dancing in his head, he did have deja vu of the time many moons ago when his parents took him Christmas shopping.

Why is it when we have these pleasurable moments our thoughts have always been filled with snow and sleighs and beautiful steeds and jingling bells? To Nick it seemed like eons ago.

As he thought about it, maybe this time was the best of all. But what if he had married and had children and a nice secure job with US Steel, not having to care about all the problems he has, not having to worry about who's trying to fuck him, and whose head he may have to bash. Instead, he'd be watching his children shopping for Christmas presents and seeing their eyes light up with the joys of this very special season—things that in their future when the years start weighing heavily on their shoulders—they will be reminiscing, as Nick is now doing.

He does have two children under foot that belong to Joey and Liz and though he never thought he would, he secretly enjoys them, even their moments of hellish actions to which children are prone.

After this grand season, a week later, comes New Year's Eve with all of its festivities and ringing in of the New Year. Nick considered making a New Year's resolution, but a horrifying thought occurred to him, maybe he should go back to church which he had not attended for many years.

How many of his past actions would be condoned by the church, and by an extension of that, what would Jesus think?

His thoughts were becoming very profound, and he pondered about the many things he had participated in that were illegal. He justified them—in most cases—by believing they were society's wrongheaded thinking, but were not in Gods lexicon.

Gambling is something that everyone does in one way or another. From the time we are born we are gambling on something, even if it's just trying to make it to the next year. Everybody gambles in some way, maybe it's just a friendly bet between friends, but because I do it to make a living it becomes a sin and against society's ill-conceived laws.

Many times I have tried to improve the conditions of other people. Never in my life have I ever ignored the plight of the poor, or neglected children, or people with crushing handicaps unable to fend for themselves

When I organized the CCC, people were outraged that I required mandatory participation. They called it extortion—protection money—and if that's what they want to call it, that's fine with me, but every ones situation was improved. Protection is exactly what it was. The CCC protected them from harassment and incarceration because of unjust laws, provided health insurance for them and their families, protected them from unfair competition, and they had a forum to state their problems and find solutions that may benefit their businesses, a credit union of sorts where loans were made available for those in need. For all that they paid a monthly premium. Because of their type of business—taking bets on sporting events—the law considered them criminals

So you see it wasn't Nick that was the criminal, it was the law and those that enforced the law that were the criminals. Yes, there were times when some force was involved, but this only happened when it was necessary to keep the organization intact for the good of everybody. We did employ punishment the same as any city, state, or national government would, the difference being, if you were picked up for some minor offense you might spend a couple of years incarcerated or at the very least pay thousands in fines. In our case, it may be just a confrontational conversation, or possibly a beating that might injure your psyche and cause some painful moments, but you will be back to work in a short time and you did not spend years in the can while your family had to fend for itself. Tell me what method would you prefer?

Maybe the thing Nick has to atone for is injuring that horse when he fixed the race at Belmont. He did not feel he had to do penance for fixing the race, but he did have deep unabated feelings for injuring the animal. But the nature of horseracing is in some way allocated to fixing races. It may be called other things. For instance, a trainer might be able, in most instances, to tell the present condition of his horse, and has a pretty good feeling whether or not his horse has a chance. This information is never disseminated to the bettors. He may decide that the horse's odds are on the short side and feels he can get better odds or a drop in class the next time out. He communicates to his jockey in some way that his mount is strictly there for a work out, and do not run him too hard. Well, the betting public did not know those words were spoken, and anybody that placed a wager on that horse were at a disadvantage. Whether they realized it or not they were involved in a fixed race.

How about a situation where two riders try not to give another horse racing room, in other words, block a participant to keep that horse from winning, that's a fixed race. What is it when a trainer runs a horse he knows is sick or injured in order to get back some of the entry fee and not have to pay a track-imposed fee if he scratches the horse? That's a fixed race. There are other scenarios that qualify as a fixed race. No, Nick did not feel badly about fixing that race.

Going back to church is one thing and becoming a better person is another thing. He did have some reservations about church. He has a difficult time believing everything the dogma of the church teaches, but he always remembered what a priest told him;

All the questions will be answered if you have faith. Becoming a better person may be more difficult.

Chapter Eighteen
Gulf Stream Attaining Satisfaction

Out of here and into Florida sunshine. Out of the cold and salted streets and slush and into the land of Palm trees, beautiful blue waters, and girl's in bikinis with tanned bodies making their way through the white sand in front of the Fontainebleau, a luxurious hotel where Nick was staying.

When he arrived at the airport he felt like he had just been transported on a magic carpet into a land of fantasy and he hoped he would not wake from this dream.

Nick casually sauntered to the car rental counter, found his reservation for a white Cadillac, of course none other than a convertible—what else would you drive in Miami?—and picked up the keys that were waiting for him.

Holly was following him down in the horse van with the two hoses they would race at this meet; Big Mo and the recently acquired mare named Rebirth. She had rested and restored this mare to what was now a healthy looking horse, maybe too healthy, this mare wanted to kick her stalls down, and demanded in her own way, to work every day.

Holly had her fingers crossed hoping she was not a waste of time and money. She would however, be alert for other viable thoroughbreds that may be found in claiming races.

For those not knowledgeable how the racing game works, here is a thumbnail sketch, Horses that are not of top quality generally will be raced in claiming races, that means anybody who wants to buy a claimer for the stated claiming price can place their claim before the race, and if you were first in line for that particular horse he is yours after the race. Better horses are generally found racing in a maiden (horses in their first start) or stakes races where a horse cannot be claimed.

Holly knew they needed another horse or two to complete her stable and to make it profitable to travel to faraway tracks. They did have a two year old that they were seasoning back at the farm and was being handled by a trusted and longtime associate.

Raising a thoroughbred and training it for the track was a herculean task and was better left to trustworthy persons of competency that you could trust. The employee she had selected at the farm was the most knowledgeable and competent member of her staff.

Upon arriving at the hotel, Nick stripped and jumped into swimming trunks and headed for the beach, unfortunately one of the frequent thunderstorms – always a possibility in South Florida was in full regalia, but Nick could care less he was so imbued with the euphoria of being in these southern climes that he went straight into the water with the threat of lightning strikes all around, not to mention the fact that there may have been sharks circling about. It was rare that a bite would occur, but a certain amount of circumspection is in order. But Nick filled with ecstasy was happily splashing about as lifeguards frantically tried to holler and whistle him back to safety. Among themselves they wandered how much sanity that this person could exhibit in what was obviously a state of exuberance. Finally Nick relented and abashedly returned to shore and profusely apologized to the two young men who took their responsibilities seriously and tried to show as much respect and courtesy to a knot head like this, that they were capable of.

Nick now properly cowed trooped to one of the sunning chairs that surrounded the pool and with the sun now shinning— as it usually does after a thunderstorm— he decided to try to get some sun to lessen the neon whiteness of his skin which stood out like a sore thumb among all the tanned and hard bodies on the deck.

Soon he was approached by one of the hotel dance instructors, she introduced herself as Judy Ray and asked if he would enjoy having instruction in a dance of his choice. This girl was beautiful in the stunning way she wore her makeup and casual dress that emphasized her extremely lithe body, curves were not hidden.

Nick had a difficult problem in getting his eyes to rise above her bust line. She finally said, "if you want to talk to me you will find my face about a foot higher than where you're looking." When he did raise his gaze he found a shockingly beautiful head of silvery blonde hair that amplified her deep crystal- blue eyes, a deepness that had to be compared to the blue water of the Atlantic Ocean. Her eyes were set rather far apart emphasizing her high cheekbones with a pert nose that seemed a little too small for the total effect. Nonetheless she was drop- dead beautiful.

"Hell yes I want lessons, are you sure you want to teach someone with two left feet?"

And so the dance lessons commenced the following day with Nick's prediction of his ineptness coming true. It made him feel like an elephant trying to keep up with a Gazelle, but dam it, he was not a quitter he would keep up until he was able to get on a dance floor and feel he was one with the music or at least getting through to the end of the tune without falling down or bothering other people on the floor who really knew how to dance. Give the devil his due! Did he really want to learn to dance, he asked himself, or did Judy have something to do with it. Probably a little of both.

Nick would very much enjoy dating this vision of loveliness, however he had nothing to offer. She was a dancer and preferred men that were suave and debonair and could move around the dance floor with grace and elegance.

These dance teachers were on the fringes of show business, each night she did exhibitions in the Boom-Boom room at the Fontainebleau as an enticement to other guests to take lessons. This is how they made a living.

Nick continued to take lessons until finally he started to show traces of competence and exhibiting some artistic skill, at least in his estimation, but he was still shot down whenever he asked Judy out.

He was going to be busy at the track, and would get around to the problem of Judy Ray later.

Nick was anxious to meet with Holly when she arrived at Gulf Stream with the horses.

The drive was pleasant and he loved the facilities at the track. This was a first class operation and the finest thoroughbreds in the country would be competing here.

He hurriedly rushed to the back of the track where the stables were and searched for the Clariden Farms' stalls.

He spotted Holly busily working on Big Mo. The big stud had just finished an afternoon workout and was being groomed. Holly believed in spending time bonding with each of her charges.

This was the last meet for Big Mo before he would be put out to stud, hopefully he would show well in the two races he would compete in and in turn increase his stud fees.

Nick believed in Holly's training methods because she cared so deeply about her horses. He truly believed that she would one day be recognized as a top trainer and eventually have a horse that will be good enough to run in the Triple Crown races. Getting that type of a high quality horse for her is Nick's job. In the meantime making enough money to support the expenses of the farm was uppermost in his mind.

They warmly greeted each other and Holly immediately informed Nick of her plans for Rebirth. She felt that the first race the mare would run in would be a $50,000 claimer. She felt that based on her past record no one would want any part of the horse. Rebirth would be stepping up in class, so she was pretty sure there would not be a claim. And Rebirth, taking home some money was a good possibility. However, if in the unlikely event a claim was posted, $50,000 is considerably more than was paid for the horse. Of course Holly felt it would not be enough compensation for the time and effort she had put into this mare, she was hoping that this would be the last time she would run in a claimer. The hope was that she would show well in a couple of stakes races and then breed her and some great foals would be the end result.

After talking about the mundane things connected with the various items that she needed for this racing meet, Nick asked if The Prick had shown up yet, Holly said, "I honestly don't know if he's here or not, nor do I care, I just want to train and race my horses and I will ignore whatever he has to say."

"Holly, the way he talked to you and what he had to say about me is not something that will go without being seen as a tremendous insult to us and our racing operation. If we allow this motherfucker to get away unchallenged then we will always be considered insignificant and looked down upon. Even the racing officials will shit on you whenever they want."

"Wait a minute Nick, I think I know you pretty well and when provoked you can be dangerous, promise that you will not hurt this man."

"I have tried extremely hard to do the Christian thing, and I truly believe that in most cases I have succeeded. However, in some circumstances the situation may demand a

165

solution. I believe an emphatic answer to what was implied by that Prick is necessary.

"What do you want to do?"

My desire at this point is to come to a meeting of the minds. If he stops talking about us as if we are the scumbags of the earth, we can go peacefully on our way and not give it another thought. But, let's assume that he does not agree to a peaceful solution and continues speaking about us in the same way he has in the past. It could develop into a set of circumstances that will have us not welcome to any major track in this country.

"Can't we just ignore him."

"What do you propose that I do, Holly, turn tail, and accept the fact that his noxious mutterings affect our earnings now, and in the future? If you want that, then I have the wrong partner."

"But I'm afraid you might be brutal."

"There are times in this life that you must fight for your survival, just like our country has for these many years. Can you imagine what would have happened to this country if we had not brutally defeated the Germans and the Japanese? In order to win the peace we had to be brutal, killing wantonly without regard to the children and women that got in the way, witness Hiroshima and Nagasaki, of course I am not advocating for, nor condoning killing just for the expression of a belief, but I think I have the right to express my displeasure of his beliefs and actions, and if necessary to exhibit a little force to emphasize my complete aversion to what he had to say in the past."

"Nick what will happen if you slug this guy and get arrested and miss this wonderful experience we are going to have here in Florida?"

"First of all I'm not going to slug him, hell he may be in better shape than me and he will be the one doing the slugging. I will figure out some form of punishment if he refuses to listen to reason, and if I go to the slammer I want you to be the first one in line to post bail for me."

"You do not have to worry about that, I'll let you cogitate in there for a while and get you out of my hair, and you'll have a chance to rest and make friends with your fellow cellmates while I enjoy these great temperatures. I'm just kidding, please be careful and be the kind of great salesman I know you can be."

"I'll tend to it tomorrow, the rest of today I will go to the betting windows and try to pay for tonight's entertainment."

Chapter Nineteen
Star struck

Thinking of that immediately brought to mind Judy Ray. Nick knew it probably wasn't her real name. Suddenly, a light went on in his mind, if there was a celebrity appearing somewhere on Collins Ave—whom Judy was in awe of—and he could cadger an invitation to their table for the evening, that just may do the trick with Judy. The invitation would have to be delivered to me while I was taking a dance lesson by a bellhop from the Fontainebleau, and if it was a top-notch celebrity that she was dying to meet, it could be the ticket to her heart and just maybe, a hop into bed. God, this sounds better all the time. How do I go about this scenario?

The Pittsburgh operation has a lot of connections with various personages and they may be able to help. Nick runs through this in his mind, and imagines he calls Vinnie or Larry and says to them, *'hey I've got this dance teacher I'm trying to date and I need a celebrity to hang with for an evening to impress her, and maybe just the thing to enable me to get laid.'* The laughing goes on for several minutes before they hang up the phone, so that circumstance will be ruled out.

He decides to call Larry and tell him about Rebirth, she will be running in a claimer and the odds will be high, maybe twenty to one, or better. "Get an across the board bet down on her (if rebirth finishes 1,2, or 3 she'll return a substantial sum). I do have a request, Elvis is appearing down here this weekend, and my date and I would like to hang at his table that evening, if we can't get a connection with him, Sinatra will follow in about two weeks, and it might be possible with him."

Larry responded with some reluctance, "What the fuck do you want to meet these two meatheads for? One is a small Prick that thinks he's tough and the other is doing so many pills he has turned into a pill. What the hell you going to talk about with either one of these sausages? They talk a different language then us, and think they are the center of the earth. I'll see what I can do, Elvis has so many hangers on that he's hard to get close to. Sinatra may be a better bet, maybe we know somebody in New Jersey, I'll ask around, somebody always knows somebody, and these so-called star assholes like to hang out with guys that are connected.

"Thanks Larry."

But as far as Sinatra is concerned, you have to be careful with him he's pretty vulgar and may insult you, we can't put a hit on him. There's a hell of a bunch of guys that may not like him, but he does do some good charitable acts and kind of redeems himself that way. If he thinks you are uno di noi (one of us) or uomo d'onore (a man of honor) he may hold you in a higher level of respect."

"Hey Larry, this is some good information, but nothing new under the sun. I heard about this guy's character before."

"Another entertainer you should consider is Dean Martin and he is from your area, a truly nice guy. And many times when Frank is doing shows in a certain place, Dean is also booked nearby, one ammonimento (be careful) he plays golf every day and he will invite you to play with him, this will flatter you but he only wants to take your money. Not because he needs the money. It's an ego trip with him.

"I can hold my own at golf, but thanks for the warning."

"For chris sake, your over-confidence is irritating. For god sakes listen to me, I said the guy plays every fuckin' day, when is the last time you fuckin' played. I'm tellin' you sometimes you are an idiot."

"Whatever happens make sure you don't go Hollywood on us, it's bad for business. You don't need any more bullshit, you're already fuckin' around with the horses and God knows what else. By the way, how you doing with that sweetie in California?"

"I'm not, she's in California, and I'm in Florida."

"Well I guess that will change, we already have word she'll be spending some time with you around Valentine's Day."

"Shit, I'm not going to deny it but how the fuck did you find out."

"Nick don't you know we know everything? that's part of our business. If we reach a stage that we don't have a clue, that's when were out of business. Hey, give us some credit! We are not going to let some guy from Youngstown have free rein when he is handling millions of dollars of our money a year, come on get real."

"Look, Larry, just see what you can do for me and I won't forget it."

Later, Upon reflection of the conversation, Nick realized his home was bugged but there wasn't a thing he could do about it. If he found all the bugs on and in the estate; they would have them replaced in 24 hours. He really did not mind the bugs, he knew they were only protecting their investment and he had nothing to hide. Knowing the bugs were there gave him the chance to allow them to hear what he wants them to hear.

That night, Nick made the rounds of a couple of clubs and then went to bed. He wanted to be fresh in the morning because the next morning he intended to search out The Prick and have a da uomo a uomo (man to man) talk and Nick expected to come away from it with some sort of understanding.

Finding where the Prick was staying won't be hard. First, he went to the Racing Secretary's office and inquired which barn was his. Nick got the barn number but they could not tell him if he was staying in a van on the course or had a motel or was staying with friends. The best thing that Nick could do is go to the barn and ask an employee where he could be located, or what time he would make an appearance at the barn.

When he entered the barn he found the Prick working with one of his hot walkers, Nick realized that he had probably been at the track since about 5:30 this morning working the horses. He was one of the best trainers in the country and you don't get that way without a lot of hard work. Say what you will about him, he was the hardest working trainer at the track and passionate about all aspects of horseracing. Of course, this is what will make it difficult for Nick to reach an understanding with him. The Prick felt that not only he had been egregiously injured, but also his horse had been permanently injured. A horse that had the potential to reach the top tiers of racing, and in turn his whole racing operation was affected. Knowing this made Nick apprehensive about the conversation he was about to have with The Prick.

Nick approached him, held out his hand in a manner that indicated friendliness, and hoped that The Prick would be receptive to a civil conversation.

"I'm Nick Lasko, and I would like to have a courteous and respectful conversation with you."

Ignoring his proffered hand he said, "I know who you are and I want you the hell out of my barn before you're carried out." This attitude was being said from a guy that was about 5'7" with grey hair—what there was left of it—eyes that were a washed-out brown, slight of build and a nose that made his face interesting because of the way it was cocked to one side. All in all, he was not a guy that made you think he could carry out any physical attacks. But Nick knew that standing before him was a wiry guy who had spent a lifetime working hard and just may be able to carry out any threats he made.

"In as conciliatory a manner as he could muster, Nick said, "I have no doubt you can do what you say you can do, but before you carry out any threats don't you think you should hear me out?"

"Look you Mick or Dago bastard, get the fuck out of here and I mean now!" Nick looked at him for a long moment and by his actions and body language he was ready to assault Nick. This is one time that he decided that giving up the field of potential battle was the better part of valor, and rather than continuing the conversation Nick turned and slowly walked away.

This confrontation took on a whole new connotation. Nick was deeply concerned about the conflict. He now knew that he would have to settle this himself, if for no other reason than for his own psyche and self- respect.

This was turning into a Billy Barone situation. He could assign this to someone else to carry out but that would not give him any satisfaction. The problem was that anything that happened to this man, Nick would immediately end up being the prime suspect, so he would need an excellent alibi at the time that whatever happened, happened. The only solution would be to obtain someone from out of town that would come in, do the job, and get out.

He called Vinnie, explained the problem, and in Italian said, "I don't want a hit, just to destroy his entire operation, a little fire would be nice."

Without hesitation Vinnie said, "We'll take care of it."

Of course there was always the possibility that the phones were tapped so the conversation went something like this: "Hello Vinnie I just called to see how you are getting along. I know that friend of yours had that awful fire at his home and his dog was burned. You know... I have a friend that I have a great relationship with, and I sure hope nothing like that would take place at his business. But you know Vinnie, you never know in this day and age what could happen when you least expect it." In other words Nick had to go around his elbow in order to get to his asshole. But, the intensifying federal scrutiny of the time made this kind of conversation normal.

At this point it was necessary for Nick to keep a high profile. He wanted to be seen, and he would always be in the company of friends. If he went to a club, he made sure the bartender knew who he was, and other people sitting nearby knew his name. By this time his dancing was coming along quite well, so any unattached woman was fair game, Nick did not care how old they were if they could dance, Nick would dance with them. He was having fun with his newfound abilities.

The Pittsburgh crowd would take care of the Prick right away, that's how they operated. If a job was there to be done they got it done now, as long as it was a simple action. If it was a hit— that's not so simple—all disappearing situations had to be approved by a Capo di Tutto Capi.

Nick was very valuable to the organization and anything within reason was approved. On the spot, he was expecting a little bon fire to take place within a day or two.

Three days later the fire was reported in all the daily papers. And reported as a case of arson. Four thoroughbreds perished and the entire stable area was destroyed.

The Prick had related the bad blood between him and Nick and told the police he had a confrontation with Nick just days before this incident.

It wasn't long before the police were trying to interview Nick without any success.

Nick had decided to hire a local attorney and referred all questioning to him. When he was questioned at police headquarters, his attorney was able to document Nick's whereabouts on the night of the fire.

That ended the interrogation, but now Nick had another reason and a steely motivation to do more harm to The Prick, until he learned to keep his mouth shut, bad things would continue to happen to him.

Larry called and wanted to know if everything was alright, and he had good news. Sinatra was going to appear at the Riviera in two weeks and Nick would be invited to attend a little party he would hold at the Joinna Hotel in the Dream Lounge after his last performance. This club was a known hangout for Cosa Nostra; he knew that mob figures would be attending.

He asked Larry if he would kindly call this bit of good news to the front desk and have it delivered to him while he was taking his dance lessons.

"Are you fuckin' kidding me? You are taking dance lessons? Get outta here! You'd do anything to get laid. For Chris sake get married and you'll have a regular piece of ass and you won't have to go looking for it."

"Yeah, and I get the same hole every night and its probably costing a fortune, hell I can stay single and hire a working girl and pay less."

"Yeah sure and God knows what you're going to come home with. You idiot, think about it even nice girls have STD's and you never know, that thing hanging between your legs will become unworkable— or who the hell knows— may even fall off." (Larry was laughing pretty hard but there was a kernel of truth in this raillery).

"Don't tell me different Larry, you know there are times you want something strange."

"I can tell you honestly Nick I will not cheat on my wife. I really am in love. You can't imagine the things she has put with all these years with me. What kind of asshole would I be if I ran around on her now?"

Good naturedly Nick said, "Let's face it Larry the reason you don't run around on her is your too ugly and no one else will look at you."

"Oh yeah, at least I don't have to take dance lessons to get someone to go out with me. Listen to me Nick, this guy Sinatra can be a first class Prick, if he gets under your skin too much, just gather up your girlfriend and walk away, and by the way he's not above hitting on your friend— that's his reputation— so don't take it personal he has friends in high places like Sam Giancanna out of Chicago."

"Sammy Giancanna?"

"Sinatra had a casino in Lake Tahoe that Sammy bankrolled, but Nevada revoked his license because of mob connections— namely one Sam Giancanna. So I'm telling you don't step on any toes. Be nice."

"Just asking Larry; is it true that Jack Kennedy is fuckin' Sammy's girl friend?"

"I don't know, but what I do know is that bastard, Kennedy is reported to have a perpetual hard on. For Chris sake don't get me started on that bastard.

"Is there anything I have to do— somebody to call to let them know I'll be there?"

"You mean with Sinatra?

"Yeah, I mean with Sinatra, Jesus Christ what else would I mean?

"Just show up, tell them who you are and they will show you to his table."

"This is great Larry, any time I can do you a favor, let me know."

Chapter Twenty
Catastrophe— dead horses

When Holly heard about the fire and four horses that were destroyed, she was leaning against a stall, as the news washed over her she felt all the strength leave her body and slowly slid down until she was sitting on the cement floor. Tears started flowing down her cheeks; the sadness that overcame her was all-encompassing. Her tears were mostly for the horses, four superb animals that had put their complete trust in their human masters, and those same masters betrayed them, callously destroying them because of the childish anger tantrums of their owners. Oh yes, she knew the one that had put those magnificent animals down, but he had reached a point that he had no other choice, so The Prick was equally at fault, if he had not been so malicious, things would have eventually died down and we all could have gone about our business training and racing thoroughbred horses and taking part in this grand and historic vocation that truly is a calling, but now she just wanted to leave this behind and go someplace and regurgitate and just keep on walking until she could get far enough away and never look back again.

And walk she did. Finally exhausted she sat down in a meadow and let all the tears flow out and cried until there were no more tears left. And there she stayed until the sun started rising, and she realized that she was crying for the Prick, Nick, the horses and herself. She felt so desolate. Unable to think or function anymore, just completely drained and completely alone with all the responsibility of this racing operation solely on her shoulders with no one to help. All she wanted to do is lay her head on someone's shoulder— and someone to say don't worry everything will be alright.

She struggled to her feet and as much as she wanted to stay where she was, her sense of duty was calling and she trudged back to the barn and began preparations for the day's activities. Big Mo and Rebirth both had to be worked, legs to be wrapped, liniment to be applied, and after the morning work outs, they had to be hot walked and washed and curried, and a thousand other things had to be done and it wasn't going to get done unless she was there to do or direct it. On top of this there were several claiming races she wanted to see, and had to study the horses that were running to see if there might be one or two that may be good enough for Clariden Farm Stables. After all of this took place, maybe she could find a friend to have an evening meal with and just maybe there will be no more tears.

Nick knew or thought he knew what Holly's reaction would be and he steeled himself for this conversation he would have with her, he was apprehensive fearing what her response would be. He knew the amount of passion she had for horses, and to have four beautiful top tier thoroughbreds horribly burned to death will probably have Holly in a deep funk and her mood would be just as horribly burning. So he gathered his courage and went to the track not only to hear Holly out, but to look at the claimers the same as Holly intended to do. He caught up with her as she was leaving to go to the clubhouse and a special box seat, reserved for trainers and owners; he approached her with much trepidation while he waited for the explosion.

As they walked side by side toward the clubhouse there was a good deal of silence, finally Nick spoke up; "I'm extremely sorry Holly, I know how you must feel.

Holly stopped walking, turned, and looked at him. "You have no idea how I am feeling," and resumed walking to the clubhouse,

Nick took the lead in this pseudo, one-sided conversation, and pressed forward to what he feared was an impending disaster, but he wanted her to know that the intention was never to harm the animals even though he was lying, he would lie if he had to. "Whether you believe it or not I did not have anything to do with that fire, it was just an unforeseen, and coincidental accident. It seems when anything unfortunate happens I get the blame,"

Holly did not respond and continued walking. Nothing more was said until they sat down in the reserved box.

"I know why you did it Nick, and I feel it could not be helped. I think I have finally come around to a way of thinking that is completely foreign to me. I guess the real world—the world you operate in— can be tough, and you must be strong to survive."

Whoa! Nick could not believe his ears, he turned to look her in the eyes and see if this really was Holly, she looked away and he could see a tear forming in those pretty eyes and in these moments he could see how attractive she really was, not only that, but the tugging on his heart was bringing a torrent of emotions to Nick's persona, and as this was going on in his heart, his head was having thoughts that were extremely subversive.

Let's just assume for a minute that he forgot about that dance teacher, Judy Ray and instead asked Holly to accompany him to the Sinatra party. The more he thought about it the better it felt and sounded.

That afternoon in spite of feeling confused about Holly, Nick claimed a horse that Holly felt would be a good addition to the stable. She recognized the sire of the four-year-old chestnut stud called Burgoo. Holly liked his confirmation, and recognized the sire of this horse that had been lightly raced and went into retirement early in his career, but had produced a couple of winning foals in what turned out to be a rather short life span standing at stud for this horse.

She felt that the horse was overlooked by many good judges of pedigree.

Chapter Twenty-One
Miami and the Nightlife

With all these confusing thoughts swimming in his head and the excitement of the new horse, he returned to his hotel and settled into the routine that was Miami nightlife. If it wasn't for a couple of new friends he had made that he met in one of the clubs he frequented, it would have been boring. These friends Bob and Toby were witty and comical to be around, but to add to the craziness, the most improbable coincidence; they were both managers of dance studios, from the Robert Morgan chain and every so often got together to spend a few days in Miami and just fucking around, hitting the various clubs and asking stag girls to dance— which they were excellent at— so they had a lot of fun and so did the girls that danced with them.

It happened that one night as the three of them were standing at the end of the bar in the Boom-Boom Room at the Fontainebleau, a beautiful and exquisite woman was sitting at the bar by herself which was unusual for a woman that gorgeous to be alone, and it looked like she wanted to stay that way because she rejected all invitations to dance, of course the idiots at the end of the bar, namely Nick, Toby, and Bob, decided that one by one they would ask her to dance.

They knew being turned down would lead to a long walk back to their seats and return with some humiliation, that would not long deter them, they decided to draw straws on who would ask her to dance. The long straw went first, the intermediate straw, went next and the short straw, went last. As luck would have it, Nick drew the short straw. This, after she had been asked and refused to dance a gazillion times, now, after turning every one down, she was showing signs of irritation.

Nick's time came, and of course Bob and Toby expected it to be a hoot as they imagined he would make his way to her and then dejectedly make his way back to his seat where his friends would be laughing and giving him the razzmatazz and in general making his embarrassment entertainment for the other patrons of the club.

However, Nick, thinking this out, decided this girl wanted something different than what was being proposed. With his new found dancing skills he had recently been introduced to Cha- Cha- Cha, he waited until a good Latin tune was being played and then walked over to this beauty and using the suaveness that Nick was noted for, lowering his voice, speaking softly, his body language rhythmic and in sync with the orchestra, he said, "I really do not mean to disturb you, and I know you have been turning down many other guys, but because you are so attractive and cosmopolitan I thought that this Latin number might intrigue you, and so I would like to offer up my services and would be delighted if you would dance with me.

She said I absolutely will, I love Latin Music."

Nick made sure, as he made his way to the dance floor that he passed his cohorts and smirked as he went by.

She was an excellent dancer and obviously knew her way around the dance floor. Everything was going in the right direction until another couple carelessly bumped into them, this sweet looking beauty that Nick was dancing with turned and said to the offending couple, "drop dead you Mother fuckers."

181

ouch; Nick could not believe that these words dropped from those well-formed lips, but other than that, the night progressed beautifully and they danced almost until closing.

Nick asked her out for the next evening and she was cooperative with that suggestion. They made plans for dinner and dancing and Nick was eagerly looking forward to the evening. Who knows; as the song goes, this could be the start of something big. He then realized he did not know her name. Laughing he said, "we have had a lovely time together, but don't you think we should know each other's name," joining in the laughter "she said I would think so, my name is Angie and I'm from New York," "He said I'm Nick from Ohio," Angie stopped for a moment and said, "I'm better with names if I can connect it to something... so from now on I will call you Cha-Cha Nick... I'll probably never forget that."

The next day he hurried to the track, he wanted another look at the horse they had claimed, he got there in time to see him work. The exercise track was crowded with other horses being trained, and Burgoo seemed to be agitated and frantic with all these horses, the exercise boy was having a rough time just staying on his back and seemed like he wasn't sure if he wanted to continue the workout. About this time, Holly walked up and stepped on to the track and asked the rider to get down, she took the horse by the bridle, and led him back to the walking ring where she just talked to him and cooled him down.

There was a quietness about her that had a calming effect on the horse. After spending a considerable amount of time with this stud, she brought him in to be groomed. Nick said, "That's not a very good sign is it?"

Holly smiled, "it's a very good sign, unless you know what's wrong with a horse you don't know how to fix it. We now know that he doesn't like other horses running with him."

"Does that mean we can cure him, now that we know?"

"No, it does not mean we can cure him. It simply means we have a chance to cure him, now that we know what his problem is. There are times when a horse has picked up a particular habit or possibly an addiction that no matter how hard you try they will never get over it, but at least in this case we have a shot at it."

That afternoon Nick was attending his dance class and the bellhop that he had been expecting arrived. In a voice that could be easily heard announced that Mr. Sinatra has extended an invitation to attend his after show get-together, with some friends.

Nick looked at Judy and said "darn it, I don't have a date would you like to go with me? It's this Saturday."

Her eyes lit-up. Are we talking about Frank Sinatra?"

Nick said, "I sure am."

"How did you get an invitation?"

"We have many mutual friends."

"I would very much enjoy going with you but what should I wear."

"I don't know because I'm not a connoisseur of woman's clothing, but I think a simple cocktail dress and high heels would be in order; let it show off your figure, of which you have a pretty extravagant one, so I do not think it will be a problem."

Judy at this point seemed very excited and ebullient. The date with Sinatra was a few days off and Nick was keeping his fingers crossed that all would go well.

In the meantime, he had to touch-base with his people back home, and Big Mo and Rebirth were entered in Stakes Races this week.

Nick was a little late this day arriving at the track, he would not make the first race, but that was okay, the first race generally had second- tier horses participating. As he rushed to his box he had to pass a booth that seemed to have a lot of activity going on. A closer look revealed Dino and Frank with several friends and what looked to be a bodyguard having a lot of laughs just two boxes away.

Nick decided to see how really bad Frank was, so he approached the box and talked to the guy who was probably the security. "Let me introduce myself, my name is Nick Lasko from Youngstown, my associates are Cosa Stessa Pittsburgh guy's, tell Frank and Dino that I own a horse that's running in the next two days and I have some information that may be helpful to them."

After hearing all the particulars they invited Nick in to the box. Frank said to him, "ain't you the guy that got an invite to my little get together after my show?

"That's true Frank and I'm looking forward to it. The reason I have approached you and Dean now is that this will be my way of repaying you. I have a horse running in two days in the fourth race and the information from my trainer is that she has an excellent chance of taking this race; we think it's a good across the board bet and the odds will be right. If it's possible try to place any large wager off track. If she comes in you owe me a drink and if she doesn't I owe you one."

"Geez, can you afford it?"

"Hell no, why do you think I'm coming to your party, I heard you were picking up the tab, I am a little worried that you may play golf with the hustler sitting next to you and he may relieve you of some of your coin, and bam we may have to reschedule the party."

"What's the name of the piece of shit you want us to bet on."

"Hey fuck you, I'm just trying to help your fucked up career that I hear is in the shit can. The name of the mare is Rebirth. I believe she will have a good outing.

When Nick got to his box he heard Dino holler out, "hey you got anything running today," Nick hollered back,

"Magnificent One in the eighth race, the odds aren't right. Keep your two bucks in your pocket."

Big Mo being a very large horse standing 17 hands 2 inches and weighing a proportionate amount was not the fastest on the break from the gate but he was the boss when running in the pack and once he reached the stretch he was hard to beat, a very long stride and great stamina gave him an advantage.

On this day running a mile and sixteenth, he got caught up in a gaggle of horses on the backstretch and entered the finishing kick well off the pace, but did get third place money which Nick sorely needed. He did have the good sense not to bet, due to the fact, that as one of the favorites in the race, the risk/reward ratio was poor.

When he got back to the stables, he found Holly livid, she was stomping around muttering profanities, and said to Nick, "Big Mo has his fore leg nicked and I'm worried about it. That Goddamn jockey doesn't know how to ride and won't listen to instructions. Sonofabitch, he came out of the seventh hole, from there it should have been easy to keep him clear of the field. I specifically told him not to go to the rail, not with this field that were all rail-riders; I knew they would all be jammed up in there. So what does he do, he's on the outside with a clear field in front of him, but no this wasn't good enough he got him into the rail as fast as he could, got him jammed up with the other rail riders, got him nicked and goodbye race. That bastard cost us about $100,000 and got our baby hurt."

Nick said, "Holly do you think there could have been some hanky panky involved. Do you think that the Prick may have had some input with that jock?"

"I don't know but it was the dumbest thing I've seen in a long time."

"Holly, I think I'll go over to the jockey's quarters and find out for myself."

When he entered he found his jockey playing pool, he was a small South American kid that seemed to be too young to be riding in top races, Jose Santera seemed to be a nice enough kid. Nick said, "Hey, Jose come over here and sit with me I want to talk to you, do you know this guy, and he named the prominent trainer the he called The Prick,"

"I've heard of him, isn't he the guy that just had the fire, and had his barn burn down."

Nick said that's right, that's what happened. Did you ever ride for him or had any dealings with him whatsoever,"

"No never, I wouldn't know him if I saw him in person."

"Let me ask you this Jose, I'm the owner of Magnificent One that you rode today. Holly, my trainer gave you explicit instructions not to take him to the rail early in the race, why did you do exactly that?"

"Well sir, when we broke from the gate the horse was a little sluggish. I was worried that we would be too far out of it early in the race, so I decided to take him to the rail to save ground. But when we got to the rail, he found another gear, and all of a sudden we got jammed up with a bunch of horses. I could not extricate him from the pack. I finally found a hole when we entered the stretch, but it was too late and I decided not to push him too hard because it seemed to me that he was not acting the way he should."

This satisfied Nick, and he said just as he was leaving, "I hope you have better luck next time."

Before he went back to the stables, he decided to check Jose's Bio, he found that this kid was a little short of experience, even though he was probably an up and comer, this did not mollify him and hurried back to confront Holly.

When he found her, he let out a torrent of verbiage, "Holly what the fuck are we doing with an inexperienced jockey up on a grade one horse in a grade one race? Please explain this to me and it better be good, because it's not the jockey that was a piece of shit but the Goddamn trainer that hired him and now I have an impaired horse."

186

Holly responded with an unbounded torrent, of her own, "You sonofabitch I'm trying to do the best I can with a limited wallet. You are always saying to watch expenses, do you know what chance we have of getting an Eddie Arcaro or a Jack Bradley to ride for us, and they are already spoken for. I'm out here trying to do the best I can examining in detail the jockeys that are available to us, while you, you bastard are taking dance lessons and trying to fuck anything that walks or should I say dances!"

"Hold it you hot headed bitch, who in the fuck are you going to put on Rebirth, she's scheduled to go in two days."

"You're calling me a hot headed bitch. Look who the fuck is talking. I don't know who I'm going to put up now, I was going to put Jose up but you seem to have problems with that."

"Listen to me; it's too late to get another jockey, so let's give him another chance and I can't believe I'm saying that. For Chris sake I've got Sinatra and Martin betting the horse on my say so. I had just talked to them and gave them a tip on Rebirth."

"Well Nick, do, and say what you want but I believe that mare is a good one and should show well. I believe I can put a monkey on her back and she still should finish in the money. I'm personally gonna bet her."

Nick thought about going back to the jockey's room and warning Jose that he'd better give Rebirth a good ride or there's always the possibility that something could happen to him that may not be pleasant, he decided against that kind of intimidation because he felt the kid was trying to do the best he could. He was a little disgusted with himself for even thinking that way; he certainly did not want to become some kind of lunatic that wanted to bully and knock everybody around because of some imagined injustice or insult, whether or not it was real.

The number one problem was Big Mo. Was he going to be okay? That night Holly called in a Vet to double check her work. At this point, she felt that it was not a serious injury, and in days gone-by, she would have handled it herself. However, with a horse of this magnitude and being his next race was a $250,000 affair, it behooved her to be very careful, very careful indeed or Nick may come roaring in here like a bomb with the fuse lit.

People were hanging around the stall that evening, friends, friends of friends, stable boys, hot walkers, exercise riders, other trainers, owners, and anybody else that was trying to get information they could use at the betting windows.

What they were trying to get, was information on whether or not Big Mo was seriously injured and if so, would Nick run an injured horse, or would he scratch him from the race. Just seeing the Vet's van pull up draws a crowd.

After spending the afternoon taking dance lessons, Nick returned to the track and went immediately to the stabling area, where he encountered a crowd around Big Mo. His temper exploded, he ran in and exclaimed, "what the fuck is going on in here? I don't know any of you people so get the hell out before I start kicking some ass," and scatter they did. Nick's reputation had preceded him

He said to the Vet, "hey Doc what's the prognosis."

"Well if this horse hears any more of this yelling and carrying on he may fall over from a nervous breakdown. I believe he will be fine, just keep it clean and with a few days' rest, he should be able to race without a problem next time out."

"Doc I sure am glad to hear that." When the Doctor left, Nick turned to Holly and said, "I'm trying very hard to be civil, but what the hell were all those people doing in here."

"Nick I was so tied up with the Doc and Big Mo I honestly did not pay attention to anything else."

"All right Holly, look at me, pay attention, you will get the word out that you're not sure if Big Mo will run or not, you may have to scratch him. When working him on the clockers track try to work him when there are few clockers around and if there are too many, slow him down tell the exercise boy to back off, but don't tell him why. If we can pull this off, we may get some excellent odds and make some extra money. It's possible that this little injury may work in our favor."

"If he wins I promise I won't holler at you anymore."

"That's a bullshit promise and you know it, Its your nature to holler, that's what you do best. I'm not even going to rate your other attributes one of which your always looking to fulfill, but you probably overrate that one too and at the rate you're going with that dance teacher; from what I hear you are not getting any fulfillment there either."

"You know Holly when you are insulting me you don't use a knife you use a fucking spear right through the heart. Oh well; that's what I pay you the big bucks for."

"Where are the big bucks you're paying me? Apparently they went right by me without stopping, because I haven't seen them."

The day of Rebirths coronation arrived and with it a lot of excitement. Both Holly and Nick decided to sit in the box seats instead of the rail. Dean and Frank, were as rowdy as ever, whooping and hollering and getting the attention of Nick, waving their tickets that they had bet on Rebirth, Nick hollered back, "you don't have a thing to worry about it's in the bag."

Nick and Holly had bet a fair bit of change on an across the board ticket and were holding their breaths. They had so much to gain from this race and it would also validate Holly as an excellent judge and trainer, that was showing great promise.

They nervously prayed, hoping that a claim had not been put on Rebirth and apparently, nobody did. This was a six-furlong race and Rebirth had the number three postposition, which is right where they wanted her. It was important that she have a good start. If she had drawn the number one hole, it's possible that she may be bumped or squeezed. You must remember that on her left was an unyielding fence so if a horse outside of her was to squeeze inward she would have nowhere to go but against the rail and race over, but in the three-hole she could get bumped from either direction and still have some leeway.

No problem! She got a great break and took the lead immediately and never relinquished it, finishing strongly.

Sinatra's box was yelling like they had just won the entire track, come to think of it with their money, maybe they did.

A warm feeling came over owner and trainer; they unrestrainedly hugged and kissed each other without restraint.

Tonight would be a hell of a party!

Frank worked his way over to their box and said dinner and celebration on me at the Dream Lounge at 6 p.m. Both of you be there. Nick looked at Holly and said, "Well, you know where you're dining tonight."

"She said no I'm not, not with my clothes."

Nick laughed, "If you hurry to town, buy what you want on me, then meet me at my hotel, and we will leave from there but if you want have the concierge of the Fontainebleau go shopping with you, they always know what's in style and what looks good on you."

"I will try to not embarrass you tonight, but I warn you, I may show up in a potato sack and you will have to live with that for the rest of your life. I will sure not look like your dance teacher, and I'm sure your friends will wonder about the quality of the girls your now dating."

At the appointed hour, Holly arrived at the Fontainebleau. She was dressed in a form-fitting emerald-green sheath dress that accented her fiery red hair, with glittering heels to match; Her necklace was simple but elegant with one large stone resting between her ample breasts, attached to a fine filigree chain, and dangling elegant earrings that matched the charming necklace.

When Nick saw her, his first thought was not how stunning she looked but what the hell did this stunning outfit cost him? When he spoke to her he said, "Holly I know I said I would pick up the tab but please tell me that the necklace is not real, or that you have had it for ages, just tell me that I did not pay for it because maybe I did not explain myself with enough clarity. The statement, picking up the tab did not mean diamonds; it meant clothes not Jaguars, Rolls Royce's, the Hope Diamond, and other things of that ilk, but you do look fabulous and I'm proud to be your escort for the evening."

As Nick drove to the Dream Lounge down Collins Ave., he could not help but feel like he was living in a dream. Hotel after hotel, each one was more magnificent then the last, lights dancing and flashing with enthralling brilliance. It was more than his imagination had ever tried to comprehend, a warm all enveloping star-studded night.

He was driving a convertible but the top was up to accommodate Holly's hair, this was the kind of night that he wanted a girl at his side, and by God he had one, and a beautiful one at that, and one that did not have an ego that had to be massaged every 10 minutes, she also could hold her own in any conversation without flinching when it got rough.

He was less apprehensive having Holly attend a Sinatra party than Judy, if the party got a little out of line as some of the Rat Packs parties or the Summit as they preferred to be called, had a reputation for, Holly would be able to handle it better.

When they entered the lounge, the waiter immediately showed them to Sinatra's party. Quite a crowd was gathered around a large table and as they approached, the participants all stood and gave them a round of applause. Dino stood and said, "these are the people that made our day at the track, gave us a 20 to 1 shot and I don't think that's ever been done before."

They danced and other gentleman wanted to dance with Holly and the music was nonpareil. The night could not have been better.

When the music was at an end, Holly and Nick stepped onto the beach, kicked off their shoes and romped and luxuriated with the sand between their toes.

Nick was reminded of the song; *Moonlight becomes you it goes with your hair*. It wasn't very long before they dropped to the sand and desperately embraced with uncontrolled passion and when it was consummated they were completely exhausted.

His last excursion in Miami with Dean and Sinatra would be Saturday night where he would escort Judy Ray to be with the Rat Pack and that would make her happy, but Nick had lost his enthusiasm for this particular outing.

His thoughts were returning to Youngstown and the big job he would have in front of him when he got home.

He had to organize the project of entertaining and winning favor with the people of Ohio that controlled the state. By doing this he also won favor with the Pittsburgh and Cleveland factions that were the ones that controlled his future.

Saturday night arrived and Judy was all a twitter. She wanted to be spectacular at this event, you never know who would be attending this shindig, and she wanted to be noticed, her last thoughts were about Nick, if she even thought of him at all, he was just the guy that was her escort to be ignored if at all possible.

When they arrived at the Dream Lounge they were treated royally and escorted to the tables where all of Dino and Frank's friends were seated.

The instant Frank spotted them he immediately said, "hey Nick, where the hell you get all these beautiful women."

"Nick responded I'm a piker next to you, I can only dream about the choices that you have.

"Frank said dream no more I would be happy to change places as long as you accept all the lawsuits that go along with all those broads that you think are so great."

"Thanks Frank, I have enough other problems to worry about, so I think I'll pass on your proposition."

After a lot of back and forth between all of the people in the party, the dancing started. Nick danced the first few dances with Judy and after that her dance card was completely filled with all of the wolves surrounding her and that she encouraged.

Nick seemed to be left out of the equation and for his part he was not concerned.

When he decided to leave the party, he went to Frank and thanked him for a superb evening, made his goodbye's and asked Frank if he would see that Judy got home safely that night, she was having such a good time that he didn't want to disturb her.

Frank said, I understand, "I'll see that I get a limo to take her home or whomever she goes home with, I'll make sure she is safe."

"Frank you have my undying gratitude.

"Frank said, Forgetaboutit."

Chapter Twenty-Two
Home and the big bang.
The end of a romance

The next day Nick was winging his way home to the cold, the ice, the snow, and the problems that he was sure were popping up.

A problem still there, was the Prick, Nick had not heard anything from him for a while and he hoped that the Prick had learned a lesson and taken it to heart because Nick had already put a substantial hole in his racing operation and if need be, his home life would be disrupted, maybe permanently.

Nick planned to send an emissary or two and have words with him and see if he will listen to reason. This is a thing that will have to be put on the back burner until after the festivities have concluded at the estate.

He arrived late that Sunday night.

As he drove past the gates and went through security, everything was in disarray as Joey was working feverishly to get this estate, to the point it resembled the picture on the invitation. The same thing was happening on the interior where Liz was in charge. The party was only two weeks off and Nick was thrilled to find things so well advanced.

Where were the dogs? Joey had them in the kennel while workmen were busy putting the finishing touches to the estate. He released them upon Nick's arrival and the affection he was shown was just amazing, he asked Joey facetiously are these the watchdogs we been raising? Joey responded with a laugh. About this time Joey's two kids burst forth and gave Nick as big a greeting as the dogs. In a million years Nick never thought he would enjoy children but he surprised himself, he really enjoyed these two kids.

Nick was expecting Jenny to arrive at any time; he had plenty of work lined up for them both. They would be the ambassadors of good will and the heads of public relations. Everybody must be called and a strong connection established with each and every invitee. Nick started on this just as soon as he could.

His first call was to the Governor, leaving a message with his secretary, said this is Nick Lasko, "Governor I wanted to call you personally to assist you in any way and to remind you once again of the Valentines party that is the inauguration of my new estate, and Governor I'm also sure that the word inauguration is not unfamiliar to you. I'm sure you realize that I am jesting and want you to know that I am on your side in any further plans you may have either on a national or on a statewide level."

Nick continued making many calls of this type throughout the day. Some, he was able to talk to, and others he had to leave messages. This was hard work and it tested Nick's skill as a communicator.

Other things kept occurring to him such as remembering to hire a Limo company to ferry guests from the Airport to the estate. He should have already hired security guards to man the front gate and security guards to protect the perimeter and the rear of the estate to safeguard against any untoward events from taking place.

Jenny's arrival was eagerly awaited. The costs were staggering and completely unforeseen, for instance china and silverware, maids and hostesses, a 16 piece orchestra that had to play continuously, all the small details including things like the type of floor wax applied to the dance floor, The arrangement of the food an hors'doeuvres, which tables will display what type of center piece. For God sakes Jenny "hurry up."

The next day Jenny called from the airport saying that she had arrived and wanted to double-check the address. Nick said, "grab a cab, give him my name, and he will know exactly where to take you and won't screw you around."

When she came through the front gates everybody was there to greet her including the dogs. All knew how much we needed her even though she was unaware of her importance up to this moment.

Nick enthusiastically kissed her, one of the few times he did, in fact he can't remember having an intimate moment with her in the past and he is pretty sure that this kiss did not reach that qualification either.

"My God Fast Nick I am happy to see you, I never would have believed in a million years, I was coming to Buckingham Palace, but in my estimation a king does live here but he has no queen yet, what's the problem Fast Nick?"

"I'm waiting for you to become eligible."

"Sorry to disappoint you, but I may never become eligible and that has nothing to do with you Nick, it's just my personal situation that may continue a long time into the future. But pray tell me, whose lovely children do these two belong."

"I probably should claim them because they do live with me but I can't do that as much as I would like to. They belong to Joey and Liz my superintendent and his wife who is head of my household."

"Jenny, we have a ton of work for you to take care of come to my office and I will clue you in."

"Jenny I know that I will be throwing you in to the middle of a very high profile festivity. You will be dealing with the highest ranking political bosses in the state and you will be talking to them as if you knew them all your life. I want them to fall in love with you just as I have, because they will all be here February 14, and I have put in charge the most charismatic most beautiful and intelligent person I know to lead the festivities."

"Fast Nick, the most full of B.S. person I have run across in many a moon but I do love your way with words."

As much as the master of the house regretted his next magnanimous decision, he never the less sacrificed his lavish bedroom to Jenny with raised pedestal bed and all. He said to himself, that dam bedroom was rather effeminate anyway.

The grand opening was just one part of the equation, getting out, meeting, and glad-handing the various contractors and builders that would need help in getting contracts with the city, state, or county was another. The Cleveland and Pittsburg people were deeply involved in this game, but probably did not have the clout that Nick would be able to wield and because of his past performances they may be in a mood to defer to Nick, knowing that he would be more than willing to divvy up the proceeds.

The time was drawing near and Nick's anxiety level was reaching unforeseen heights, he knew that there was always something that had been overlooked, for instance there was nobody to announce the guest's arrival at the entrance. Frantically he searched for Jenny, when he found her he advisedly said, "Jen we don't have a greeter at the entrance.

Jennifer said, "Take a deep breath and calm down I not only have a person that will make the announcement at the door but he has a bit of an English accent."

"Goddamit Jen where the hell you been all my life, with the crew I have put together this may go down as the premier event of the season. That brings to mind the reporters, do they have enough access?"

Nick it's up to you to notify the media. Nobody here knows how much publicity you want."

Joey interjected, "Nick your past reputation may bring some hindrance to you."

"Joey you have known me for a long time and of course my past now plays a part in everything I do, but I am becoming more and more known for all of the good deeds that I have accomplished in the past few years, and many people are better off because of me, orphans, homeless, just people down on their luck that needed a helping hand, I've even had business men come to me for a loan because the banks would not give it to them and they were in danger of going bankrupt, I literally saved their businesses, several that will be attending our party have been helped by me, Joey I could go on and on talking about the things I have done."

"Nick, I know from personal experience how you have turned my life around," Joey responded, "and the many kind things you have done that people have no idea that you accomplished."

After talking about these good things, Nick's mind was turned back to The Prick; he decided to send one emissary to have a conversation with him. He was back on his farm in Pennsylvania so Nick had heard, and was still crying about everything. It was time to step up the pressure.

Nick called one of his very trusted men into his office and carefully coached him on the things that had to be said to The Prick. When this man confronts the Prick it has to be in a fashion that will be unexpected, the emissary will say what he had to say and get the hell out before the Prick has a chance to call the local constabulary. If for any reason he refuses to keep his mouth shut and not cooperate, that gives Nick's associate, license to take the steps that are necessary.

"Anything we do to him will have to be given the go ahead from Pittsburgh. But look at me, no matter what Pittsburgh says it is not okay to put the finger on him. Once you have the okay from Pittsburgh, non chiamormi solo andare Avanti e fare quello che hai delle cosa da fare, (do not call me, just go ahead and do what you have to do), ricardo non hit senza famiglia saranno coinvolti, (but remember no hit and no family will be involved), otherwise do what you must."

This guy was becoming a real irritation to Nick and he wanted this solved and the problem to disappear.

He felt The Prick was doing more to destroy him, Nick Lasko, than he was to The Prick.

Nick's thoughts were more and more turning to the ultimate solution. But the mere mention of this type of solution made Nick shudder with dread.

After thinking this thing through, and realize the penalty for murder is the chair or spending the rest of his life incarcerated.

After all, I have done to this man, destroyed everything that the man has and it still doesn't alleviate the nastiness, than what option is left? There are only two options; kill him or live with the fire and dripping vituperation coming from his mouth.

The final subjugation; Nick would have to concede that he had lost. Of course, he could continue the McCoy & Hatfield feud by bringing a lawsuit for slander, now doesn't that sound smart, keep it alive so we can give him a forum to issue his proclamations against Nick.

The magical night arrived, and the snow arrived about the same time, in fact, the weather was so bad that the limos were having a difficult time getting up the drive. Snow was piling up, and of course one of the things that was neglected in the planning of this party in the off chance there was snow, we should have had a crew on hand to shovel snow. Corrective measures had to be taken, and we pressed the security guards into service and now they were snow removal specialists.

The home was built in such a manner that the limousines arrived under the porte cochere, and enabling the guests enter unencumbered by the snowy weather. Once their wraps were removed they were announced by Jeeves the— almost English butler—and properly introduced to the other previously announced distinguished guests.

It did not take long until the party was in a full-blown fantasyland of food, drink and music filled the estate. The Ball Room dance floor was crowded with swaying elegantly dressed ladies and gentleman, the vocalists couldn't have been more spectacular, singing old and current favorites that set a time-tone which transported the dancers to by-gone times, when smoothness and moving with panache and grace was the opulent style of the day.

At the peak of the festivities the master of ceremonies rose to introduce Nick Lasko.

"Without further ado the man that made this memorable Valentine's Day possible, a drum roll please, Nick Lasko."

Nick proceeded to verbalize his welcoming speech.

"This dance is a success because of your attendance.

"Tonight has seen the coming together of the most influential and forward looking people of the state of Ohio."

"I think everybody here knows how hard I work for not only the Democratic Party, but also the many independents and those Republicans that will compromise and move this state forward toward a better future and have the welfare of our citizens at the core of their values."

"You know the one intrinsic thing we all have in common is our constant need for campaign contributions, because without them we have no way of getting our message to the voters. I have been very blessed to have had the wherewithal to fund many of your campaigns and that is something that I look forward to in the future, God willing."

"In order for me to continue the path I have chosen, you must all do your part, and when I say your part, I mean to try to help me by giving some of your time to me. Nothing hurts me more than when I make a phone call to your office to have a secretary say to me, I'm sorry the congressman or Senator, or whatever the case may be is too busy to speak to you at this time or the response may be, 'I'm sorry the senator or the congressman is not in at this time.' nothing could possibly be more of an aggravation and by the way this also applies to a constituent even more than me.

We are talking about votes here people! After all isn't that what it's all about? Give me and your constituents as much time as is possible and believe me you won't regret it. What I'm trying to say is, give the people that count as much of your time as humanly possible."

"I happened to have been in South Carolina, and I had an incident occur that I never forgot. I was attending the State Fair in Columbia— and there's nothing more that I enjoy then a good old fashioned fair. I was browsing through the exhibits in one of the many buildings that were showing the fruits of the labors of the people that made those unbelievable pies and cakes, when I came upon this little guy standing in the middle of the aisle handing out campaign literature sweating profusely, reflecting the heat that was typical of a South Carolina October. It was on a Thursday when the Gamecocks were playing their football archrivals Clemson; Today is what they call Big Thursday because the big game of the year was being played simultaneously in conjunction with the State Fair.

Eventually I found myself in a conversation with this Gentleman who spoke to everybody coming by, and even though I was not a voter in South Carolina he found things interesting about me and gave yours truly as much time as he did the voters. He impressed me with his loquaciousness and his ability to find something interesting in everybody he talked to, and shaking hands with everybody that passed by, he was the personification of a person that was deeply interested in you. It didn't matter if he was sweating and had been standing on his feet nonstop for several hours. You could see in his eyes that this is what he lived for; you could see that this is where he belonged. I later found out that he was one of the most successful members of the State Senate reelected by a landslide every time he ran."

"In the short time I talked to him, we became such good friends that I expected he would invite me over for dinner. Well happily that never happened because I had no room left after filling up on those sausage's and peppers that they sell at the fair."

"The next fella I want you to hear from is our beloved Governor Michael DiSalle."

The Governor got up and gave the standard opening remarks and kept it short and said let's get back to the festivities.

Nick tried in his most genial manner to get around to everyone and he was successful in that endeavor.

The weather outside was frightful and the snow had piled up while the party was in full blast. Nick had peeked outside and did not like what he saw. He knew that the airport would be closed and roads would be impassable. He felt that the limos as heavy as they were could make it to the hotels.

He prevailed on his staff and they started calling hotels and motels to book rooms for as many guests as they could accommodate, and the rest would be staying the night at the estate. Many had rooms booked but their accommodations were too far away. Some had to be sleeping on the floor, but they would have blankets and plush carpets to sleep on. He promised all that Santa Claus and Mrs. Claus would make an appearance and would prepare a sumptuous breakfast.

That next morning seemed like a continuous party from the night before, many laughs were had and the cooks that prepared the morning repast was a potpourri of the staff and the guests all getting together and doing crazy things to the food but it all turned out well and everyone was fed and finally sent on their way.

Nick was completely exhausted and probably not be interested in another party anytime soon.

The parties' over but the work has just begun.

Chapter Twenty-Three
For Sale

The marble halls of government were calling in a loud formidable voice. Nick was finally able to operate on a scale that he had not thought of in his wildest flights of fancy.

The job ahead was to contact any employer that had to work with the government on contracts.

Setting up a corporation and starting a legitimate business, had been a problem in the past. Now he would be paying local, state, and federal taxes, not to mention F.I.C.A., and unemployment tax, and various insurances that would protect him if he were sued. Of course, he would never have to use the latter because he had his own insurance that was more effective, efficient, and quicker to take action.

Jennifer was an extraordinarily valued associate, and he would love to keep her on with the new company. He called her into the office and offered her a position as chief financial officer at a salary that would make a whore blush.

Jen said, "An offer like that comes once in a lifetime, but I will have to turn it down. There are things about me you may not know."

"Jennifer you must know by now that I am in love with you. Do you think that I would have carried a torch for this long if I had not had you thoroughly vetted? I already know about your ex, and he stills pays the high maintenance upkeep of the life style you live."

"Well, Fast Nick I am surprised that you know about that, which means that my privacy has been invaded, but that still means nothing compared to what I am going to inform you of."

"Jen, I cannot think of anything that serious that would make me change my opinion of you."

"Your opinion of me has nothing to do with what I'm about to tell you, even though I value it highly."

I have two beautiful children that are in my ex-husband's custody, and I have visitation rights once a week, I love them very much, and do what I can to spend time with them."

Nick felt a sense of shock and foreboding, "Jen this is something I did not know."

"Fast Nick you know it now, I lost in a court battle because of money! I'm sure you have said this before; The golden rule, he who has the gold rules. The Judge saw it that way, and I lost the custody battle."

"Jen I do not believe that story, there has to be more to it because no court in the land would take children away from a loving caring mother."

"Fast Nick you are able to discern many things about life, and you are right about this. If I must admit what the real problem is, it will show what kind of a piece of shit as a person and mother I actually am."

"I met and fell in love with a well-known actor and carried on a long-term affair with him. I was under the illusion that we would be together for the rest of our lives, and so I filed for divorce willing to leave a loving husband and two beautiful children for a pig in a poke, that's how blinded by love I was."

"Please continue." Nick said this with a touch of anger rising within him. How can the temerity of a person trump common sense, and the conventions of society?

"Of course right after the divorce, the actor dumped me just as easily as you would an old shoe."

"At this time of my life I had no income, no money, no prospects, and no self-respect. It was at this point I ran back to my ex and offered to eat any self-respect I had left, and do anything I could if he would just take me back, and put it all behind us. He looked at me as if I was a filthy and used rag and closed the door in my face. He was the man I was waiting for when you met me in Las Vegas— and yes he stood me up. He never wanted to see me again, but every month like clockwork he sends me a check. He informed me that he did not want the mother of his children going penniless."

"I truly respect his values, but everybody deserves a second chance."

"No, not in his world, not a person of his high moral character. If you can understand this, you will know, I will if necessary spend the rest of my life trying to make it up to him, and if at all possible to be with him again, because you see Fast Nick, he is the one I love and I always will."

Hearing Jen's confession devastated Nick, this was something he had not foreseen and did not want to think about now.

This was a blow he could not easily swallow, and he spent what seemed like a millennium in a funk with various thoughts running through his head trying to think how he could get her to change what her feelings were. He knew he could, with the right connections, win her children back for her. He could supply the money that her ex was now providing, hell he could even have the ex-disappear, but you know, none of this could make her love him until she made up her mind to have feelings for him, so, currently it was hopeless.

The incessant ringing of the phone broke Nick's malaise; the emissary that Nick had sent to handle The Prick was calling.

"Not over the phone I'll meet you at the Brass Rail. Can you make it in 30 minutes?"

"You bet I can."

He turned to Jennifer, and he asked, "Is your flight back home all set."

"I leave tomorrow, and I hope that I didn't spoil things for you. I still value your friendship, and I trust that you have appreciated my efforts on your behalf."

"I couldn't have pulled this party off without you. I appreciate it more than I can tell you."

Nick said his goodbye's to Jen and while doing this was feeling emotions that filled him with remorse, knowing this unrequited love was at an end, and could never be.

The Brass Rail was an iconic meeting place in Youngstown, and when you used the phrase— meet me at the Brass Rail— no further explanation was needed.

Walking into the restaurant, he immediately recognized the emissary that he had sent to confront The Prick. A very well dressed and mild looking gentleman that had a reliable reputation for carrying out his given mission. However being mild was not one of his characteristics.

Getting right to the problem he asked him, "Did you take care of the problem?"

"I broke his jaw and the last time I saw him he was being picked up and taken to the Emergency Room."

"Any witnesses?"

"None."

"Will it work?"

"I don't have the slightest idea. But if I were you I'd leave him alone unless you want him whacked."

I do not want that.

"Than just go by it Nick, don't become obsessed with it. He's a little Mother-Fucker who won't be able to talk for a while, plus you have destroyed his racing operation to the point where it's going to take him years to recover to a position of eminence in the racing game— if he ever does— and at his age, it's doubtful."

Nick was inclined to agree but with an ominous sense of foreboding. Realistically what could the Prick do except complain?

He had to get back to establishing his business. The important thing now was get in contact with Cleveland and Pittsburgh and let them know how things were progressing. He notified Stefano Guliano and Angelo Vilanotti, which now was Capo's with the two competing segments, and thanks to Nick, keeping the peace was essential, because Nick was paying a healthy Vigorish to both of them. Nick kept bringing in more money as time went by; they had no inclination to upset the apple cart at least not at this time.

Nick knew that each in their time would make a run at all the businesses that Nick had established. Greed was not a respecter of genius and certainly Nick could lay claim to that. But he was not a full-fledged Italian and even though he was half-Italian, that half was not Sicilian and Cosa Nostra had a pertinacious streak when considering elevating a member to associate status.

He wanted a high profile business address and felt that the Public Square near the old Palace Theatre would fill the bill nicely.

He did not at this time know that in the not too distant future, down- town Youngstown would become ghostly, and a disconcerting sight to see the emptiness of the environs.

What Nick was doing absolutely fit right into what the Mafia was always trying to do; win favors for their pals, make them prosperous, and eventually shake them down for more and more as time went by.

This was now the easiest thing in the world to do.

When somebody came to them requesting a contract from the state or municipality generally involving large sums of money, the next call the organization made was to Nick. He was able to put substantial sums of money in their client's pocket, The Mafia would have those patron's forever indebted to them.

Nick was a registered lobbyist, the real purveyor, the one who actually was the source and connected personally with the Mafia and clients, so the clout was all with him.

Of course, the amount of work and dedication that was required and the masterpiece he put together was prodigious, many times he was dealing with not one legislator but a whole raft of them, especially if there was a committee involved.

When he was able to put the whole thing together, he felt as if he had painted a Rembrandt.

His fees were extravagant and were based on the amount of money that would be involved in the contract, and the amount of kickbacks that he would have to provide, and who was included in the payoffs. Generally, the more powerful the legislator, the greater the vigorish. In the off chance that a legislator was an honest and idealistic politician, Nick would have to use other tactics that would be of significant concern to that particular person— possibly a donation to a favorite charity, or winning specific legislation for his constituents. Whatever the case may be, Nick was more than equal to the job.

As time went on, except for mostly minor problems in Nick's various enterprises, things were running smoothly. One evening he received a call from Stefano Guliano from Pittsburgh asking for a meeting with Nick the next day. "Okay Steve, pick the time."

"How about lunch."

"Okay, make it at the Capri one pm, do you know where it's at."

"I'm not familiar with it."

Ron Chicone

"On the north side, go to Belmont Avenue, past Saint Elizabeth's hospital continue north about a mile or so. It will be on the right."

Nick could not figure out what Stefano wanted, if a Capo was coming down, it couldn't be good.

The next day was overcast and rainy, the gloom of the impending arrival of winter.

Nick's mood was as miserable as the weather, especially meeting Stefano.

When Nick arrived at the appointed time, Steve had not arrived yet, and in fact, kept Nick waiting for over a half hour. At this, he had a feeling of impending misfortune.

Steve came ambling in acting unconcerned and relaxed. "Had a hard time finding this place. Look Nick this is a little public; I'd like to have some location with more privacy."

"No problem there's an office downstairs I believe the manager will let us use it."

They ambled down the stairs to a well-appointed office.

"How are things going in Pittsburgh queried Nick?"

"Look at me Nick! The Feds are cracking down all over the place. We have a couple of people turning states evidence, but these are low level Soldatos. We are not going after them so much as we are their sponsors; you have to watch everything you do.

Jesus Christ you can't even whisper out in the streets anymore."

"So how can I help you?"

"Whether you know it or not we are entering into the Juice Racket, (drugs)

"Goddammit I was afraid of this."

Nick that's where all the money is! All the high society rich and the niggers and spics are in this shit as if it was candy."

"Hold on, I took an oath that I would never get involved in anything that I would pull more than six months in the can.

210

This crap you're doing could start out with twenty years for the first offense."

"Believe me, in years to come this junk will be legalized just like liquor was, but the street value is so high that you don't have to do truckloads to turn a healthy profit."

"Okay Stefano, why in the fuck do you need me?"

"Nick you are the man with all the connections. We have shipments coming in from all directions, the Great Lakes, jet planes, both private and commercial, cars and trucks coming up from Florida, Georgia, South Carolina, North Carolina, Louisiana, Mississippi—and we need to protect these shipments. I hear tell you are the guy with all the power in the halls of justice, and the State House, and the Highway Patrol, and the Coast Guard."

"Steve listen to me, you have heard wrong, yes, I have some influence, but what the hell happens when I approach these power brokers with a request to get involved in drugs. Sure, we can make the pay-off so large we could sway them over to us. But one little squeak from any of them and I'm in the slammer for many years." "We have a pretty nice set up now. We are wielding power in just about any business you want to name, and none of us has served a day in the can because of it. But get involved in drugs and we are all going to be serving time, and I don't look good in a jump suit.

"Look Nick, we got some stuff that we are bringing up I-75 all you have to do is make sure the patrol is not patrolling when we are hauling or at least not stopping certain types of cars or trucks and your end of it is going to be six figures."

"First of all I'm not going to do this, second who do you suggest I go see if by some ungodly occurrence and some unknown fuckin' reason I decided to do it. I have a horror of spending the rest of my life in a penitentiary. As far as I'm concerned it's not going to happen."

"Nick, mi ascolta, si opera in questo stato, perché VI, permettono anche, farete questa cosa perché VI chiediamo.

(Nick listen to me, you operate in this state because we allow you. You will do this thing because we ask you).

Quello che chiedono è per me di tagliare le braccia e le gambe, siete miope. (What you are asking is for me to cut off my arms and legs. You are being short sighted). I am personally disturbed that you are trying to get me involved in something that everything in me is yelling don't do it."

Listen Nick, this is not a request. Choices are not with you. Capisce.

"I'll tell you what Stefano, I will confer with some of the other Capo's in Pittsburgh, and see where we go from here."

"Fuck you Nicholas. The only one that counts is sitting right here beside you."

"Goddammit Stephano is that a threat."

"No, that's a promise"

Nick raced back to his office and as soon as he could, contacted Vinnie on the phone.

"Vinnie, I have an important subject to discuss with you, and if it isn't solved, could destroy my whole operation and cut deeply into the vig I am providing to you people up there in your fuckin' penthouses."

"I'm all ears Nick."

"Since when is Stefano running things in your backyard and then stepping into my front yard and wanting to run my operation and tell me what to do? This is after everything I went through to set this operation up. Does he have any idea what I had to go through, in fact, do any of you have any idea what the fuck is going on, and what kind of gold mine we have? I don't think so.

"Hey partner, kudos are yours."

"All of you believe you are doing me some kind of favor by letting me work my ass off getting people on my side, using my personality, all my skills, all my knowledge, and fortitude."

"Hey settle down, I don't want to be the bearer of bad news, but things change."

"You may not know this, but do you have any idea how much abuse I've taken from some of these legislators wanting to know why they aren't getting a bigger share of the pie. I even had one guy tell me that if he didn't get a bigger piece he was going to rearrange my face. I acted as if I was frightened and humbly told him I would see what I could do.

He said, "That's not the way it's going to work. If I did not come up with the juice," he said, "he would throw my Dago ass out of his office if I ever showed up again." Of course, this is a guy that we need, and I bowed and scraped my way out of his office. I then took a portion of my cut and gave it to him."

"These are the things I have to do to keep everything rolling.

"I appreciate the humiliation that you suffered in that situation. I do not think I could have been that understanding."

Now Stefano comes around and tells me how he's going to run things from now on, and he's talkin' about Pot, Meth, Coke, Blow, Horse, (Heroin) and Iron(Crack)— all of this shit I've tried to stay away from all of my life."

"For Christ sake slow down for a minute you're talkin' like an asshole and not using your head. Nick there are things in this life that we have to confront, and other things that it's best to attack from the rear or attack obliquely and this is one of those times that the rear or oblique option is preferable. This is serious enough that either you come over here or I will come over there. What's better for you?"

"Vinnie come over to my place. At least here I'll know who's doing the bugging, It's either Pittsburgh or Cleveland or both."

"Nick, if you can get loose tomorrow I'll be there in the afternoon."

"You got it Vinnie; let's get this ironed out once and for all! Do not take any associates with you."

"Nick at this point was getting bad vibes, and he did not know what Pittsburg was about or what they were thinking.

Nick's natural suspicious nature was now kicking in. If they're changing the business and going into drugs they would not want anybody around who is negative. That means maybe they finger me and take me out of the picture. Why not? It wouldn't be the first time or the last.

They would have somebody step in to take my place.

Of course, they would have to deal with the unfamiliarity problem with the various influential people I have groomed, but they had enough shit on them that if they did not cooperate they could stuff indictment after indictment at them.

Meeting Vinnie was usually a pleasure for Nick. He genuinely liked him. Vinnie was the kind of guy that knew how to get along with people and always tried to give the best advice possible. This was the reason he was made the consigliore for the Pittsburgh faction.

They sat down together the next day in a room that Nick had cleaned and cleared of any bugs, so it was a secure area

Nick said, "Vinnie give me the low- down on this drug racket."

"Look partner this is what the game is coming to. The money is too large to be ignored. In the past, we tried to ignore it, but if we don't get into it, the other groups will become dominant in our own territory and it won't be long before we cease to exist. Nick, you don't have a choice. You go along, or you don't exist anymore."

"Vinnie I was pretty negative when Stefano was here, is it possible they have already fingered me?"

"Nick I don't have knowledge of that—and if I did, I wouldn't tell you—but this thing is so big they are not going to let anything or anyone get in the way, so if I were you, I would be always looking behind me. Don't be like Satchel Paige who once said, "Never look back somethin' may be gaining on you.""

Remember my friend, something or somebody is always trying to gain on you."

"If you have a lot of jack, they will be standing in line to take it from you. In your case, the only way I can see they can take it, is to obliterate you. So Nick, you either go along or get along— one or the other— no in between."

"For God sakes Vinnie this is going to destroy us. The Feds have a hard- on when it comes to drugs."

"Listen to me Nick, the pressure is already unbelievable. They are cracking down with a vengeance. Ever since Bobby Kennedy became so powerful under the president, he has put unrelenting pressure on the Cosa Nostra, and we were the ones that got the sonofabitch elected. We handed two states that I know of to the Kennedy camp. Hell he was fucking one of Sam Giancana's girls.

With all the hullabaloo in Cuba, they've been talking to people that we know, about getting rid of that cockroach in Cuba, They want us to do the dirty work, and they take the credit. These people are two-faced bastards, and now they are trying to put us out of business. These are times that try men's souls." The real losers are going to be those dirty bastards the Kennedys.

"Jesus Christ Vinnie, all of this was damn clear when he was running for election."

"Shit Nick, the fuckers father worked with us for years, and he was the one that came to us for help. What were we supposed to think? The Kennedy's are too young and have always lived a rich and protected way of life, they don't understand the forces they have unleashed. The Cosa Nostra goes back hundreds of years and has faced dozens of repressive regimes, and they think they can stamp it out? Not in their lifetimes, and their lives may be unusually short."

"Hey Vinnie you're making it sound like my lifetime may be very short too."

"Look Nick there are no guarantees in this business, remember dying is easy, living is tough. If I were you, I'd walk lightly on tiptoes when you're talking to Stefano. I know I wasn't much help. You are an extremely self-reliant person; You will figure out what to do. By the way Nick, what was the name of that senator who told you to get your Dago ass out of his office?"

"His name was John Scully, but it was nothing, we got it straightened out."

"We like to know his name just in case, you know what I mean."

After Vince left, Nick had a lot to mull on. The general tone of the conversation had been unsettling, and he was now in a quandary. What the hell should he do?

Nick's answer was received a week later, when he picked up the newspaper in the morning. Headlines blared out, Prominent Senator Murdered in his office. The article went on to explain that his demise took place early in the morning while he was drinking his coffee. No one heard anything.

Nick immediately picked up the phone and called Vinnie; he was extremely upset and knew he could not say much over the phone. He said, "Vinnie, what the hell is going on?"

Vinnie replied, "What are you talking about?" Remember that this is a broadcast station."

"I haven't forgotten, but I'm upset, which is an understatement. There was no need for what happened. It was all over, and a particularly useful servant is no longer there, if you get my drift."

"Nick some things you can say and some you can't. In our language, when you use insulting phrases to describe or be discourteous to any of our people then you must face the possibility of retaliation."

"Retaliation is one thing but the extremity of the retaliation was overdone."

"Nick there are times when the proper action must be taken when a disservice is done."

"I would have thought you would have learned your lesson; the Prick is still shitting on you. If you had listened to us in the first place that problem would have been solved."

"I must admit that the Prick has been a thorn in the ass, but it's kind of eased up now that he's racing second- tier horses. For now, I'm going to ignore him."

Ending the conversation, Nick picked up the phone, and called Stefano, "He said Steve give me the dates, and I'll see what I can do."

"Nick, Lei sarà una gradita aggiunta per i nostri fidati luogotenenti" (You will be a welcomed addition to our trusted Lieutenants).

After Nick received the dates he started giving thought to who in his repertoire was a viable person with connections to the highway patrol, the only name he could think of was a Capo in Cleveland. Anthony Vilanotti with whom he had some contact with in the past. When Nick had him on the phone he said Tony, "This is Nick Lasko from Youngstown. Do you remember me?"

"Yes I do, what is the problem. "

"Tony, my problem is what somebody from Pittsburgh wants. He is Cosa Tessa. Can I send an emissary to you? He will inform you of the particulars."

"Of course you can, I have a restaurant called Vilanotti's in Murray Hill. He can see me most anytime there, but why don't you come yourself?"

"We could sit down and have some of the best Dago Red you have ever drunk, and enjoy the best pizza in Murray Hill."

"You know what, that is the best offer I've had in a long time, you can expect me there tomorrow, sarà che essere conveinent." (Will that be convenient)?

"You bet it is, ci vediamo domani." (See you tomorrow).

217

Nick had hired a competent secretary who was enrolled at Youngstown State University studying business law. Alicia Gatti had graduated from Rayen High, and now at a more advanced age, after a disastrous marriage, she decided to go back to college and finish her B. A. Nick made a deal with her that she could take all the time she needed to attend college. She would be paid an hourly wage based on the number of hours she was able to work.

Because she had a solid handle on the law, her training was invaluable in handling the enormous volume of paperwork Nick had to fill out. It was truly gargantuan. When he had to leave the office for an extended period. He was assured that he left it in capable hands.

On his way to meet Tony, Nick organized his thoughts. He had to sell Tony on putting him in touch with the right people or Tony could act as the go between for Nick and Steve.

He did not want to be in this position, and he knew this would be an awkward conversation with Tony. But in this business you had to have a gigante set di palle (giant set of balls).

Entering the uncommonly beautiful restaurant, Tony was actually doing the greeting. Imagine if you can a top Capo in Cleveland greeting and leading you to your table. If you have a complaint, maybe you would like to file it with him. On top of that, Tony had an impressive background. He had played professional football in the Canadian League.

Going about 6'2"and 240 made him quite an impressive human specimen. Maybe somebody whom you might think twice before issuing a complaint. In actuality, he had a genial disposition and was more than willing to listen to any complaints. He would fix them immediately, and many times a free meal was a probability.

But don't let the guise fool you. If you crossed him in any way you would be foolishly entering a danger zone and he did not get to where he is letting fools run over him, but he had a balanced view of day-to-day problems and usually came up with a Solomon view of the situation. The thing that kept him at the top of his profession was being a clear thinking problem solver.

Tony came over to the entrance as soon as Nick made his appearance and with a wide smile shook hands, as he did he said, "this was a pleasure to have you grace my restaurant with your presence." He led him to a special table that was situated in a private spot away from the general hubbub and din of the diner.

Tony said, "I have given a lot of thought to the day I spent with you at your beautiful estate. I thoroughly enjoyed the surroundings and your hospitality. I would have enjoyed keeping in touch, but with our people the way it is, may have started too many tongues wagging."

"Nick let me introduce you to my wife, Dawn, who is the real manager of this establishment. She will be taking care of us as we talk."

"I mean no offense, but Dawn, your wife, is certainly beautiful, and knowing your personality Tony, you deserve it and I don't mean that gratuitously.

"Sometimes I spend too much time talking to the clientele and she has a way of getting me back to business. Without her, this restaurant would not exist."

"You know Tony you are such a wide- open gentleman, I wonder how you got into this thing that we have."

"Nick, sometimes it just the way we grew up. You know in this country there was a lot of discrimination not only to the black folk, but us Italians to. So, to make a living we did what was around us, and became tough and worked our way into a better situation for our famiglia. To stay viable we had to do some things that were not too nice."

"The people that we surround ourselves with are nothing more than good friends and we all belong to a club that has political ramifications, and we call it Our Thing or Cosa Nostra."

"Aw, but Nick, that is not what you came all this way to talk about, so tell me what can I do for you, but before we get down to business I am a horse racing buff and I go out to Thistledown Race track as often as I can."

At this point his wife who had just brought our wine interjected, "Passa troppo tempo e denaro in quel posto." (He spends too much time and money at that place).

"You see that's what I was telling you, she's always watching over me, thank god someone is.

Hey Nick give me a tip on a horse."

"Tony if I had one I'd bet on it myself. The truth is that I have been so busy that I haven't talked to my trainer in a long time. The only communication I get is, send money."

"Tony I'm sure you know that the way our thing is headed, is into total shit. You know what I'm talking about. I highly resent it, but I'm stuck. Stefano came to see me and asked me to do a favor involving this new thing, it has to do with the highway patrol."

"Tony you know that I have connections all over the state, but seriously weak when it came to the patrol. Now Tony, I'm skating on thin ice because I was decidedly negative when speaking to Stefano which did not go down well with him. I was informed I did not have a choice. In fact, it was a tossup whether or not they had me fingered. So I looked around and the only one I knew that had a long time association with the patrol was you, so I'm coming to you for help."

"What is the help you need?"

"On a particular day there are certain types of trucks and cars that will be traveling I-75, they need the patrol to look the other way."

"Nick, believe me there is nothing I'd rather do than help you out. There are other things I can help with, but not the patrol. However, I will give you a contact number of a friend of mine. There may be a way, but I will not be involved. If I were you Nick, it would behoove you to be careful, the Highway patrol and the troopers that dedicate their lives to it make this an outstanding organization, and there has never been a hint of corruption associated with this group."

They continued to have a pleasant repast of Italian delicacies and homemade vino. Nick had figured out that Tony was not going to be his salvation with this problem. So it was up to Nick to come up with a solution.

He decided not to contact the number that Tony had provided Tony had made it clear that this was something he did not want to become a part of, and Nick wanted to honor that stance.

Okay where do we go from here? A lie may be his best bet; he decided to inform Stefano it was all set, but any vehicle that broke the law no matter what it was would be stopped and searched and that was the best he could do.

The emphasis to Stefano was to inform his drivers to obey the letter of the law. If they did not, they were on their own.

Stefano upon hearing this was not happy with this rendition of the way this was going down, but it was the way it was, and the way it was going to be for now, but his estimation of Nick was downward.

The problem: if one truck is confiscated, we are talking one million dollars. Not an inconsequential sum, and if that happened then maybe Nick's life could be in jeopardy.

Nick thought, "maybe I should be thinking about putting the finger on Stefano." If he wanted to, the logical way would take the path of threatening the Pittsburgh people, In other words Nick's services would no longer be available until they put a hit on Stefano.

Another way to get a bullet through his head was to go to the Cleveland group and offer his services exclusively to them if they put a hit on Stefano. Nick was just daydreaming.

There was one more option, do it himself. Put a bomb in Stefano's car and the hit would be completely anonymous.

Nick was thinking of possible options, if by some chance, one of those trucks or cars were confiscated that day.

If this occurred, his life would not be worth a whole lot, and this whole thing would become the survival of the fittest, so whoever got to whomever first, was the winner.

What a way to win, by becoming an assassino (murderer). This is a thing that all of his life he had tried to avoid. Just thinking about it made him realize he was sinking more and more into the morass of the Mafia and this was just a step away from being an assassino di una persona. (Hit man)

As it turned out no car or truck was stopped on the appointed date. Nick sighed with relief when the happy news was related to him.

While he was in Cleveland, it would be an excellent opportunity to see Clariden Farms and Holly.

As he was driving over to Chardon, he reminisced a little about better times before this drug thing took hold. When he stepped out of the car he immediately spotted Holly working a colt in the ring, she was not having an easy time of it. This colt was either not happy or too happy because he was rearing, kicking, and generally raising hell. He finally reared so high he almost went over backward and Holly came sliding off and landed on her ass with a thump, and here comes the hero Nick, to the rescue. Actually, the colt got to her first. The horse seemed to be a little non-plused as he trotted to her and nudged her with his nose, saying in his own way, "Hey, are you okay, I was just having a little fun, I never thought you would actually fall off."

Nick finally arrived and helped her to her feet, asking, "if she was okay."

"Of course I'm okay; it's not the first time or the last I've been dumped off a horse. How about you trying it Nick, " He readily agreed. Nick had ridden horses most of his life and was a pseudo accomplished equestrian. Holly watched with some sense of foreboding as Nick quickly swept up the reins and proceeded to work this colt around the track until some of the spunk was out of the colt. He then pulled up in front of Holly, handed her the reins and said, "Here you are, I believe he's ready for you."

"Damn it Nick, I did not want that colt run like that, He's just a baby, and you could have easily injured him."

"It looked to me the way you were riding him was infinitely more dangerous. I felt you needed help."

"Okay what the hell do you want?"

"I just stopped to see how things were going and if you needed anything."

"Hell yes I always need things, but you are never at the office, and you do not return any of the messages I leave."

"Well I'm here now so let's have at it."

"Let's start with how much money you owe me for all the little shit I have to raid my piggy bank for, and then I have a list of the things that are needed around here."

"Okay but how about that colt, what's the story?"

"Actually he was an Ohio bred, and raised just a couple of miles down the road on a friends farm that also runs his horses at Thistledown. This colt seemed to have a lot of *moxey* and spit and vinegar about him, and that intrigued me, so I brought him over here where I could work with him and see what he had. Right now, the jury is still out; I have not made up my mind yet whether I want him in my barn. His pedigree is not that impressive, very ordinary."

"He would be available at an attractive price. We need to add to the menagerie, but we need to make intelligent choices. "

"There is an auction is going on in Lexington at the beginning of the year, what do you want to do."

"I'll probably be too busy to go, but Holly I would like you to attend and maybe pick up one or two prospects that we can get ready for the summer sessions. Tell me how Big Mo is doing with his studbook."

"His dance book is close to being filled, of course we won't know for a couple of years how productive he will be. If we can get a few stakes winners out of him, the stud fees will skyrocket, and then we will be on the path to nirvana."

Chapter Twenty-Four
High School Football

When Nick arrived home many urgent messages were awaiting him most of them from his CCC Group. He called the president and asked what the problem was. The president, a really nice guy that many times seemed a little overwhelmed with the problems that came up within the group. He said Nick, "it looks like the fix is on with some of these high school teams, but its spread beyond the confines of Youngstown."

"How bad is it?"

"It seems to be in the bigger cities."

"Who is being compromised?"

"It seems, somebody is compromising the referees."

"Do you have or does anybody have an inkling of who these crooked refs are."

"Not at this time, but I'm going to continue to ask around."

"You do that, in the meantime give me the names of some of the bigger games being played that our members are taking unbalanced bets on."

When Nick got the names of the teams that were likely to be involved in a fix he decided to take matters in his own hands and devised a scheme that would hurt the guys that were doing the fixing.

The games that he focused on were playing in three of the largest cities in Ohio. He sent two emissaries to contact all the referee's that were working these games. He arranged a meeting in a Banquet room at a large bistro in Columbus, using the name of a well-known newspaper to get them there under the pretext of interviewing them for a series on the problems of high school referee's.

Nick was going to run this meeting personally and was looking forward to it. He took it to heart that they would corrupt a clean sport like high school football, that he himself had played and take the game away from the hard working, spirited and prideful players, that had this tremendous school spirit that all the players felt, and went out and gave it all they had, then see it taken away by bad calls from a crooked referee.

Nick would see to it that this would not stand. He would make sure that they paid for past transgressions, either with the forfeiture of monetary gains that they had acquired in the past, and fines induced by the CCC because of their nefarious activities associated with these football games. These fines may be accompanied with a painful interlude in their lives, probably with time spent in the hospital. Where they could cogitate in mournful, painful repose for a few days.

Nick thought about the wisdom of taking bets on high school games, that in itself would give raise to shenanigans that would be highly unethical and lead to everybody getting hurt, not only the kids but also the parents and other interested spectators.

Nick decided to try to eliminate the practice of the CCC taking action on high school games. Hopefully this could control ugly circumstances like this from taking place.

The night the meeting took place was a gleeful moment for Nick. He was there early with four of his trusted associates. Two of them he stationed at the door and two stayed with Nick on the podium. About half of the ref's came in on time and the other half straggled in late, seemingly without a care. But before this meeting was over they would care very much.

Nick got up as soon as everyone was organized and seated; he had the two associates at the door lock them.

The attendees were a little puzzled that beverages and pastries were not in evidence which was generally par for the course in a meeting of this type.

He explained to them that they were invited there not by a newspaper, that was only a ruse to get them together, to talk about fixing football games. As that was said, two of the refs started to walk out, and the two associates of Nick's grabbed them roughly by the shoulders and carelessly threw them into their seats and then calmly walked back to the doors.

Almost in unison the referees cried out, "what in the hell is going on? "

Quietly Nick said, "I'll be glad to tell you what is going on."

One of the refs was not going to shut up, so once again an associate walked over and back handed him enough to start his Nose bleeding, Nick feigning concern said, "we are sorry for that," and Nick walked a napkin over to him and again apologized.

"Now I think everyone can see that this is a rather serious get together and there will be no further interruptions or further actions will have to be instituted."

"My name is Nick Lasko from Youngstown. I represent the CCC which is composed of many small bookmakers around the state of Ohio."

"It is in our best interests and the best interests of our clients to run as clean a bookmaking service as is humanly possible. I know that the service we provide is illegal but so are a lot of things that all of us do every day, for instance every one of us bet on a golf game or a poker game at your house."

I could go on and name a thousand other things that we do, that is illegal, anybody remember prohibition, or how about shopping on Sunday. But you know, the really terrible thing was, if you cheated at that golf game or that poker game or any of the other things we ordinarily do in our everyday life, you become that piece of shit that we all despise."

"Sitting in this room right now are people that can be referred to as pieces of shit. Sitting in this room right now are guys that we can label as scum of the earth."

"You may not realize the harm you have caused not only to the players but the Bookie's that lost tons of money on these fixed games and those guys that we call bookies, are people that have family's to raise, bills to pay, mortgages that have to be paid and I have people sitting right here in front of me that could care less, what do they care if other people have to struggle to meet their obligations as long as they get theirs."

"Well, let me give you a clue, I care very much, and you sonofabitches are going to pay. You're not fucking around with the local authorities when you're fucking around with me. Just looking at you makes me sick, so getting rid of you permanently doesn't make me sad."

"Tonight you will have a choice, tonight you will tell me who has been fixed for the games this weekend, not only will you tell me that information but also the people that are behind the rigging of these games, if that information is forth coming then maybe, just maybe, you and your family will not be affected by the actions you have chosen to take. However if this information is not given to me I promise you, that you have no future."

"Now after this meeting many of you have not been actively involved in the fixing of games, will feel that you have been mistreated in this get-together, and that will have been true, but all of you have been in some way connected to this cheating scandal."

"If you refereed a game and you knew one of your associates were calling infractions that never should have been called, and you did not alert the proper authorities then you are just as guilty as the sonofabitch that has made those calls."

"So don't tell me you are as innocent as the pure driven snow. Now let's get on with the show."

"I want to interview each of you individually, see that table in the far corner, that's where we will conduct the direction of your future."

Nick did interview them individually and found to his satisfaction that only two were corrupted.

Nick informed them that they would not make any infractions against the team that was supposed to lose.

One of them said, "Nick these guys will kill me if I double cross them like this."

"Well I'll kill you if you don't double cross them."

"Give me their names and I'll see what I can do. In the meantime each of you bastards will donate to the CCC the amount of money given you as a pay-off for the filth you caused. There will be one little difference. The amount you donate will be fifty percent greater than the amount you received. If the amount you donate is less than you received plus fifty percent, I will have your homes stink-bombed. If you think I will not know how much you owe, you will be sadly mistaken. And corrective action will have to be performed. Its your call.

After obtaining names and as much pertinent information as he could, he immediately called the ringleader, a guy by the name of Clifford Barnes, a woman answered the phone and Nick asked for Clifford,

She said, "He was not there,"

Nick asked, "Where he could be located."

She responded by saying "he could be found generally at his favorite sports bar called Gilligan's in a small town called Lodz."

Nick realized that this town was only about 50 miles from where he was. The four associates were still with him so they motored over to the tavern. Along the way they acquired a baseball bat. To be expeditiously used if there was extraneous action to be taken.

Nick counseled his four employees on how he wanted the bat used. "First and foremost the bat stays in the car. We would handle things with words or physically with our fists. The bat would be a last option. If it became a situation we could not handle, the options open to us would be to leave or possibly escape, which may be a better and more accurate expression of what we may have to do, and wait for a better opportunity."

"However, if we can take care of this tonight, than we may be able to save a ton of money for our members this weekend."

"When we enter the place and we see that the circumstances are not conducive to our style of persuasion inside of the bistro, than we will encounter him outside, and then we use the bat but only to injure not to permanently disfigure him."

The five of them entered the bistro and stepped up to the bar, ordered drinks for themselves and told the bartender to get a drink on them for Clifford Barnes. When the bartender poured for Clifford, Nick was able to identify who he was.

He was an obese balding bastard and had the look of sleaze oozing out of his rumpled, stained, white shirt.

Clifford waved at Nick in a thank you wave for the drink, he then realized that Nick was unfamiliar to him so he strode over to take a closer look.

"Thanks for the drink but do I know you or am I supposed to know you?"

"That's a negative to both questions Cliff," Nick responded, "but the reason I'm here is to engage you in conversation concerning certain football games that I have a very strong interest in observing what the outcome of these games will be."

"I suggest that we take a seat at one of the tables where we will not be overheard."

Upon hearing this Cliff stepped back and looked Nick up and down and then turned and looked over his four assistants, with some hesitation, he finally led the way to a standalone table. As Cliff made himself comfortable, he said, "Is there something I can do for you?"

For a long moment, Nick stared at him and was silent until Cliff again spoke up and, asked, "Is something wrong?"

Nick leaning very close and speaking softly and deliberately said, "you bet there is something wrong. First let me introduce myself, I'm Nick Lasko from Youngstown, if you have never heard of me, ask around and you will be informed of who I am."

"I am intricately involved with a group called the CCC which I organized and created some time ago. This is a group of bookmakers that have banded together to better control their way of life, and this thing they have chosen is their way of making a living. Now it has come to my attention that you and some friends have decided to corrupt a segment of our enterprise that compromises the way that our group earns a livelihood. Not only that, but the very thing that is venerated by the youth of our country is being undermined by you and your friends."

"These young boys work their butts off for the chance to play football in front of their parents and relatives, and make their community take pride not only of them, but also their school, and then you steal all that away by having referee's make improper calls that take the game away from the rightful winners."

"Cliff responds by saying, I don't know what the fuck you're talking about."

Nick says, "Let me show you what I am talking about, you fat cocksucker." He motions to one of his men who immediately comes over to the table while the others stayed by the bartender in case he decided to call the police, and kept their eyes on the few customers in the place.

Nick says to his man, "Clifford here says he doesn't know what the fuck I'm talking about; I wonder if you can show him what I'm talking about."

Nick's muscle picked him up like a rag doll and tossed him over one of the tables, then took a chair and broke it over his back. Nick stepped in at this point before his guy did some permanent damage to Clifford.

Nick leaned down and whispered in his ear, "this weekend the teams that you have attempted to fix will be unfixed or you will receive another visit from me and my associates, and the next time I won't buy you a drink and by the way you haven't finished the one I bought you," Nick threw the unfinished portion in his face and then started walking slowly to the exit.

He turned back to Cliff and in a soft voice said, "Cliff, in order to repay monetary damages you have caused, a little stipend will be expected from you. One of my people will be in touch."

As he was leaving he passed the bartender and said, "If you call the police it will be the end of your business."

Nick was extremely glad to get home that night. It's as emotional and tiring for him as it was for the people he had to threaten.

The two mean watch dogs were jumping all over him when he got home and he stumbled into bed after stepping over two wild, fierce and dangerous dogs, oh yeah, ha-ha.

Waking up the next morning did not relieve him of the anxiety that he felt in the last couple of days. He wouldn't know until all the games were played and counted how things would come out, he could only hope for the best.

After breakfast he hurried to the office and started calling members of the CCC and letting them know that they should not take any more bets unless the money was coming in on the side that they could use the new action to help balance the books. What he means by that is; every bookie wants an equal amount of money on each team, that way he is assured of making his vigorish.

The weekend came and went without a major catastrophe. But it pays to be vigilant and remember, where money is involved, scammers are sure to show up.

Nick advised all members of the CCC to stop taking action on high school games, they are too easy to fix. Maybe an exception can be made for good customers that you know well and you would be doing it strictly as a service.

Chapter Twenty-Five
Palm Beach

January has arrived and the thrill of the holiday's was over, as winter set in, thoughts of palm trees and such, and warm southern nights with a full moon and the milky way in full bloom started to invade his reverie.

There was a place in Palm Beach that he had heard of called the Patio Club that had a roof that opened up in the evenings for dancing under the stars, could anything be more romantic?

Nick had been so busy with his career and all the problems that entailed, that his love life had taken a back seat.

He was getting the itch to make his debut as a newly minted dancer. It's been a year since his lessons and he wondered if he still remembered the dances and the steps he had learned. He decided that Palm Beach, not to be confused with West Palm Beach, would be an excellent place to spend some time. It had one of most elegant hotels in the world called The Breakers and what the wealthy called the Season, was in full swing, anybody who was anybody was there.

The names that spent the winter season in Palm Beach was staggering, established old money families was the rule, and new money in most cases, those that earned it themselves were to be regarded as something to be tolerated. De rigueur not a real part of the Palm Beach scene.

Most of the balls were charitable in nature and of course even new money was welcomed, however in many cases new money had not acquired the niceties and common courtesies that being brought up with wealth entailed. Generally speaking, those that made it themselves tended to be louder and more outspoken and opinionated, after all they were brought up in the rough and tumble world of business.

Jews, Forgetaboutit they were not invited at all no matter how much money they had, The Jews had to establish their own club and eventually became just as snobbish as the Wasps.

All in all this entire place had a long standing reputation of being the playground of the rich and famous, names such as Vanderbilt ,Pulitzer, Rockefeller, Whitney, Kennedy, Flagler, Morgan, Livermore and others of this ilk, like the gathering of Eagles, consorted with each other in the exalted confines of this community.

When Nick decided to visit Palm Beach none of this had been made clear.

What he knew; all the most famous people in the world vacationed there. This was a society that was completely foreign to Nick's type of existence.

Getting away from all the problems, and harrowing avenue's that the organization was taking, and trying to make him an integral part of a despicable drug trade was what Nick was trying hard to ignore. He did not want to inform anybody where he was. Of course, they would speculate that he probably went to Florida, but not to Palm Beach, not in a million years.

So this place would be the perfect foil for him. Alicia Gatti his secretary would be the insulation between him and his normal world.

He left the world of ice, slush and salt and arrived at the West Palm Beach Airport in an entirely different world, sunny, warm, and blue skies welcomed him. His attitude immediately improved.

Taking the limo to the Breakers in Palm Beach, his eyes took him to the yachts that were anchored in the bay and he wandered how anyone could afford these luxurious playthings. He would love to own one.

His mind briefly flicked over the drug trade and then dismissed it when he thought about the amount of time he would spend in a penitentiary, all for a boat, no thanks not for him.

He checked in and enquired about any parties or dances that were being held here?

All the staff at the Breakers reception desk, were very cordial and informed him of all activities and directed him to where he could find out more, they told him, the Chamber of Commerce and the Palm Beach newspaper that has a section called the Shiny Sheet and carries a tremendous amount of weight among the elite of this closed Island, has the entire goings on of social life in this exclusive community. He particularly wanted to know where The Patio Club was located because he would be there this evening.

Full of energy he toured The Breakers Hotel and found it fascinating especially the Circle restaurant and breakfast room not to mention the many ballrooms that were in each wing.

After talking to some of the guests they informed him of a restaurant that was a Palm Beach tradition located about a block down North County Rd. on Royal Poinciana Way called Testas. He decided to try to get the full experience and walk to this restaurant and found it exhilarating.

Testa's had outdoor tables where you could watch the passing parade of Palm Beach residents and tourists, you could easily tell the difference, Palm Beach residents had a panache that was not readily apparent on the touristy interlopers who were wearing sandals and shorts.

The Palm Beachers dressed with a casual elegance, surprisingly the men did not wear socks and looked great in white trousers with blue blazers, the women were startlingly stylish wearing beautiful wide brimmed hats that matched their ensemble. You could tell they hadn't walked very far because all wore high heels.

But it was not just their clothes but the way they carried themselves, a riveting haughtiness and smart casualness that belied the presumably vast amount of wealth they represented.

Nick knew from considerable amounts of experience that the accumulation, preserving and sustaining of wealth was a job that created huge amounts of angst.

Raising a family surrounded by luxury was not an easy job, trying to keep their children grounded.

He noticed that not one of these visions of loveliness looked his way, that was his clue to look in the mirror when returning to the hotel, what he saw was not very flattering. Having just debarked from a plane flight and wearing comfortable clothes that were a trifled rumpled and certainly not the tailored Youngstown look that was a bit on the flash and glitz side that would probably not be in the best of taste here where they had a flash all their own.

He decided a shopping trip would be desirable. He inquired at the reception area where the best shopping area was and in unison they responded, *Worth Avenue,* Probably the most exclusive shopping street in the world, Nick mused, "probably the most expensive in the world."

His musings were confirmed when he entered the first store and found prices that he had never seen before, was this the Palm Beach experience that he had heard people talking about. No, it wasn't, because as he tooled along the lengthy three blocks this Avenue was composed of, the experience kept getting more expensive. After consulting with the various sales clerks, he was finally able to select a representative Palm Beach wardrobe. Being slender and handsome with thick curly hair made him look like he had just stepped out of G. Q. Quarterly.

Shoes=$600

Ron Chicone

Trousers=$300
Blazer=$1400
Shirt=brought a nice one with him, otherwise = $200
Socks= not necessary otherwise $25

After succumbing to the Palm Beach experience on Worth Ave. He wondered what he was in for tonight when out dancing at the Patio Club.

For Nick, he could now, after having his stroll on Worth Ave. truly appreciate a Palm Beach girl the way they dressed, the way they walked with their head held back and high heels hardly touching the sidewalk and seemingly unapproachable, but don't bet on that because Nick was intent on approaching a few tonight.

At the hotel, there were several messages from Alicia, "please call the office I have a message for you from Stefano". Reluctantly he did, but Alicia had already gone home for the day. So tomorrow is another day, I'll call tomorrow.

Dressed and motoring down North County Road in the requisite convertible, he felt exhilarated, the evening was the kind you dream about with stars so big you could reach out and touch them and soon he was entering the Patio Club. It was just as beautiful as he thought it would be. The décor was decidedly raffish bringing the outdoors inside. Because of the sliding roof they were able to control the interior gardens.

As he made his way to the bar his eyes were scanning the crowd and an orchestra was softly playing Begin the Beguine a rumba. Nick's feet could hardly stay still.

Before he got to the bar he had to brush past a group of girls sitting at a table near the dance floor, Nick stopped and boldly said to all of the girls at the table, "if you would kindly excuse me for my impertinence, but I just this day arrived in Palm Beach and I am under the spell of this music, and dance I will, with any one of you that would be of a persuasion, and would dance with someone that has just come in out of the cold snow and ice of the far north." There was complete silence, not

238

one uttered a word and an embarrassing silence ensued for it seemed a rather extended length of time and finally Nick said, "I'm sorry to intrude on your conversation please except my apologies," as he was turning to leave one of the girls spoke up, one that was exceptionally beautiful with dark almost black hair and eyes to match but seemed to be the one least likely to dance with a bold stranger, she had a haughtiness about her that cried out, please do not disturb me you are not in my league.

She arose from her seat and said, "It would be enchanting to dance with you and yes you are bold but pleasantly so."

Nick could not believe his good luck, she led the way to the floor and Nick knowing he had not danced for quite a while stepped gingerly until the rust disappeared. It did not take long. The next dance was a foxtrot, *Dancing in the Dark*, Nick always remembered Fred Astaire and Cyd Charisse dancing this number and in his mind's eye he was Astaire and she was Charisse, he asked her name and she whispered "Maria Elena" but never said her last name, he asked, "and your last name is?"

She said, "It's not important, let's just enjoy the music." And suddenly he realized she had a slight foreign accent spoken with a soft, lilting, mesmerizing, reticent quality.

For all the world he felt he was transported to heaven in this time and place and as the night wore on, the magic was all around him, and it was like floating on a cloud.

Finally the night was coming to an end, as all things must. Nick went to the bar to order drinks and when he returned to her table, suddenly like the proverbial nymph on gossamer wings she was gone, she was ethereal, did she exist at all? Or was she just a figment of his imagination? Did this really happen? Yes it did because the essence of her fragrance lingered with his senses.

Nick was desperate to find her again, wanted to find her again, needed to find her again, it seemed he asked most everyone in the Club who she was but most expressed an ambivalence or guarded response to Nick's questions.

Returning to the Breakers, Nick's mind was racing. He would find her even if he had to hire private detectives to do this, but what clues could he give them other than her first name and a description of what she looked like, that was a pretty sketchy picture to give to P.I.'s.

That night Nick slept the sleep of the dead and awoke believing that he had a fantasy dream.

For breakfast, he went to the beautiful and unique Circle Room at the Breakers and engaged other occupants of the hotel in conversation. And started to get an education concerning the snobbery of Palm Beach. He was finding out that many of the balls and storied parties here in this very private enclave were by invitation only. A list that was widely disseminated but not official was called "The 400". This list gave the names of the most esteemed and venerated residents of Palm Beach and of course people that were on this list received these valued invitations.

However there were balls that the only requirement was a tuxedo and money, for instance the Red Cross Ball required a ticket charge of about $700 a person. It was frowned upon if you attended stag and not being a favored recipient of an invitation the seat or seats you were assigned were far removed from the stage and dance floor.

Actually, Nick could receive an invite to many of the parties being that he could bring to bear pressure on the Governor of Ohio to use his influence and contacts to shake loose invites to closed parties. He had no interest in attending these parties if he was going stag, and he had no acquaintances that he could interact with, but if he could find Maria Elena and she would accompany him to these happenings than that would throw a different light on it.

Nick on this evening would return to the Patio Club with a stop at Kelley's bar that drew an awesome crowd a notch below the upper crust but much friendlier, this was a place for conversation and making friendships.

Before he embarked on this evening of pleasure he would have to touch base with his secretary Alicia and he was sure it would not be pleasant. Alicia promptly answered the phone and a little on the frazzled side said, "I'm so glad you finally called, Vinnie and Stefano have been frantically trying to get in touch with you, I have deflected their seemingly urgent calls by saying I was not privileged to know where you are. You never told me because you did not want to be bothered while you were enjoying a well-deserved rest. They have bombarded me with questions that I answered the same way, I don't know."

Nick thought about getting in touch, but decided to make them wait another day. This would be his way of letting everyone know that he was not at their beck and call whenever they wanted him.

He intended to start conveying he did not work for them, and if they wanted something done, maybe kissing his ass would be one way of getting it accomplished. The other conveyance, if you wanted it done, he would do it, if you wanted it done now, do it yourself.

It could be dangerous in taking this unpredictable path, but he was angling for more respect, actually in the long run this method may be less hazardous and may be able to extricate him from the drug trade.

Sitting at the bar at Kelley's he struck up a conversation with the gentleman next to him and eventually a friend of his joined the banter, subjects that were discussed seemed to center on the parties and characters that were a part of the P. B. scene.

Nick asked the two gentlemen, "how they knew so much about these things?"

They said part of what we do is to act as escorts for wealthy woman of a certain age. Many times their husbands or boyfriends or live in lovers are too busy to take them to a particular party that they want to attend, so we act as the stand in for their companions."

Nick asked, "doesn't that create a certain amount of jealousy?"

They replied, "not at all, you see we are gay and not interested in their girlfriends." Nick asked, "are you paid well for that line of work?" One of them replied, "Well, yes in a manner of speaking, my full time job is an art Director at an art gallery; I receive commissions on any art pieces that are sold, the women that I escort will make their purchases there and refer their friends to the gallery."

Turning to his friend, Nick said, "that is certainly interesting and how are you compensated?

He said "my rent is taken care of, and small loans I receive are never repaid, so you see we are compensated, but not in a vulgar way by an outright monetary charge."

So in a way everybody has a racket, or to put it in a gentler manner they have an innovative way of earning a living.

A question that he was dying to ask; *did they know of any girl named Maria Elena.* He figured that with their knowledge of Palm Beach that there was a good chance that their familiarity with heiresses and debutante's may bring the name Maria Elena to mind. Both of them looked a little startled and asked "how do you know Maria Elena?" Nick replied "I met and danced with her at the Patio Club just last night."

"Well then you are one lucky dude. She is probably the most sought after debutante on the Island. Her family owns one of the mansions on South Ocean Boulevard just past Mar-A-Largo the Mrs. Marjorie Meriwether Post Estate."

"Well pray tell what is her last name?"

"Actually her first name starts with Contessa Maria Elena and continues to Gabriella.

"Are you telling me that she is a Contessa and a descendent of the European Gabriella's?"

242

"That's what they say."

"Who the hell are "they?""

"The people that matter and know everything about everybody."

Nick was dumfounded.

He said, "Do you mean the first girl I meet in Palm Beach is a fuckin' Contessa. Jesus Christ I don't have a Goddamn chance in this game."

"She is being pursued by every guy that has a dick in this town and they would buy heaven and hell to have her."

"What clubs or places does one of her station in life generally frequent and spend time at?" Nick inquired.

"Nowhere in particular, she seems to be a rare commodity and seen infrequently. The party scene does not appeal to her unless there is an outstanding orchestra playing, her one love is dancing. You might try going to the Royal Poinciana shopping center, in the back, on the water way, is a very private supper club that is located there called The Celebrity Room, every Tuesday is First Nighters night. A top act and celebrity opens there on that night during the season. Your chances of meeting her and speaking to her there will be nil and none. First of all you will have a difficult time gaining entry; second of all, she will be escorted and surrounded by very protective friends and third of all having met you just once, is there some reason she would want to see you again."

Nick replied, "I can't think of one reason except I am an exceptional dancer, and Nick should have added "dreamer".

He returned that night to the Patio Club with the hope however slim that Maria Elena would return, but alas that was not to be. He did meet another girl that made it an enjoyable evening of dancing and she made it known that an invitation to her place would be entertained if he would ask. But at the moment he had too many things on his mind, one of the things was Maria Elena, but the other was getting back in touch with his people in Pittsburgh. Tomorrow morning he would take care of that.

The morning arrived and Nick called Vinnie who he would much rather talk to then Stefano. His secretary answered the phone He said, "Joyce, this is Nick, may I talk to Vinnie," she said, "hold on I'll trace him down." Soon she came back on and said, "Nick give me your phone number and I'll have him call you."

"Not a chance, I'll call him back."

"Hold on he just came in."

"I thought that was the case, Joyce you can't shit a shitter."

"Sorry Nick, I just listen to the guy who's writing the check."

"Well tell him you're not getting enough if he wants you to pull shoddy tricks. If he wants you to be an actress, than get you a ticket to Hollywood."

"Hey Nick cut out the shit where are you," Vinnie said.

"Vinnie, I had to get away for a while, I really feel like I'm being set up. With this new thing you have, you and cohorts will be making a ton of money. But let's see if I can guess who will pull as much if not more time in the slammer than any of you."

"I have spent more time and effort setting up the thing that I have and you are asking me to destroy it in one bad call and I know that everybody in the organization will be protecting their own asses and fuck Nick who is he? He's not one of us. It brings to mind a phrase used in an old time movie when the kid trying to get rid of a broad that was getting the Champ's attention, Jackie Cooper told Wallace Beery in the "Champ" give her a buck and the breeze, and I'm the broad in that movie."

Vinnie said, "hold on a fuckin' minute Nick, give me a chance, nobody wants to cut you out of a thing. But listen we can't continue over this thing, we got to have a face to face meeting. And what fucking movie are you talkin about? Jesus you're talking in circles. Tell me where you're at and Stefano will hop a plane and see you personally and parlare faccia a faccia come uomini." (Talk face to face like men).

"Okay Vinnie, Goddamit I give up, I'm in Palm Beach and I'm staying at the Breakers."

"Hell Nick I know a little about that place and you better come home or you're going to wind up without a pot to piss in. You'd be better off in Vegas."

"Look Vinnie it doesn't matter what Stefano has to say I ain't coming home. For God sakes I danced the whole night with a Contessa. I mean a real Contessa her name is Maria Elena Gabriella, she is related to the Gabriella's ruling royalties of Italy I think."

"You think? What the fuck is wrong with you? You're thinker isn't thinking too good anymore. Somebody is setting you up for a classic sting and you don't even know it. You better come home before they take you down the primrose path and make a bigger fool out of you than you already are."

"No, Vinnie this was for real."

"For real? Get away from me before your shit rubs off on me."

"Okay, Okay, think and say what you want but what I'm telling you is the truth."

"Get behind me Satan. The great Nick Lasko has swallowed it hook line and sinker and he's being reeled in and can't wait until he's fleeced. Yeah, maybe they'll promise marriage to this Contessa and you can go to Italy and get married and she will meet you there but guaranteed you'll be the only one at the Alter without a Italian lira in your pocket and no bride either, but what the hell you'll be a Prince of a guy."

"Go fuck yourself Vinnie, the only Contessa you ever met was in a whorehouse."

"Hell Nick, you ought to open one, maybe you could get this Contessa to work for you."

"Goodbye Vinnie, I would have never thought so but I think I'd rather talk to Stefano."

"Listen to me Nick, I know we were only kidding, but even if you did meet and dance with a Contessa, what does that mean? Nothing, you will fall in love with absolutely no chance of anything else happening, it's something that will never have a chance of coming to fruition. It cannot happen. I know you think of yourself as a big time Lobbyist but let's face it you are still a racketeer, and Countess's don't marry racketeers. Si capisce signor camorrista."

"Che sei mio padre? (What are you my father?) Not to worry Vinnie it's just a fling and my ego has been massaged. Have you ever danced with a Contessa, Vinnie?"

"No but I have danced with plenty of dogs in my day."

"Man I don't doubt that."

His next problem was dealing with Stefano; at this point he had no idea what he would tell him. He guessed it would depend on what Stefano said and what his attitude was like.

Worry, worry, worry, why did life have to be like this. Every day was a new uneasiness that would fester in his consciousness. Well, what the hell this is the path he chose.

In the beginning all he wanted was a simple bookmaking operation where he could take bets, pay off the winners and have a lot of true friends that he could go out with and have a beer and did not have to look behind himself wondering when it was his turn to take a bullet in the head.

That night there was a new place to visit, The Chesterfield Hotel, containing the Leopard Lounge, an iconic Lounge that has one of the most unusual ceiling paintings, showing nudes, and one male nude with a hard phallic, okay if that word is too hard try cock, still too hard, well it was and is, and of course a conversation starter.

This place had an ambiance all its own. The people that populated this bar were generally Palm Beach wannabe's, a great place for people watching, actually the number of very beautiful women was surprising and many of them using their charm and wiles on very rich old men and most of the rich old men did not look that interested. A piano player played and sang beautifully, and it added to the enchantment of the Leopard Lounge.

However, Nick knew he had to return to reality tomorrow when Stefano arrived, but before he would leave this enraptured Island, he would have one evening at The Celebrity Room and one more shot at seeing Contessa Maria Elena Gabriella.

This was Saturday, in three days it would be First Nighters Night, and Nick would not leave until he attended the Celebrity Room, a membership only club. They told Nick he would have trouble getting in, but he had found in the past that it's wonderful what a greased palm could do.

Stefano arrived early Sunday morning at the airport in West Palm Beach, Nick was there to give him a ride to the Breakers, but Nick had a surprise for Stefano. Just south of the breakers there was a beautiful old Episcopal church that was called Church of Bethesda by the Sea and had intrigued Nick, he did want to attend there before he left. Stefano arrived early in the morning and Nick felt they could make the 10 am services. When they pulled up to the church, "Stefano bellowed out where the fuck are you taking me."

"Shut up fuck face and quit swearing, we are going to church, we are just in time for 10 o'clock services."

"Kiss my ass this is not going to happen."

"Yes it is, even if I have to drag your ass bodily into the sanctuary and make a scene that this church probably has never seen before."

"Goddamit Nick I'm Catholic I can't go here it's against my religion."

"No it's not, that old dogma changed a long time ago, besides Episcopalian is as close as you can get to Catholic in the

247

Protestant church, besides this is a gorgeous church and it will do us good before we begin our talks."

"How long has it been since you went to anything resembling a church" Nick asked?

"Fuck you, I go to church dam near every Sunday."

"Stefano how can you say that, when you are standing on holy ground and being deceitful in front of the Savior himself."

"Cut out the bullshit Nick, if we are going to go in then let's go in and get this over with."

This inspiration of Nick's seemed to have worked out well because when they finally got around to discussing business the foregoing events seemed to iron out the rough edges of Stefano. Nick also knew that the Mafia was inherently religious and the things they did they believed were on the side of God. Many times the church itself was more than a little involved in the inner workings of the Cosa Nostra; Priests had been known to act as consigliore for the organization, even liquidations that were ordered by a Capo DiTutti Capi would have been looked upon favorably by God, they thought.

Finding a place to hold this discussion was a little difficult, Nick's first thought were some small rooms in the North end of the Breakers but he then thought that a dollar to a doughnut they were bugged probably by either the hotel or other meetings that had been held there and somebody wanted information on that group, so he ruled that out. One of the big ballrooms would have been perfect but they were always working on getting these rooms ready for the next event so there was staff going in and out.

He remembered Testa's and the tables outside and conversation was prolifically bountiful there, virtually impossible to pick up any one conversation.

As they took their seats, at a typically crowded outdoor segment of Testa's, he could tell that Stefano was enjoying this very ambient way of a delightful breakfast, especially being engulfed in tropical breezes and your eye's being enchanted with the sight of the towering Royal Palms lining the street not to mention the beautiful girls flowing by on the sidewalk.

Brings to mind a song that Jimmy Durante use to sing, *Beautiful girls walk a little slower when you walk by me*, all of this was being enjoyed in the utmost way by Stefano.

So Nick had set the stage for what he hoped would be a fruitful discussion.

"Nick, you and me have got to come to some kind of an understanding concerning our business, you know we are not asking a whole lot, on occasion looking the other way. After all you have all the connections Nick and it was with our support and protection that you were able to operate like you did. You know we were very accommodating when you wanted to organize the CCC group and I'll tell you why; they are too small they don't contribute enough for all the trouble we have to go through sorting out their petty squabbles, every time the local authorities pick them up on whatever Goddamn trouble they get into, we have to send an attorney down to bail them out. These guys are not all little boy Lord Fauntleroy's, they get into all kinds of bullshit scrapes, knocking the shit out of their wives, dealing in the numbers racket without being sanctioned, doing a little coke and weed and who the hell knows what else. Plus the local Cops ain't gettin' any grease so they target your members. By the time you cut up the take with Cleveland, take your cut and give us a pittance, were losing money."

"Some of what you're saying is true, but you know that anything you have to put out from your pocket is reimbursed from the CCC treasury."

"Stefano interjected. Sometimes it's not the money it's the fuckin' trouble that we have to go through. If we charged by the hour the CCC couldn't afford it."

Nick said, "Look, Mr. Guliano I didn't notice you or anybody complaining before this new thing came along, and now you're trying to intimidate me so that I'll go along with this bullshit that you guys are getting into."

"Another thing Nick, most of the contractors and people who want or need something from the government we turn over to you and you line your pockets with the vigorish and we don't know how much your keeping and how much you're giving us. That's how trusting we are."

"Oh; Stefano how can you sit there and keep shoveling the shit at me, you know exactly how much vigorish I'm taking in, you sono le tue fonti (have your sources) and you don't trust me that much, non lo fai nessuno più di tanto." (you don't trust anybody that much).

"Yes it's true that we do keep tabs on people that do services for us, but you are a special case. You have mountains of ambition and who knows where you will wind up one of these days."

"That's just the thing I been trying to tell you Stefano, if you put me in a situation that destroys my credibility with my benefactors, than I will not be able to help the organization in the future."

"Here let me give you a scenario, let's assume you come to me and say Nick I need to get a ship cleared on Lake Erie, what that means is I contact somebody that has jurisdiction over the Coast guard, who the fuck that would be I have no fuckin' idea, but I do know that the feds have something to do with it, so that's not even possible, I'm good but I'm not that good. On top of that you have this guy called Danny Greene that hates Italians although John Nardi is the reason he still lives. Nardi who is a Capo in Cleveland is his sponsor, Danny's the boss of the International Longshoreman's Union, and if he figured out that stash was coming in on a particular ship, goodbye stash."

Stefano said, "we know the bastard and he's high on the list. (May 17, 1977, Greene's longtime ally and Protector John Nardi was killed by a bomb. On October 6, 1977, Greene went to a dental appointment at the Brainard Place office building in

Lyndhurst, Ohio. The automobile parked next to his exploded, killing Greene instantly.)

"I do have an idea that can be of great help."

"Stefano, listen to me, you have to clean up this money you're getting in. Where are you going to put this money? You can't put it in a bank the Feds will want to know where the hell it came from. So you have to have businesses that can be manipulated to show greater earnings that really never occurred."

"Okay were talkin too much here, Stefano, I should be leaving next Wednesday we'll talk when I get back."

This thing that Nick is talking intrigued Stefano and he decided not to push on Nick at this time.

Nick returned Stefano to the airport to catch his flight Monday morning and was relieved that Stefano was not badgering him on what his obligations were to the organization, he realized that he had caught Stefano's attention with his potential proposal to wash money. Which meant that Nick had pushed a hot button; this indicated that they had a problem with the government?

Now he could relax and give his attention to this dream he had met at the Patio Club. Going to extreme lengths to learn more of this girl that everyone thought of as a Contessa, he eventually extracted the information by consulting the Chamber of Commerce and The Palm Beach Post and the editor of the Shiny sheet an adjunct of the Post, Finding out that she was for real and did enjoy an evening out at the Celebrity Room, where he fully intended to be Tuesday evening.

His attendance Tuesday evening at this prestigious Supper Club he was hoping would not be compromised because of the very popular entertainers appearing there.

Xavier Cugat and Abbe Lane were very popular stars during this period and seating would be limited. Nick knew that calling for a reservation was out of the question; he was not a member and of course would be refused, what he intended to do was bribe the maître dee with copious amounts of coin of the realm. He knew that everybody had a price; all he had to do was find the price point where his quarry would garner some interest in getting Nick seated. A table would be out of the question because of the amount of patrons that would be there that night, but Nick wanted a seat at the bar where he would be more comfortable because he was a single male unaccompanied by a companion.

The evening that Nick had so anticipated finally arrived. The Celebrity Room was not more than two miles from the Breakers. It was a beautiful drive ending in one of the most gorgeous high-end shopping centers in the country and why not, after all it was located in the most sought after town to live in the U.S.A.

Nick pulled his rented Cadillac Convertible fashionably late as he intended to be, into a small round drive in front of the Club and felt that the Cadillac did not make enough of a statement judging from the amount of Bentley's and Rolls Royce's that he could see.

The doorman opened his door and called for the parking attendant, asking "if his companion would be arriving in a separate car."

Nick responded, "That he would be joining friends and did not expect anyone else to join him."

Nick walked confidently into the front reception area where several servers were patiently waiting for the late arrivals. One of them approached and asked "if he could be of service". Nick said "are you the person that is in charge."

Pulling himself up to his full height and taking a step back, he said "as a matter of fact he was, "Nick held out his hand and said, as he moved closer and more confidentially, "I have a difficult situation that has arisen and I felt you may be of some help to me. I am rather new to Palm Beach and did not realize that this beautiful establishment was a member's only club, and I promised to meet a friend off the record, if you know what I mean? Certainly I am embarrassed to find out this is restricted to a certain clientele." Nick put a $50 dollar bill into his hand and he proceeded to say "that he is exceedingly disconcerted and it would be appreciated if he alleviates his distress by seating him at the bar." There was a noticeable hesitation and Nick without hesitating himself placed another $50 in his hand.

This time, without hesitation he asked Nick his name, and said "he was honored to have him as a guest this night, and if there was anything further he could do, it would be his pleasure to serve."

While Nick was being served at the bar he looked at his surroundings, beauty filled this club especially the ceiling where a huge painting that had been created by Robert Bushnell a well-known artist, hovered over the dancers. The orchestra that absolutely glittered with dazzling lights while the dance floor was blanketed in what seemed to be moonlight and may have been; set a mood that you felt to the very core. Behind the orchestra was a patio wide open to the waterway overlooking the yacht basin in the intercostal body of water.

The whole scene could only be described as the most romantic place on earth this night, and Nick was filled with the excitement of seeing Contessa Maria Elena and hopefully having one last dance with her before he returned to his life and she to hers, of course this was her life and Nick did not belong.

It was not long before he saw her sitting at a featured table encircled with friends and upper echelon entourage,

She; more glamorous than ever was the highlight of the table and one by one the handsome young men that engulfed her rose and danced with her, all were far better dancers than Nick and they floated and whirled around the floor like delicate butterflies while she laughed and had a wonderful, graceful, exquisitely fulfilled evening.

Nick watched in longing and silence for what seemed a very long time, and finally turned and finished his martini and with a last look at the Contessa, and with the music playing, he made his departure, realizing that his little dream and yearning for something that could never be is finally over.

Returning to the Breakers that evening and expecting to be depressed by this recent episode, he was suddenly overcome by the supreme joy of living.

Here he was, in one of the most upscale locations in the world, where he had danced and been entertained by a Contessa. He owned a racing stable, had friends and contacts in the highest echelons of power both in a social sphere and in the underworld, and he was able to go between this orb of influence to benefit friends and customers that may need a favor, and on top of this, owned an estate that made its own statement of supremacy, and he was in excellent health.

He had always distained smoking, nicotine, alcohol and pills of any kind. With a great amount of forethought he had installed a workout room in his home that he used habitually when he was there.

This is not to say that occasionally he would light up a stogie or have a social drink or a glass of homemade dago red wine when he was with friends.

As these thoughts ran through his mind he realized that the reason for his direction and path in life was largely determined because of where he was born and raised. So thank you *Youngstown*, you were a tough teacher but if you were willing to listen and learn, these immigrants that populated this town would give you an education a college could not give.

Chapter Twenty-Six
Back home in Youngstown

When he arrived at the tiny Youngstown airport, he was rudely awakened to the fact that it was still January. It was cold and dreary and depressing, but for some reason he was glad to be home. The elegant palm trees were another world away.

Joey picked him up in the van, and the ever-profuse and teeming potholes gave the ride home that feeling of "yes, you are back home."

His contingent of greeters waited as he burst through the front doors: Liz, the two kids, John and Marie, the two dogs, F. Scott and Zelda—and they were all a little rambunctious and a really nice reception for Nick, which he enjoyed.

Problems with the CCC group surfaced as he was alerted by Stefano to some of their activities that Nick knew about but tended to ignore, allowing the members more leeway. But the revenue from sports betting had fallen off as they spent more time hawking the Bug (numbers or policy racket), which tended to have a bigger profit margin.

Nick would have to see the members individually because you never know who was listening if you made a phone call.

It was possible that a large meeting could be held if he could be assured that only members would attend. The problem is the media would get wind of it and be hanging around outside the meeting room, waiting to interview the members as they were leaving.

The eight-hundred-pound gorilla in the room was the I.R.S. They were becoming obnoxious and were pressing many of the members for money, claiming that they were making more than they were reporting for income tax purposes. Of course, this became a Catch-22 situation as gambling was not illegal to the federal government, but if you reported income from gambling operations, that would be prima facie evidence against you under local and state laws.

An anti-gambling bill came out of Congress, called the 1961 Wire Act, which made the transmission of information for gambling purposes illegal. Of course, the line (point spread) on all the national games came over the phone, which was illegal under the Wire Act. This bill put a serious crimp in the gambling business. Members of the CCC needed to know what the point spread were on the various games being held around the country. Not only football, but baseball and horseracing, were very critical to have up-to-date odds on the thoroughbreds at the many races in operation simultaneously. If you were operating a horse racing room, you were dependent on having a direct wire to Las Vegas.

Eventually, this problem was alleviated when Vegas established a direct premium wire to the various horse rooms around the nation.

Here was the problem that the I.R.S. presented to the participants in the business of gambling:

Assume that you were taking in $100,000 a year and did not have a job. What could you do with that money? Absolutely nothing—could not put it in a bank, no home, no car, could not negotiate a loan—about the only thing available to you was to give it away. It would behoove the recipient of the money to earn it through legitimate businesses and pay taxes on the money.

Assume you opened a bistro, and the bistro brought in $50,000 per year. By putting in your ill-gotten gain as part of the income from your business, you would be able to report it to the Government so you could pay taxes on it and it now becomes legitimate income. Of course, with that business came additional problems of the hiring and firing personnel, consumer satisfaction, supply problems, not to mention potential lawsuits and a host of other matters that you would have to take under advisement.

Let's simplify and solve the problems that owning a business would create for you. That's what Nick wanted to do on a much larger scale by making the members of the CCC a part of partnerships in various businesses. Each member would contribute as much money as they wanted laundered, the contributions would be sent to a foreign off-shore bank, eventually finding its way into legitimate businesses in this country.

Their contributions would come back to the participating members minus taxes and other expenses that are a part of doing business. It would be now termed "clean wealth assets" that would have no restrictions on the use of this money.

Nick would have to communicate this proposal in person to every member individually face-to-face, in that way all conversations are kept very private. Besides the matter of joining in the partnership, there is the matter of paying the CCC remuneration for the money made from the Bug (numbers racket).

After members have been informed personally, a meeting will be held for all members inclusively so that they will be properly cognizant of the new requirements of the organization and penalties for non-compliance.

Nick gave it a lot of thought, but he finally decided to bring the Cleveland boys into it because they were Ohio people and more centrally located.

Knowing he would ruffle the feathers of the Pittsburgh group.

He did hold Tony Vilanotti of the Cleveland faction in very high regard, and Tony's general outlook on things tended to mirror his own. He felt that he was trustworthy and could get things done smoothly.

He called Vilanotti's restaurant and eventually talked to Tony.

"After informing Tony briefly and not in too much detail, he told him of the need for about five men that had a good command of the English language.

Tony said, "Hey, paisano, where the hell around here can I find five guys that can speak English let alone intelligently? But I tell you what I will do, I'll round up a few guys, and you can come up and interview them here in my place. I have a banquet room that you can use. Pick five that you feel could do the job."

He made arrangements with Tony, interviewing a host of potential agents and finding five guys that could carry out this responsibility in a reasonable way. The next thing was to get them back to Tony's the next day and have them undergo training in all aspects of what Nick wanted to have the members understand. They would have to be knowledgeable in the issues that the members would bring up: he schooled them in everything from the way they dressed to how to respond, including what their reply would be in a negative situation, or if a positive retort was received, what their answer should be.

Basically, the message they would carry to the members: creation of an investment they would be encouraged to participate in that would alleviate their concerns with the I.R.S. The hardest part of the message they would impart to them was the fact that they would have to start paying homage to the organization on income they are receiving from the numbers. The CCC in the near future would be holding a general meeting that would clarify the revolutionary changes taking place. Attendance is mandatory.

Nick called the president of the CCC and informed him of the actions he was taking, and out of respect for his position in the CCC, he asked for his indulgence in this matter.

"Nick you are the man; you are the reason that this organization exists. I know that what you are proposing is for the good of all of us. So buona Fortuna." (The best of luck).

The agents had their work cut out for them. Traveling the entire state of Ohio and finding each member would be an exhausting job. Any member that they could not contact in a timely manner would then have to travel to see Nick individually in Youngstown.

In the meantime, the income from the numbers would have to start coming in immediately, and this was going to cause a riot, if Nick had to guess at the reaction. He also knew that they would not report the real amount that they were taking in or claim that they were not handling the Bug. Nick knew that would be bullshit, and he would see that they would contribute anyway.

He set up the meeting for next summer. He wanted to avoid the major sporting events like the Triple Crown, the Masters, and the beginning of the fall football games. This allowed Nick time to investigate potential investments that would fit the intended purposes of the new Corporation that he had attorneys working on.

Nick had to change gears and start looking for businesses with the potential to take in a massive amount of cash money without raising suspicions of the I.R.S.

The business that came to mind was golf courses; they were primarily cash cows in an era where the ubiquitous use of credit cards was limited, and the courses were a growing and vibrant industry. Nick knew of just the place to own these businesses: where else but Myrtle Beach, a growing capital of the golf industry, where he had spent many hours indulging in a sport that he wished he could allocate more time to.

And when you thought about golf, you naturally thought about the capital of golf: Myrtle Beach and the Grand Strand.

Chapter Twenty-Seven
Myrtle Beach Time

- The advantages of having and owning golf courses in Myrtle Beach:
- Weather: very mild winter temperatures
- Abundant restaurants
- Touristy places that some would call tacky, but Nick would call entertainment
- The Grand Strand, sixty miles of beach
- Within striking distance of the major population centers of the country: New York, New Jersey, etc.
- A great destination for Canadian visitors in January, February, March
- Proximity to the Romance cities of Culture and History: Charleston, Georgetown, Savannah, the Low Country, Beaufort and Jekyll Island, etc.
- Plenty of accommodations: motels, hotels, condominiums

In other words, a better place for this type of business did not exist.

Nick arrived in the spring of the year and, after finding suitable lodgings, introduced himself to the officers of the Chamber of Commerce, who were very instructive on the nuances of this area after checking Nick's credentials.

Nick's interests were in finding golf courses that were for sale and large tracts of land that would lend themselves to the construction of golf courses.

A starting point would be finding the right real estate agent. He was pointed in the direction of two agents that were well thought of and very successful with a forthright manner and were very direct with no bullshit: Joan Lyons and Linda Baker. Joan was a lovely blonde with green eyes from Cleveland, Ohio, who still thought a creek was a crick. She worked with a pixie of a girl that looked all of sixteen, who was from a small town in South Carolina and had a southern accent. Her interpretation of a group of people was y'all and anybody that she was having a conversation with was included in that group.

Each realtor was very driven, and sexuality exuded from them. Make no mistake, though, money was the gruel on which they fed. Hard work was just a description of their character and part of their nature.

Johnny, the representative of the Chamber, said to Nick, "I know of two ladies that are very successful real estate pros; believe me, I don't know if they know anything about large tracts of land, but I know that they have larger balls than any man I know. If you are ready for a wild ride, I'll introduce you to them."

When the ladies arrived at the Chamber and were introduced to Nick, he could immediately sense the exuberance in their manner. You could tell just by being around them that their mood was electrifying as they commenced, after the intro to Nick, pinning him down to exactly what he was looking for. He enumerated, first of all, acreage. Any one parcel would have to be about one hundred eleven acres and may involve more than one parcel. Also of interest were any existing golf courses that may have a potential of foreclosure due to money problems or mismanagement that would make them attractive to Nick.

The reason behind this thinking:
- The infrastructure had already been installed.
- All licenses and authorizations by city, county, state and federal had been secured.
- Services such as electric, water, cable, roads was already useable.
- Watering systems have already been established and installed.
- Personnel, such as it was, would probably be retained and that would be determined after they were properly vetted and retrained.

Location was of the utmost importance, and already established courses were located closer to the center of town. Newer courses were built farther away as land became limited in prime locales.

The downside:
- The infrastructure, because of a lack of money, had been allowed to deteriorate.
- Personnel were inadequate.
- In arrears on most if not all the bills that had become due and payable.
- More than likely money was due on taxes to the city, county, state and federal governments.
- Back taxes on payrolls, unemployment, disability insurance, and, of course, penalties that would be due for non-Compliance.
- Suppliers standing in line for the money owed them.
- Insurance on liability and other risks that had been allowed to lapse.
- Unpaid mortgages.

- Pending lawsuits were always a possibility.
- The clubhouse would have to be completely refurbished.

There would be a multitude of other problems that were unforeseen at this juncture, but if there was any one that was better versed in solving problems than Nick, he probably did not exist.

The two ladies pushed on trying to pinpoint the amount of money he would have available to fund all these impossible dreams.

Nick could not give them an amount because he himself did not know, but he did tell them it would be substantial.

What they wanted to tell him was "money talks, bullshit walks." Hell they had heard this crap before, and it was all some asshole trying to make out and get laid, acting like a big shot and probably did not have a sow to his name but wanted to impress them.

The two of them made some excuses and got the hell out of there as fast as they could, telling Nick, "they would get back to him after they had a chance to go through their files."

Linda thought: *files my ass, I've spent all the time that I'm gonna on that loser*. Joanie, on the other hand, decided to give the information to their secretary to check this Nick Lasko out. She told her to make a few phone calls to persons that Joanie knew in Cleveland—her hometown, a city she knew well—that consisted of lawyers and shady characters from Murray Hill that was a hot bed of La Cosa Nostra and may have a handle on this Prick. The only reason she did this was because the guy was kind of good-looking and maybe, just maybe he was not a bullshit artist.

It was not long before her secretary rushed into the office and proclaimed, "Nick Lasko was a well-known lobbyist, has connections with Mafia types, and may be La Cosa Nostra himself with connections all over the country. It would be best if she did not get involved with the likes of him." Of course,

Joanie couldn't wait to tell Linda. When Linda got the news, her eyes lit up, and Joanie's eyes, which were already green, now had big dollar signs in them.

Joanie immediately called Nick and informed him that they had a big day scheduled for him tomorrow, and the property he would see, she could assure him, was highly prized and much sought after.

Let it be clear that Joanie and Linda had no idea what the hell was available and no idea of where they would take him. Land sales were not their area of expertise. But to hell with that—they were now the experts and the high connoisseurs of Myrtle Beach Terra firma. This was now their realm and kingdom, as far as golf courses for sale were concerned, and they would call every course in the area if they must to ask if they were interested in a sale to moneyed interests.

The golf courses did not seem to be a problem and as they delved into this end of it. They found there were many courses with money problems, and the corporations that owned them—were more than willing to entertain a sale to a qualified sucker—errrr, buyer.

These two girls did their homework that night and were very prepared when the morrow came.

Meeting for breakfast, the girls were much in awe, believing they were having breakfast with, in their minds, the meanest, baddest Mafia guy in the country. Nick was puzzled by their deferential manner when addressing him and finally said, "My name is Nick, use it." Almost in unison, they said "*Yes, sir!*" He looked at them in a perplexed way and decided to let it go, but it did make him feel old when they kept calling him "sir."

Nick said, "We will have to go in your transportation, all I have is a two seat 'Vette," and away they went to the hinterlands.

The problem the girls had was finding where this property was located, not being experienced in huge tracts of land sales put them in a position of trying to read maps that showed the land parameters with symbols that they had no fuckin' idea what they meant. When they saw acreage vast enough, whether or not it was for sale, it was presented to Nick as pristine land that was not as yet listed; but it was the real thing, and off they went traipsing through the brush and swamp land in their beautiful clothes, explaining to Nick that they had not anticipated participating in a hike over hill and dale in fields that were unimproved.

One other problem that they related to Nick was that they had not confirmed the outlay in dollar terms on this beautiful piece of real estate. They had not, as yet, pinned the owner down to a firm situation. One thing they did know is that anything was for sale if the price was right.

After an all-day excursion to parts unknown, the girls were swathed in clothes that were covered in briars and burrs and mud. Nick for his part was delighted with the expertise that these women showed, and how they plowed ahead apparently unafraid of alligators, snakes, spiders, and other things like mosquitoes and sandflies.

That evening the ladies commenced doctoring their various bites and scratches and throwing their clothes away. They started a search for blue jeans and visited the sporting goods stores to buy boots that would be apropos for woods and swamps, not to mention finding a real estate pro that could teach them how to read those Goddamn property maps.

The next day dawned dark and rainy, not a day to be slogging around in some damn field that hadn't seen a mower in months, but a great day to visit golf courses that might be on the block.

The ladies selected two courses that were potentially available; in each case they were unable to contact the owner or owners, so they talked to the general managers using a ploy about out-of-town architects gathering information concerning golf course condos and the potential that they would present.

They explained to Nick that they had to make up some excuse to see and survey the courses without the employee's being aware that the place may be for sale.

Nick was puzzled, but enjoyed being an architect for the day, he talked about Roman Corinthian and Doric Columns, used in the construction of potential condo's, and the agents didn't have a clue as to what he was talking about. Hell, Nick didn't have a clue as to what he was talking about.

For Nick, time was growing short, he had to get back to Youngstown to prepare for what he knew would be a difficult general meeting with the CCC group.

He said, "Ladies, I have appreciated your time and effort, and I believe that we have made some progress. Now that I have a feel for Myrtle Beach and the opportunities it possesses, the next step will be to set up a meeting with the principals involved, and I, for my part, will bring knowledgeable people to bear on this situation. I know that this will take some time, but it will be very fruitful to your pocketbook, so be patient and multiple rewards will come to you."

Nick was looking forward to getting back to Youngstown and facing the challenges that awaited him, but not without some amount of foreboding.

Chapter Twenty-Eight
Bringing the C.C.C. to heel. Problems and more problems

As soon as he returned, he contacted his secretary Alicia and picked up his ubiquitous messages. He then arranged for his five emissaries to meet with him at his home.

His home. No place on the face of this earth did he enjoy more. Joey and Liz, their children, and the two dogs, were his famiglia. He did wish that he had someone to share his ups, and downs with, but that cannot be. Everything he did or any actions that were undertaken had to be kept to himself. His failures and successes were his alone, and no one could share in this life of his. How sad?

This was the price he paid for the life he had chosen.

Many times he asked himself: if he could do it all over again, would he take the same path? His answer was always the same: *yes*. If he was able to fast-forward to a time in his life when the old man with the scythe was standing beside him, would his answer be the same? Probably not, but the old man with the scythe may be standing next to him now. In his business, the possibility that he would die by some unknown adversary was an excellent odds on bet, but there was one good thing about that prospect: just like Marilyn Monroe, he would be forever young.

Why, oh why, was he pondering this now? Is it possible that his subconscious was telling him something? Maybe it was saying "for Christ's sake, find a good woman and settle down." Every woman that he fell in love with did not love him. The only one he still wanted was Jennifer Lake, and that was an impossible situation that could never happen. She would never love someone in a profession like Nick's. He still found it impossible not to think of her.

Oh, well, everything in this world wasn't always fair. It seemed that true happiness was for all time just out of reach—each time it was in your grasp, it slipped away. He wondered if it was the same for everyone. Hell, maybe it was; maybe everyone in this world was unhappy, and they just made-believe that they were enjoying their life, even when it was all crashing down.

Yes, everyone was facing the prospect of death, and it was in most cases not easy. Think of the things that happen to people: Cancer, heart attacks, operations, various diseases, things that make your life a living hell like Alzheimer's disease, arthritis, knee and hip replacements, all kinds of accidents that leave permanent scars and injuries. Then there are other things like inept politicians that cause us to lose our jobs, take your money away in the form of higher taxes, and the ever-present inflation—you know they are scamming you, but the only choice you have is to go to the ballot box and vote for the next crook to take his place.

Maybe happiness is not what we think it is. Maybe it is the struggle, maybe it is the reaching out for something that is a step out in front of you, or maybe it is the next accomplishment that we worked for and sweated blood for, whether or not we achieved that triumph or feat or exploited an unattainable talent that we never knew we had. Maybe that's what happiness is.

As he waited for the five messengers to arrive, he was thinking about all the things he had to do: contacting the Cleveland and the Pittsburgh outfits; getting in touch with Holly and finding out what she's up to; getting a handle on the members of the CCC; staying in touch with the members of the Ohio State legislature—thank God they were on summer break; then get together with his auditors and find out where the hell all the money was going. It just seemed that no matter how much he brought in, it disappeared in a fortnight. Of course, this new venture in Myrtle Beach was going to be a huge undertaking.

He received a communication, which was given to him by his secretary Alicia. The Attorney General from the State of Ohio told her that Nick should get in touch with him as soon as he could and this was concerning the incident with Senator John Scully. Nick knew the Attorney General well; they had dealings in the past and had a good working relationship.

With alarm bells ringing, which was part of the security system that Nick had installed, he knew that the five gentlemen he was expecting had just arrived. Joey let them in, and they roared up to the front entrance in a black limousine. *Jesus Christ, could they have been more obvious? Somebody, somewhere was sure to have my home under surveillance Let's make it easy for them—how about a black limo in the afternoon with five sinister-looking guys in it? That would do it.*

They trooped through the huge Gothic front doors with two large German Shepherds trying to be their friend; these were my two "vicious" guard dogs, F. Scott and Zelda, *Oh, well, not everything works out as planned.*

"Benvenuti a casa mia." (Welcome to my home.)

"É con piacere che accettiamo la vostra ospitalità accerttare." (It is with pleasure we accept your hospitality.)

Nick had Liz prepare a large luncheon for these behemoths. When he had originally selected these men, one of the requirements is that they would be of imposing stature.

As they took part in Liz's culinary delights, they were intelligent enough to not speak of the real reason they were there. Every time Nick thought they might slip, he held a finger to his lips and pointed to the walls as if the walls had ears. After everyone was satisfied, Nick led the way to what he thought was the one secure room in the house. This was the area that he had thoroughly checked for listening devices, commonly known as "Bugs."

Each in turn gave Nick their report, and the overriding theme they ran into was: hostility to the new proposals, especially to sharing of proceeds as concerned the policy game. Most of the members were ambiguous to the laundering of money.

The representatives replied that the members must fastidiously adhere to these edicts or face the wrath of the organization, which in its own way could be injurious to their future health as members of the CCC.

In a few cases, they were met with outward hostility from members threatening bodily harm and an outright refusal to not attend any meeting that was planned. Nick immediately asked for and received all the particulars in relation to these members.

Once he received all of the reports, Nick asked each of his emissaries how they were doing and was their famiglia "in good spirits." He tried to know a little about each guy who had performed and accomplished a well-done job. He knew that this was a hardship on their families, and so he inquired if there was anything he could do personally for their loved ones. This was not something that he would do to insure their loyalty. He was truly interested and concerned for their welfare.

Nick felt that good deeds done in this universe would be returned four-fold in the future or the next universe.

There are exceptions to every rule—for instance, The Prick, but the only reason he was still alive is due to the largess of Nick. Did he feel bad about the torment that he caused him?

Yes, he did, but he was at wit's end with this guy? Never did he run into a guy that was as stubborn as he was.

That was not the problem now; it was closer to home and much more serious. If he allowed the affiliates to go their own way, that would mean the breakup of his cash cow, not to mention the vigorish that was going to the different factions and kept them happy. If the money stopped flowing, the steel union may become upset because of the mortgage they hold on Nick's estate, which allowed Nick to sleep inside at night. *Oh, shit*, he thought, *let's get busy and get that silver tongue working.*

He knew that when he got through to the CCC affiliates on the phone, the rhetoric would be brutal and threatening, but no matter what, they would attend this meeting. The first thing he had to pay attention to was the communication from the Attorney General. This message seemed out of the normal course of events, so it was causing him a great deal of consternation.

John Scully was the senator that Pittsburgh faction had removed, all because of a phrase of disrespect to Nick that he had relayed to Vinnie. Once again, Nick learned the same valuable lesson that seemed he had to learn over and over: keep your damn mouth shut. He remembered his mother's mantra, *"Let your mouth run only when you have put your brain in gear."* Sometimes you never seem to learn; you just go on committing the same fucked-up mistake until finally the mistake is so tragic that it makes you withdraw into yourself. Of course, that is a consequence that will hinder your personality in the future.

You eventually become more guarded when holding a conversation, even with those you trust.

Getting the Attorney General on the phone was no easy matter, but the connection was eventually made.

"Mark it's been a long time since I have talked to you. What's been going on?"

"Nick, some rather disturbing news was relayed to me about this ongoing investigation of John Scully. Your name has now entered the investigation, so you will incur some scrutiny."

"How did my name enter the fray?"

"His secretary claims she overheard him threatening you."

Nick wanted to say, "*That's true, but it was nothing,*" but upon reflection, he decided the less said the better. After talking about many other things—and, of course, what the A.G. was most interested in: the coming election—Nick said "Mark, keep me informed."

Mark responded in pleasant tones, "I will try as best I can, you know that, Nick."

This was a thing that he had to put out of his mind; he knew this investigation would be a long, drawn-out affair. He also knew that the Mafia would not be connected because it was a hit and run affair, but being that he had been threatened by Scully, it looked like they would focus on him. He would hire an attorney when they contacted him and wanted more information.

His more immediate problem was straightening out the members that wanted to absolve their obligations to the CCC and go their own way. That was not going to happen, not if he had anything to say about it, and obviously, he did.

He called the President of the CCC and requested him to pick a meeting time and place and inform the members.

He said, "Consider it done."

He called the worst offenders first. The message that he conveyed to each of them was direct: "I did not appreciate the way you treated my emissary. Apparently, the message he brought to you was disregarded and cast aside like a piece of shit. You indicated to him, that it was your intention to not attend our next meeting, and you intended to go your own way and not pay the fees that we had suggested. Now when I looked through the membership lists, I saw your name listed as a lifetime member. As a matter of fact, if you are wondering, all memberships are lifetime, and by God, unless you die or retire, that's exactly what you are: a lifetime member."

"Wait a min—"

"Shut the fuck up."

"Now listen to me carefully. I am of the opinion that you are one of a few members that some sort of disciplinary action should be taken, and if I don't see a subdued, flexible and well-mannered person at this mandatory meeting, then by God, you will receive a visit from myself and members of my staff to give you an attitude adjustment—and you will not have pleasant memories of our adjustment procedures. And please do not try to interrupt me in this conversation, because there is nothing that I want to hear from you except when I ask the question, do you understand me? All I want to hear is '*yes, sir*'."

"Now if this is not sufficient, then you can take one of the two options that are open to you. One is to resign your lifetime membership. The second, I'll let you be the arbiter of that. If you don't know what those two options are, then I hope you have had a good life."

"Look for your notification of the time and place of the meeting in the mail and have a good trip."

The president of the CCC decided to hold the meeting in the ballroom at Idora Park, a nostalgic historic structure that was opened in 1910 and had seen the likes of Guy Lombardo, Tommy Dorsey, Glenn Miller, and other legends that included names from the Twenties and Thirties such as Jelly Roll Morton, Louis Armstrong, Edie Duchin, and Jack Teagarden.

This venue was exactly what Nick wanted; Idora Park was where Nick cut his teeth on assuming manhood.

Having a one-dollar pitcher of beer at the outdoor Beer Garden even though he was only fifteen made him feel like he was a big guy while he was struggling through his teen years. If you were really adventuresome, everyone would light up a cigarette, hoping that nobody you knew would see and tell your parents. Because if your mom and dad found out, that ass of yours would get a good tanning.

Little did he know that one day he would look back on those years as perfectly wonderful and a joy to behold forever. So, going back to Idora was a trip down memory lane. It seemed so long ago that he was there.

Planning for this meeting was of the utmost importance. First and foremost was seating. Nick wanted the hardcore members down front where he could see their reactions. Next, even though he did not expect unplanned demonstrations, he wanted muscle scattered throughout the ballroom and all entrances and exits secured. Nobody got in or out without the proper credentials. He wanted security personnel in the parking lot. Car bombings were a common occurrence in Youngstown, and Nick would have none of that.

He contacted a source he had in the Youngstown Police Department. The one officer he could trust was Harold Lattanzi who was born and raised in Briarhill and was a neighbor of Nick's. Being only nine years junior to Harold and both of them born and raised as neighbors, Nick knew that Harold was absolutely incorruptible and was genuinely embarrassed by the way that the Y.P.D had been compromised by the dominant faction of this police force.

Harold would refuse to go on actions that he knew were illegal, or if not illegal, then not in keeping with the high standards that an incorruptible police force would use. Because of this, he was constantly under pressure from his superiors to conform, making him wary and always on his guard because "the finger" may have been put on him.

The number of murders by the Mafia in Youngstown was appalling, but what was even more appalling was the number that was never solved. Or, if they were solved, they may have involved an innocent person that the Mafia found expendable.

The Y.P.D. solved the problem of Patrolman Lattanzi by assigning him to the Juvenile Department; however, he swung a lot of weight among other officers that thought highly of him.

Because of his adherence to the letter of the law, Nick generally consulted Harold on various problems concerning other officers. He could ask for certain officers to be assigned to venues where Nick needed competent professional help, and Nick felt that clean patrolmen would be needed at Idora Park before, during, and after the CCC meeting. Harold assured Nick that he understood what Nick was trying to tell him. He had already heard talk on the grapevine about the subject of the meeting. Nick wanted to ask him where he got his information but decided that it was enough that Harold had confided in him. Realizing that Harold knew he was skating on thin ice, he had to think not only of himself, but of his family. This was the reason he never became a whistle blower.

Nick was mostly concerned with bombings that may disrupt the proceedings. His fear was more with disgruntled members of the CCC and not with the Cosa Nostra; he hated to think that after all that had been done for these people that they would conspire to disrupt the proceedings by injuring other innocent bystanders. Looking back on the phone calls that he had made to dissident members, he realized that he had been a little on the brutal side when expressing his views.

The members were not always nice guys, and many would not be averse to being unusually vindictive. So he would be a fool to let his guard down. After all, shit happens.

If all he had to worry about was the Mafia, then he would not have to worry about bystanders, because they would target him, not people that had no involvement.

The members of the CCC were not Cosa Nostra and did not adhere to the same principles the Mafia had, which superseded the society at large. One of their ideologies included: do no harm to famiglia o innocente taht astanti significava nulla di male (family or innocent bystanders that are not involved).

The day of the big and fearful meeting arrived, and Nick had done all he could to alleviate and meet any potential problems that may be in the offering.

As members started filing in, they were scrutinized by employees. They did not have machines that were able to check guns and hardware, so they had to use the old-fashioned tools of sight and feel—in other words, patted down. If there had been women that were members, they could have raised questions about the methods used.

Nick had prepared a speech that he felt would appeal to all segments of the CCC.

The speech

"Today is going to mark another milestone in the evolution of our continuing search for improving our organization."

"Today I will explain a new concept that will, in most cases, alleviate the challenging directives of the I.R.S."

"You are already familiar with the problems that occur when you fill out the many forms that are required by the government that allows you to live in this country of non-interference. In this instance I am speaking of the Internal Revenue Service and all the other taxing authorities, city, state, county, etc. And the various entities that control our lives, and go on to proclaim they want you to live in a free and independent way. Go ahead; I will wait until the laughter dies down."

The government does not condone the way that we choose to make a living, which on the face of it is ridiculous. There is nothing wrong with gambling, and if the government should face up to the fact that gambling is what every citizen in this country is involved with every day of their lives, from the moment they wake up in the morning to the time they go to sleep at night, even if it's just driving the car to work, that in itself is a challenge and a gamble, need I say more."

"What I propose is a corporation that will be actively involved in the operation of golf courses, initially, and may branch out into other forms of businesses."

"On a voluntary basis, you will be able to buy stock in this corporation. I expect that after the initial investment, whatever your level of investment is will be the amount returned to you after taxes and expenses. All the investment returned will be essentially income that can be reported to the I.R.S. because it is legal investment income and takes away any problems with the government that may have been your bane in the past. A prospectus will be mailed to you with applications. Any questions can be answered by calling my office."

"One of the most controversial elements of this meeting is the proceeds from the numbers."

"Gentlemen, I completely understand that you feel the efforts you have put into building this segment of your business was yours alone and had nothing to do with the CCC."

"Well, you are wrong—Flat ass wrong. In talking to the different sections that really are the people that allow us to operate unencumbered in our little fiefdoms, and I'm talking about Cleveland and Pittsburgh guys who, before I came along, had a war going on over Youngstown. The number of murders was incomprehensible."

"Whether you knew or not, the fight was over the numbers racket primarily. Now, when I came along, I tried to work with both factions, and I think you know what kind of risk I took. Finally, I was able to organize this organization, and we never talked about the numbers, which really was centered in Cleveland, Youngstown, and Pittsburgh."

"You and I showed them the advantages of having a cohesive group where everything was shared, all the various costs that are a labyrinth of programs that benefit you, let me emphasize YOU."

"Well, that was all well and good in the past, but things change. Our benefactors have found that the amount of revenue from sports betting has fallen off in direct proportion to the increase in your concentration on the numbers."

"It was told to me that after the costs involved in protecting the members from litigation and even getting involved in your divorces and all the bullshit with hospitals and doctors and problems some of you were having with customers, and we had to send collection guys to help collect the money, they found that there wasn't enough voguish to make it worth the conundrums they were faced with."

"Let's think about this, partners of mine, when you consider all the entitlements we have with this organization, then how can you say you want to go your own way and leave one of the finest alliances of its type in this country."

"Personally, I would feel denuded without their support, and the cohesion that I feel is behind me."

"Let me continue to address a subject that I personally abhor, and that is the subject of drugs. It has come to my ears that some of you are now purveyors of this type of offensive, horrendous, hideous scourge among the youth and weaker segment of our population. There is not one amongst you that would want your children or relatives to have this type of addiction, one that in all probability has no known cure and can only lead to a life without consequence and a living hell not only for those addicted but for those that care for them."

"So with all probity, I appeal to your sense of righteousness and morality that when the matter of drugs rears its ugly head, you in all seriousness should walk or run the other way."

"There are many ways to make a living, and when we choose the right way, we can go through life with our heads held high. Remember, we must all answer to a higher authority— whether or not you believe that, but it may happen."

"There are some people that have an addiction to gambling. I have never known one of our members to turn their backs on a person with this type of problem, and all of us would rush to his or her aid and furnish as much help as we were able to give. For us to feed from the unfortunate among us is to eventually have so much disgust for ourselves, it will eventually lead to our own downfall."

"Now on to the lighter side of this message. The new corporation that will be formed will behoove all of you to participate. Yes, initially, it will take some startup money, but I don't know a soul here that cannot afford to do this thing. If you need help financially, may I again say 'call my office'."

"Before you depart from these premises, will you please stop by my desk and give me a pledge of how much your initial amount to the new corporation will be, and at that time, you can express to me or the President of the CCC your concerns in a lucid and civil manner, and we will address your particular problems. The new corporation that will be formed will behoove all of you to participate. Yes, initially, it will take some startup money, but I don't know a soul here that cannot afford to do this thing. If you need help financially, may I again say 'call my office'."

"That's all I have to say, so may God bestow his blessings on you, and as they would say in Ireland and as an ode to all the golfers out there: may the wind be always at your back."

Nick anxiously counted the money that was pledged. Most of the members signed for the tentative assignation of the initial amount of money, and they became the founders of this new corporation. Those that come in at a later date could expect to pay a substantial penalty. However, they would have a little time before that happened, and they will have a chance to see the prospectus before committing any serious amount of capital.

Nick's next job was informing the Pittsburgh and Cleveland boys of the inauguration of this still-unnamed new corporation and finding what level of interest existed. It was important that he had a handle on the amount of capital he could expect. This allowed him to give the real estate agents in Myrtle Beach an idea of how much volume of capital they could anticipate.

Now the lawyers had to go to work, and it would be a strenuous and voluminous far-reaching document encompassing city, state, county, and federal law regulations, together with the Security Exchange Commission and the National Association of Security Dealers and any other sock-it-to-them organization that the devious mind of man could devise.

He wanted this corporation to be unchallenged and above any disputable argument in a court of law.

Chapter Twenty-Nine
The Beauty of Bermuda

After months of work and frustration putting together this huge undertaking and collecting money from the investors, he was finally able to arrange a trip to Bermuda. This is where he would incorporate and establish bank accounts for the corporation.

He was familiar with the Island, spending a small amount of time there as a guest of the Castle Harbour Hotel for one spectacular weekend in the past.

The Hotel seemed to exist only in his dreams; the eminence of it precluded any reasonable expectation of reality. But reality comes to all of us. The Hotel was torn down some years later, and when it's long gone, it's like somebody tore a piece of your heart away. Of course, at some point, hopefully you will reach the twilight of your life, and you can never return. There's no going back. You can only reflect on the halcyon days gone by. This time will live in your memory, and in Nick's case, he had no one to share it with.

Years later, as thoughts of his second visit to Bermuda haunted his reverie, visions of a dark-haired, black-eyed, brown-skinned beauty floated in front of eyes that were now fading with age, but in his mind, he was dining with her again in the spectacular reincarnation of the 1920s and 1930s dining room with a dazzling display of a chandelier.

On this visit to Bermuda, he was changing from just a guy from Youngstown to a world classicist.

This visit to Bermuda was not intended to be a vacation; this was going to be work, visiting the various banks, and deciding on the right bank that would fit his needs. Of course, he would have to play the beautiful and challenging golf courses that were unique and found only in Bermuda. He also wanted to enjoy the world-renowned Tom Collins drink that was endemic to this Island.

Oh, okay, how about a working vacation?

Let's face it, Bermuda has a way about it that lends itself to contemplation and self-gratification. Have you heard about the pink sand beaches? No? Well, hell, you haven't lived!

Instead of taking a leisurely trip on a ship, he decided to fly, saving some time, but a leisurely jaunt on a luxury liner sure sounded good. He arrived at the L.F. Wade International Airport that once upon a time was Kindley United States Air Force Base.

A limo picked him up—not that it had any resemblance to a limo, it was just a small car a little larger than the normal toys that were on the road. Road may be too strong of a word for the small tight, curvy paths that were prevalent in Bermuda.

It was not a very long ride to the beautiful Castle Harbour Hotel that would be his castle for a short while.

The next few days he set a hectic pace, interviewing various banks, and financial institutions, and becoming familiar with Bermudian law. The bank he finally selected was an old established traditional bank with headquarters in the Isle of Mann and was a very proper British establishment.

Empirical Corporation of America was the name that he decided on for the new firm. Empirical's meaning of experimental or pragmatic and this new business venture certainly would fit the category of either one. The acronym would be ECA.

After this trying day, relaxation was uppermost in his mind. He had understood there was a very unique place that, once experienced, would never be forgotten. It was a bistro in a cave in the side of a hill that overlooked the blue translucent ocean. The opening of the cave was very large, and the stone that made up this dazzling freak of nature was flecked with nero, azzuro, giallo, and breccia of dorado. Most of the seating had an unimpaired view of the coastline, including tables located on the flagstone patio. That evening, as Nick reflected on the events of the day, he struck up conversations with other patrons at the bar. It seemed that most of them were natives of the Island, and it made for an interesting night.

As Nick strolled out of the bar to the patio, a huge moon was rising, and stars seemed to form an extravagant necklace in the blue-velvet sky. There was only one thing missing: a woman that was every bit as velvety as the sky and just as deep, mysterious and unfathomable.

He believed he had met her that day—a receptionist in one of the banks he had visited. In their conversation, he had not said more than a few words to her, but she had just enough of a languorous indolent manner in her general approach that in no way was she servile to you. This made for an attitude that made you feel inferior, as if she was saying, "Please do not ask for another favor or I will show you the door." She was super-efficient, and the other employees showed deference to her. Nick made up his mind that tomorrow she would be with him at the Cave.

After an early morning walk and jog along the pathways that were made for ambling and gazing upon unexpected sights—in Nick's case, an old English Fort more than likely built in the 1600s that had still not been relegated to the standard of the reality of tourism when they take an old diamond-in-the-rough and try to improve the unimprovable—Nick took a lazy swim in an azure ocean and a leisurely breakfast.

It would be best to approach this woman in the morning before the cares of the day had set in and everything was still fresh. Nick had no idea what her situation was: married, in a committed relationship, actively looking, or would be totally uninterested in Nick. Regardless, he would employ his most beguiling personality and let the chips fall where they may.

What Nick did not know, in the Bermudian culture, you were looked down upon if you dated or became too friendly with an outsider, which would especially include tourists. One thing in his favor, he was here to establish a business relationship, and that may carry some amount of weight when trying to win a date with this charming lass.

Strolling down Front Street in Hamilton, the capital of Bermuda, Nick could feel his excitement increasing. He passed by the towering sleek luxury ships with their contingent of excited passengers coming and going, the heavy traffic on this main thoroughfare adding to the excitement that was Bermuda.

As he got nearer to his destination, he found his heart racing a little, and he thought to himself *"what the hell is the matter with me?"* He questioned whether this striking girl would jump at the chance to go out with him, a total stranger to these Isles? Besides the cultural differences, this girl was probably of African ancestry, and in Nick's world, to date a black girl was a "no-no', and in her culture, to date a white guy was a disgrace, God forbid, one that may be a tourist.

Nick turned easterly onto the street that housed the imposing bank, which was one of the biggest structures on this street. Now was the moment of truth. He perambulated up the stairs hesitantly with a reluctant gait, asking himself what the hell was he going to say when being confronted by this girl who he knew to be slightly haughty and indolent in her manner?

The doors opened, and before him sitting behind a grand desk sat the dark-haired, black-eyed beauty with the daunting presence. She rose to greet Nick, and it was only then that he realized she was not just a receptionist, but probably an executive of the bank. The features that he had not noticed when he first saw her were now pretty evident, especially how tall and slim this lady was.

Being flip was generally Nick's style, but inherently he knew this was not going to be a home-run with this very proper, statuesque and serious lady.

"Sir, how can I be of service today?" she said. "I believe this is a return visit to our offices for you."

"If you will forgive my intrusion," Nick replied, "I don't believe you gave me your name yesterday, and I must have names if I find it necessary in the future to communicate with your bank."

"My name is Tzania, and I am known as Zany."

"Well, Zany, my name is Nick Lasko."

"Yes, I am already familiar with your name. You opened an impressive account with us yesterday, and it will be my pleasure to give you the kind of service for which our bank is noted."

"Zany, my request is out of the ordinary. As you may know, I am here on this beautiful island by myself, and I find that enjoying all the delights that this island offers by one's self does not translate to an enchanting visit. With that in mind, it is my request that you accompany me to a very unusual place that I have stumbled upon but that you are probably familiar with. It's called The Cave. It has to be the most extraordinary and remarkable pub of its kind that I have ever seen. Would you honor me by accompanying me this evening and possibly making this a most unforgettable Bermuda evening?"

"Mr. Lasko, I must inform you that I am married but separated and presently dating a man that may or may not enter my life on a full-time basis."

"For the moment, can we keep it on a part-time schedule, while I have you join me for dinner at Castle Harbour?"

Zany thought about this proposition for a few moments. Her first instinct was to say no! But upon further consideration, against her better judgment she decided to accept the invitation, but with a few caveats.

"Mr. Lasko, I will join you at seven p.m. for dinner, but remember tonight I call the shots and whatever will be will be, but there will be no tomorrow."

"I think I can relate to everything but no tomorrow, an explanation may be required?"

With a look that may be described as amazement, she went on to say; "I pictured you as a man of the world, am I wrong?"

"I may appear that way, but I'm really a small town guy trying to get an education. Please elucidate."

"Let me lay it out for you, and you can take that anyway you like."

"I have a life here in the Islands. You have a life in the States. Our life, and I'm speaking of you and I, ends tonight because you will return home in a day or two and I will stay here. So what we have is tonight. Is that enough elucidation for you?"

"I just wanna say I have been elucidated, and if I did not have a million things to do back in the States maybe I would stay here, marry you, and have a passel of kids and live happily ever after."

"Believe me, Mr. Lasko, living on this island is no fairy tale. A person that comes here for a small amount of time only see's the beauty, but your life here is governed by the government in everything you do, even to the color of your home. By the way, living with me would not be a fairy tale, either. I guarantee it."

Nick went on to say, "I will look forward to having you by my side at dinner tonight, and that will be the beginning of a

287

memory that will last for years to come. What the future holds will be left to the ages."

Nick was waiting in the reception area of the Castle Harbour Hotel when she arrived. Those long legs just seemed to unravel as she got out of the car, and as gracefully as a cat, leisurely entered the hotel lobby. Nick, just as unhurriedly, took her gently her hand and with a great amount of enthusiasm said, "You look stunning tonight," he realized as he stood next to her with her white ensemble and white high heels that she was taller than he was.

The overall effect made her dark skin stand out while Nick's complexion was pasty white. Her appearance was electrifying. Nick was actually dumb founded by the elegance and brilliance she exuded this evening.

Every eye in the lobby turned her way. For some reason, he had this irresistible urge to place a white rose in her hair, but he knew the effect would be over-the-top.

They made their way to their table following the waiter. The other diners were not discreet in their obvious admiration of this picturesque lady. It made Nick feel a little reticent, as if making his first appearance in the presence of an emerging exquisite butterfly. Attention centered on this couple.

The servers, caught up in the examination of this twosome, and preferential treatment, seemed to be accorded them. Then Nick realized, she had been recognized by the staff, and in Bermuda, a high official of one of the leading industries in the Islands was held in high esteem.

They ordered from an intriguing menu, deciding on char-grilled spice-rubbed cornish game hen served with golden fried potatoes and sautéed curly kale, smothered with a tamarind and Bermuda Black Seal Rum barbecue sauce that seemed to be a little extreme for a boy from Youngstown that had been nurtured on pasta and sausage.

He said to her, "Zany, have you noticed the stares that are coming your way?"

Coyly responding, Zany replied, "They are used to seeing me with another gentleman, and there is a natural curiosity that will give them many hours of gossip. On a small island such as this, gossip is the preferred method of communication, and by tonight, the other gentleman will know all about my 'dalliance' with a person not of this enclave."

Nick, naturally curious, asked; "Not to be obnoxious, but what is your nationality?"

"I am half African and half Portuguese," Came her proud response.

"That certainly sounds exotic. Tell me more about yourself. How did this heritage come to be."

"My mother immigrated to the Azores with her parents who were actually from a tribe not far from Johannesburg. They were trying to escape from forced slavery or eventually being involuntarily indentured to one of the plantation owners. There was also a real possibility of being sold to a slaver and taken to some Godforsaken place that would hold unimaginable terrors. The mere thought of that sends chills up my spine."

"My grandparents ended up working on one of the ranches, and my mother was enticed into a sexual encounter with the owner's son who was Portuguese, quite wealthy, and very aware there was a stigma attached to having a liaison with a black woman that produced a child. When I was old enough to attend school, he sent me to live with a really sweet black woman in the Cayman Islands."

"I fastidiously attended all the schools that were available to me, knowing that my future to be of any consequence would depend entirely on me. I eventually received a Masters in Banking and received an offer to work in a British bank, which I jumped at, and have diligently worked my way up the corporate ladder."

"You see, Mr. Lasko, it makes no sense I should be seeing you on this day and risking my reputation. Everyone knows me, and of course, it will be all over the Island tomorrow. What the hell was I thinking when I accepted your invitation?"

"I can tell you what you were thinking: you just met a truly interesting guy, whom you had checked out very closely before accepting his application to establish a banking relationship, and found that the amount of money he will be able to put into the jurisdiction of this bank may be truly astounding in its proportion to the total assets of this banking institution, which in turn will bring it to prominence as one of the most outstanding financial institutions not only in Bermuda but the British Isles."

"You also know that I am closely allied with or possibly a member of an organization commonly referred to as La Cosa Nostra, but you may not know that I am a contributor to almost every charitable organization known to man and a major backer of various political parties that have some modicum of clout in issues that may come before heads of state, which means that, at some future date, I may have some use to your employer. "Now, have I got that about right?"

"Much of what you said has more than some truth to it, but as to my superiors giving me the green light to date you, you are a little off-base. This was entirely my decision, but they expressed no objection and looked upon it as favorable, given some of the things that your background revealed."

"After scrutinizing the information that was available to us, we knew that doing business with you would be like navigating a minefield.

"Now may I suggest that talk of business be taboo the rest of this beautiful evening? In these gorgeous surroundings, it will become distasteful, especially when we are about to experience a delightful and tasteful encounter with epicurean hedonistic delights. And let's make this a night that will live in our memories forever."

Nick was in complete agreement. The conversation took an entirely different bent and she was very interested in Nick's life, so he told her about his dance lessons and she became very animated wanting to know "If he knew how to Samba." She said you know Mr. Lasko I traveled to Brazil not too long ago, they speak Portuguese and I'm proficient in that language, and their national dance is Samba, and I so wanted to do that dance but I was afraid of making a fool of myself so much to my regret I never danced it, I just sat salivating thinking of doing that dance."

"Mr. Lasko, is there any way you could teach that dance to me this evening? I will willingly become your fool."

"That's an offer too good to pass up. I may not be able to teach you more than the basics, but by the end of the night, I guarantee you will be dancing the Samba."

She exhibited an amount of enthusiasm that was hard to comprehend. "I know just the place to go," she said, "with a fabulous Latin orchestra that will and can play anything I ask of them."

When they left the dining room, she was walking quickly and pulling Nick along. Nick, caught a little off guard, ended up stumbling along behind her. They went directly to her car. "I hope you don't mind, but I know my way around. I'm anxious to get there, and if you're a good boy tonight, I'll think about taking you home after the evening fireworks."

"I didn't know about any fireworks."

"I'm not talking about the kind they shoot off in the sky. I'm talking about the ones that are shot off at sea level, and you will provide the ammunition."

Chuckling, Nick said, "I just hope that the fireworks don't start before we are ready for them."

"If they do you will just have to reload and start a new holiday with a new set of fireworks and teach me a new dance. One that is sensuous and intense and hopefully instead of fireworks it will be more like an astonishingly beautiful finish to a memorable evening."

"I love the way you think."

291

Nick was able to teach Zany the basics to the Samba, and with his expertise in Latin rhythms, Zany did not want to leave the dance floor. From that point on, it was dancing, dancing, and dancing. Finally, the orchestra wrapped it up, and it was time to go to the Cave.

Exhausted was an understatement. As he left the club, he was walking on unsteady legs, but Zany was still percolating like the evening was just beginning. Nick grabbed the first table he came to on the flagstone patio of the Cave and looked forward to enjoying a Bermuda Tom Collins. They settled down to catch their breath and recharge their batteries.

It wasn't very long before Zany spoke, "Mr. Lasko, look at that moon."

"Zany, why do you insist on calling me 'Mr. Lasko'?"

Zany replied, "Because that's who you are, and that's who you will be forever more."

The night continued, and the conversation was titillating. They walked to the shore together. Removing their shoes allowed their toes to be engulfed in a moonlit glistening diamond extravaganza of pink sand. There were other celebrants on the beach that were dancing in the sand while a three-piece combo played Reggae.

Embracing on the beach and swaying to the beat of the music, their lips hungrily devoured each other. Bodies entwined and seemed to be one with the rhythm; the stars, the moon, the sand, the universe, and the heavens, all coalesced as if some giant heavenly entity was the maestro directing this grand play.

Clothes were a distraction, and so they were discarded. Naked, they entered the warm Caribbean waters while the other beach goers gave not a glance. They made love as if this was the last time they would see each other, with wild abandonment. The moon made a pathway to the stars called a moonwalk, and they took it."

Two days later, Nick was winging home to face the ever-present problems that made him never want to leave the islands and Zany, an unforgettable sojourn, and If possible, he would return. However, experience had taught him that rarely, if ever, can you go back.

With these emotions ruminating in his mind, the plane landed in Youngstown. He became slightly depressed as he viewed the landscape devoid of palms and excitement and beautiful beaches. The closest thing he knew of as a beach town was a hamlet called Geneva on the Lake, and it was losing its pizazz.

When he arrived at his estate, the famiglia was still intact, and this seemed to brighten his day.

Alicia was frantically trying to get in touch with him; a subpoena from the office of the Attorney General was requesting his presence to testify in the ongoing investigation of John Scully. Nick was alarmed at this turn of events, and it would be beneficial to him if he could find the best attorney available. He thought of the lawyer he had in New York for the racing commission, Jerry Hamm, but when he contacted him, Jerry informed Nick that his docket was too crowded to be able to give him the proper attention that the Scully case required. At this point, Nick was undergoing a severe case of nerves, not knowing where to turn at this moment; everything he thought of had its drawbacks: if he called the A.G. and prevailed upon their past relationships, it may be too presumptuous. He inherently knew that in a situation where the AG may be his inquisitor and protagonist, that it may make things worse. If he called the Pittsburgh boys for advice on selecting a lawyer, they may be willing to throw Nick in the trash and take the heat off of themselves, somehow making him the responsible party for the murder of John Scully.

As these thoughts were racing through Nick's mind, the ugly head of fear started awakening. If this got into the papers, all of his contacts in government would start running for the exits. As it turned out, it had already hit the paper, and his contacts were already jumping off the nearest bridge. Well, they may not be jumping, but they were contacting their attorneys. Their motto had become "don't call me I'll call you."

Fear was rampant in state and local governments; anybody that had contact with Nick would possibly be in jeopardy, maybe not for the murder, but in favors that may have been completed through nefarious means. This is a case of "following the bouncing ball," and where it stops, nobody knows. In other words, it's a case only involving Nick as far as anybody knows, but these things have a way of spreading their tentacles. Before you know it, they could be investigating everybody for everything under the sun.

Tony Vilanotti was a name that came to Nick, probably because his instincts told him that even though Tony was a high-ranking Capo Capi in the Cleveland Mafia, there was a certain honesty about him that Nick sensed. More than likely, he had attained his lofty position because of his inherent rectitude, Solomon-like judgments with his feet firmly planted in a down-home attitude.

Calling Tony was a decision that was the right thing to do as far as Nick was concerned; he knew that Tony would give him the best information that was available.

Reaching Tony by phone was not a chore; he was easily accessible. Nick did not have to go through a secretary or a consigliere because Tony was almost always available through his restaurant.

"Hello, Tony, this is Nick."

"Nick how the hell are you—long time no see! When you coming up to have some vino and some conversation?"

"Well, Tony, I wish I was there right now, but you may have heard that I have a problem with the Attorney General and I need a little help. It's in the way of a recommendation."

"Listen to me, Nick. Any time I can help, I'll be there with you. What do you need?"

"I need advice or a suggestion for a counselor that would not be affiliated with this State in any way."

"I know of a possibility that lives in South Carolina. At one time, we had a need for an attorney that did not have a dog in the fight, and I'm talkin' about Ohio. We looked at several possibilities and picked another guy. I remember this 'Joe' guy because he was scrupulously clean, and at the time, he may have been a shade too clean. I know of the problems you are having, Nick, and you're going to find that people you thought were your friends will now be avoiding you. You have also become non essenziali a certe persone" (nonessential to certain people).

"The man's name is Joe North. Whether or not he will take a murder case so far from his home is open to conjecture. Whatever happens, it's going to be costoso" (expensive).

"Hey, Tony, they haven't charged me with anything yet. All these guys that are running away from me now may not think that was the wise thing to do later. By the way, how is your wife, Dawn, doing?"

"She's right here by my side—il mio lato migliore (my best side). Nick, I know you will be going through a rough time, and money may be tight. Remember, if you need anything, I'll be right here."

"Tony, you'll never know how much that means to me."

Nick now started to interview lawyers by phone to kind of "feel them out" about their attitudes toward going against the State of Ohio and the AG, in particular having Nick Lasko as a client.

His mood deteriorated as he communicated with a passel of attorneys and didn't get the answers he wanted, not that he expected any that would have satisfied him. Most of the well-known lawyers did not want to take his case for two reasons. One, he had a very mysterious vocation that may have been comprised of anything up to and including Mafia, which opens another can of worms that possibly included gambling, loansharking, drugs, and fixer, so why not murder? He may be potentially a hit man, which brings us back to the hit on John Scully. Two, their reputations were on the line. They also had a natural fear, if the mob or Nick did it to Scully, what makes them think it couldn't happen to them if they lost the case or did anything to displease Nick or the mob. A couple of the younger, newer attorneys would chance it, but the experience factor made Nick turn them down.

He decided to turn to Joe North. What the hell, he'd give him a call and see what the fuck comes of it. Nothing to lose and probably nothing to gain, either. After all this guy was from some hick town in the south, even if it was Columbia, the capital of South Carolina. This wasn't New York—hell it wasn't even Youngstown! *Shit*, Nick thought, *I must be getting desperate. Well, hell, Tony Vilanotti gave him an endorsement, so he can't be all bad.*

Speaking to Joe was an occurrence that Nick was not quite ready for. Joe seemed to enjoy asking questions, and Nick was usually adept at avoiding answers. It went something like this: Robbin, Joe's secretary answered the phone and referred what she felt an incomprehensible call to Joe.

"Who are you?"

"I'm Nick Lasko."

"What do you want?"

"An attorney to represent me."

"Why?"

"I've been subpoenaed by the State of Ohio."

"Why are you calling me? Aren't there any attorneys in Ohio?"

"Hey, fuck you, I don't need a wise ass right now, I have enough of them trying to fuck me up here. But come to think of it, what the hell is one more."

"Calm down, Mr. Lasko, I did not mean to upset your fragile psyche; maybe you don't need an attorney as much as you need a psychiatrist. What did they subpoena you for, using too many expletives?"

Nick: "Sonofabitch, where did you get your degree, Podunk University in Podunk, U.S.A.? Or are you moonlighting as a stand-up comedian at your local comedy club, and you're trying out your new routine on me?"

Clients were in Joe's waiting room, and his secretary Robbin was busy buzzing Joe. He told Nick, "Listen, I will have to get back to you. Give the particulars to Robbin, and I will call you back as soon as I can."

Robbin took all the information and relayed this to Joe. When he had a chance, he looked it over and knew immediately that this needed attention. He did not know who this Lasko character was, but he called him back within a short time.

"Nick, I'm sorry I was so flip when we talked, but I was pressed for time. You see, I had a golf game booked for this afternoon, and I was a little fractious when we talked earlier."

"Well I don't want to hold you up. Let it not be said that ol' Nick held up a golf game."

Joe responded, "I've called my group and explained I would be a little late."

Joe's interest had now reached the tepid stage, and he inquired of Nick, "Apparently, this Subpoena has something to do with the murder of John Scully. Through the newspapers, I am familiar with the case, but how are you involved in this situation?"

"I do business with many of the legislators in the State of Ohio, and John became angry about something that was so minor that I don't recall what it was now. He got a little nasty with me, but it was nothing that we couldn't paper-over. When I left his office, I didn't give it another thought. His secretary overheard the entire conversation, and her perception was such that she thought John and I were in a heated argument. But, it was nothing more than John speaking in an agitated voice, blowing off a little steam. At no time was I rude to him, there was no reason to believe that I would have taken retaliatory action. On the contrary, when I left, my thinking was 'what can I do for John to let him know that I had no hard feelings'."

"Nick, at this point, I don't know if I can take your case or not. I would have to call around and gather more information."

"Mr. Lasko let me give you some free advice: if I were you, I would try to contact an attorney in your area, because if you hire me, it will be extremely expensive because of my time and travel expenses."

"Okay here's a plan: Call around; find out if you want me as a client; and if you do, I will come to see you at your office, and if not, we'll call it a day."

"I do not need to call around. All that is required is a hefty advance payment and a credit report. Do you have a problem with that?"

"If the payment is in the realm of possibilities, I don't see it as a problem."

"By the way, what did your foursome say when you said you would be late?"

"They said 'fuck you, we'll see you on the back nine'."

Alicia called and gave him the information that a lady by the name of Joan Lyons from Myrtle Beach wanted to get in touch with him, and it was important.

He had several calls from CCC members, wanting Nick to return their calls. Also, John Black from Cleveland and Vinnie Solerno from Pittsburgh were waiting patiently for Nick to get in touch with them.

The first call had to go to Vinnie. When they were connected, Vinnie said, "What the hell is this Subpoena that we have been hearing about?"

"Hey, Vinnie, this is bullshit and don't worry about it. I'll take care of it." Nick was not about to say too much on the phone, but what he wanted to say was: *You stupid motherfuckers are the cause of this! You are the impediment and the brake on the wheel of progress and the source of me losing all my connections in the State, and that causes all of us to lose money.*

Where the fuck are your brains? Every time you have a problem, your solution is to kill the poor bastard. In this case, your ego got in the way of an intelligent decision, and Goddamit, I wish I didn't have to deal with you anymore. But, all he said was, "Listen, Vinnie, I'll get back to you, I'm already working on an attorney that will take care of it."

"Nick, I know you will do the right thing," Vinnie said in a voice that was mollifying.

Next, John Black: "Jerry, I'm sorry I did not get in touch with you earlier, but I've been out of town and had many problems to get solved since I've been back."

"Look, paisan, I didn't call to cast calunnie (aspersions) your way. I just called to tell you that we are one hundred percent behind you. I have faith in your judgment. Non prendere qualsiasi merda da loro." (Don't take any shit from them.)

Nick went on to call the members of the CCC and assured them that the money they had used to buy stock in ECA (Empirical Corp. of America) was entirely safe and being held in a bank in Bermuda. If for any reason he could not go through with the purpose of this Corporation, then all monies would be returned.

He called Joan Lyons, who was very excited to hear from him and told him of the perfect golf course being offered right now in North Myrtle Beach. Nick said, "Hold on, Joan, something has come up, and I'm not able to break away at this time. You will have to ice it for the time being."

While Joan was crestfallen at this piece of unwelcomed news, her motto was "what is meant for you will not pass you by." Nick knew that this Myrtle Beach caper was a home run. He also knew that his income would be drastically reduced because of that Goddamn subpoena, so the quicker he got hopping on ECA, the faster it would put him in position to be able to call all the shots, including the stipend he would receive as Chief Investment Advisor.

Next on the agenda was contacting Holly, and touching base on any new additions to the string and what was going on in general. Nick all-in-all was upset that the expenses of running this farm were greater than he thought they should be. He knew getting a world-class string of horses was not going to be easy. Of course, if the influence-peddling was still going strong, then the farm would not be such a big deal as far as money was concerned. However, until he got this subpoena cleared up, he had no way of knowing if he would be able to resurrect his business.

"Holly, I'm glad I was able to get a hold of you. I needed to know what we have in the string. I know I've been very busy and unable to stay in contact with you the way I want to, so tell me what's happening."

"I have added two studs to the string beside what we already have. They are young and still in training, but hopefully will be ready for the Gulf Stream trip. We also have dibs on a foal with the poppa being Big Mo and a mare with a pedigree sporting 'Citation' and a lineage that goes all the way back to Twenty Grand. I made a deal that the next foal will be on the cuff with us."

"Anyway, we now have Big Mo, Burgoo, and Rebirth."

Nick interrupted; "And Empirical and Zany. This is my mandate."

"Only if the names are accepted by the racing commission."

"Holly, tell them that Nick Lasko has suggested these names, and if you have a problem, tell them I will personally call them." Now, Nick needed to clarify what was happening. "I'm sure you know that I'm having a problem with an investigation by the Attorney General, and I have virtually lost my influence in the legislature. So, the money is now a problem, and the only thing I'm asking is to be very judicious with the allocation of funds."

"Nick, I can only do so much, and I'm watching every nickel that goes out. If I can reduce expenditures, you know I will. Nick, I want you to know that if there is anything I can do, I'll be right there. I know you, Nick, and I believe you're being railroaded. You are not a killer, 'cause if you were, the Prick would no longer be around."

"Holly, if I meted out any retribution, it was always necessary and deserved, but never have I ever eliminated God's creatures. Hell, I don't even hunt or fish!"

The appearance for the subpoena was before a Grand Jury in November to process an indictment for aiding and abetting the murder of John Scully. When Nick found out this was an appearance before a Grand Jury in order to secure an indictment, he suddenly realized it had nothing to do with the murder—it was about getting information on the influence that Nick was exerting over the lawmakers. Once the information was obtained, it could be used as a hammer in the next election.

As a matter of fact, the possible Grand Jury indictment was only presented to Nick to provide a hammer on him. This scenario would play out in this fashion: The AG will at some point tell Nick that he would drop the possible indictment if Nick would give out the information the AG wanted to hear. He felt that Nick, in order to save his own sorry ass, would willingly give the information that the AG wanted.

That was never in the cards, and Nick realized that once a strong objection was made by Joe North, and possible indications of what was transpiring were given to the newspapers in the state, he was pretty sure the AG would back down.

Nick decided that now was the time to travel to South Carolina and have a meeting with Joe North. After that, he would swing by Myrtle Beach and look at that golf course that Joanie Lyons was trying to tell him about.

Joe provided Nick with an appointment the following week, and he then called Joanie to tell her to expect him in about a week.

After Nick's mind had worked through the various scenarios, a great sense of relief was felt. He now knew the AG was coming from left field and did not have a leg to stand on. This was pure and simple a fishing expedition.

After meeting with Joe, it was decided a strongly worded official letter to the AG would be sufficient to get the indictment crushed. Joe did have one tidbit of information obtained through nebulous contacts: a prominent owner/trainer from the east would testify in front of the Grand Jury and disparage Nick's character and other things that he may have been involved in. His testimony would not have been used in an actual trial, but before a Grand Jury, it would probably carry enough weight to have Nick brought up on charges.

Just maybe it was time to act on what the Pittsburgh people had suggested a long time ago. It would be a rub-out of the guy that Nick called the Prick. He had never been associated with that type of thing in the past, but when you have an angry bear charging at you, would you not shoot him if given the chance? Especially if this was not his first foray on you. The only thing that would give Nick satisfaction is if he did it himself and did it face-to-face. For now, he would not dismiss this thought but put it to the back of his mind and allow it to ferment, and when the time was ripe, he would do the actual confrontation. Until then, there was business to conduct.

Thinking of the foregoing, Nick decided to call Pittsburgh. He contacted Vinnie on the phone and updated him on the many things that had taken place.

Vinnie was truly glad to hear from Nick

"Hell, yes, come ahead! I'd love to see you; it's been a long time." It was always a pleasure to hear from him, and they had a lot in common. Vinnie said, "Nick, I hear that you're going to be on your way to Myrtle Beach to consummate a deal on a golf course. Listen, my boy, do you mind a little company? I need a break, and I'd like to play a little golf."

Chapter Thirty
The Charleston Experience

"Hey, Nick, I hear that when you drive to Myrtle Beach, you will be coming close to Charlestown. I know of your great love for history, so if you would, stop for a night, and enjoy a very unique experience. I know of a place, a bed and breakfast called The Battery Carriage House Inn, and it's in a section of Charlestown that is very historic. I'll tell you what: I'll call ahead and have them be expecting you. And when you and I get to the beach, I'll be waiting to hear all about it."

"Vinnie, that sounds like the best idea you have had in a long time—maybe ever."

The drive to Myrtle Beach was uneventful. The route used was a new Highway I-26 that brought him to that grand old city of Charleston that he had heard so much about. The history that abounded around this city was unparalleled in the part that it played in the foundation of our country.

He searched and found the section called the Battery where magnificent, very old antebellum homes were located. Adjacent to the Charleston Harbor where Fort Sumter, the place where the Civil War—or as the Southerners would say: the War Between the States—started.

Given Nick's predilection for beautiful homes and history, there happened to be several bed and breakfast inns on the Battery, and he decided to find the one that Vinnie had told him about and stay there.

Little did he know that the one selected was known for several formidable ghosts. Yes, Ghosts.

Battery Carriage House Inn was well known for the spirits that seemed to be at home and in their element at Carriage House. The drive into the Battery, except for the traffic, made him feel like he had just entered the nineteenth century. Exquisite, delicately styled *Gone with the Wind* homes lined the streets with huge live oaks, making a frame that complimented the ramparts.

Cannons on Charleston Harbor gave the feeling of having just returned to 1860, and of course, this was the home town of Rhett Butler wasn't it?

He walked up the walk that somebody had just sprayed with the scent of magnolias, climbed the stairs, and walked across the great veranda where he greeted and was greeted by several occupants of rocking chairs, idling the time away as they must have done in times gone by.

In the reception area, he was met by a beautiful girl, a flower of the south dressed in clothes of the period. As he checked in, she said, "Mister Lasko, I have a very special room for y'all that is available. It is room number ten; if you wish, I can assign it to you."

Nick asked, "What makes that room so special?"

"Well, I hope y'all know that Carriage House is especially noted for the so-called specters and haint's (this is a word that is used in Gee-Ghee or Gullah dialect that can be found in the Islands of South Carolina and Georgia) that seem to infest this place, and room number ten can come alive with what ah call spirits and is particularly active in that respect."

Nick, seemly under a bit of consternation, said, "Wait a minute. When you talk about specters and haints, are you talking about apparitions, phantoms, spirits, ghosts?"

"Yes, and things of that nature."

"Wait a minute—do your other guests know of these things?"

"Well ah would assume they generally do."

"Well how about the other guests sitting in the rocking chairs on the veranda? "

"Mister Lasko, this is the weekend, and our new guests have not checked in yet. So you see, there are no guests here at this time. Furthermore, there are no rockin' chairs on the veranda."

Wait a Goddamn minute, Nick thought. *What the fuck is going on? This girl that looks like she just stepped out of 1860 and is dressed in a Scarlett outfit is telling me I did not talk to anybody on the veranda because there is nobody here, and I'm supposed to take her word for it and believe that I was talking to apparitions? I'm a sonofabitch—I ain't buying this. Okay I'll play along with this little drama and see what comes next.*

"All right, tell me little girl, what's your name?"

With a smile, she said, "My momma said I look just like Scarlett O'Hara and named me Scarlett."

Nick looked around and did a double take. Under his breath, he said "sonofabitch". Then said, "Don't give me any more crap; what is your Goddamn name? "

In a rather small voice and stammering said, "I'm tellin' y'all the truth, it really is Scarlett."

Trying to contain his obfuscation confusion and his anger, Nick lowered his voice because he realized that he had caused an apparently vulnerable and impressionable young girl to become alarmed at Nick's fierce attitude.

He said in a more subdued voice, "Scarlett, I'm sorry if I have alarmed you, but I've got to try and understand what just happened here. Please be aware that the mystification I feel would, and could be an occurrence that anyone that had experienced what I have at this time— namely talking to people that aren't there— unreal!

When I came in here, your patio was occupied by people with whom I exchanged greetings, and then you informed me they didn't exist. If this is a game, let's end it now?"

"No, Mister Lasko, y'all have mah poor soul in a quandary. I'm sure ah do not know what you are referrin' to."

"Okay, Scarlett, you said you will assign me room number ten. Well, then, let's get on with it, and while you are doing that, please take a piece of paper and put your first and last name on it in the event that I need to contact you in the future."

"Mister Lasko, I will be happy to do that, and ah hope your heart is lifted by your stay here at Battery Carriage House."

Nick decided to put the foregoing events out of his mind and go for a walk on the Battery. It was a gorgeous Carolinas evening and thoughts of all the things that happened right here where he was walking took precedence over the previous events. However, as he passed the veranda, he noticed that there were rocking chairs there but not occupied. Scarlett was either funning him, or the guests had decided to go elsewhere. He wondered if he should go back and confront Scarlett with this information and thought "to hell with it." He did glance at the piece of paper where Scarlett wrote her full name. He was interested in knowing what her last name was. It read Scarlett Mullins, and the handwriting was beautiful as if she had been schooled in a different era. He was glad that her last name was not O'Hara—now he was just being silly.

The sailboats on the bay were nothing short of spectacular with the moonlight playing its glow on them, brightening and darkening as the clouds scuddered past on their heavenly journey.

At this moment in time, he was engulfed in reliving our country's past. If you were very quiet, you could hear the rumble of cannon, the rattle of musket fire, the yells, and screams of men. With clairvoyance, he saw the wagons bring in ammunition and more men as they clattered on their journey along the cobblestone streets.

This type of thing exhilarated Nick—just the thought of standing in the same location all this history took place.

Nick made his money outside the laws of government, but first, and foremost he was an American patriot. Laws in this country keep changing. There was a time it was legal to consume any narcotic if you had a mind to. In fact, Coca Cola contained cocaine. At one time, there was no income tax, then there was, then there wasn't, and then there was. At one time, you could drink and make alcoholic beverages and then you couldn't and then you could, and now you can drink it, but you can't make it. At one time, you could own gold and then you couldn't, and then you could. So Nick felt no compunction to give up what he felt was the right thing to do, and the things he did now would one day be legal with the government actively promoting it.

He walked slowly back to the Carriage House Inn, and as he neared this beautiful historic place, he thought about the recent hi-jinx that he had undergone. He had never encountered a ghost before, but being his mother was Italian, and being in the presence of Italian culture, there was much talk of apparitions and such. Nick had never given much credence to that kind of gossip; it was just something that you gave lip service, or sat late at night on the curb under the streetlight telling ghost stories to your buddies and swearing they were true.

However, this situation that he has encountered gave him food for thought. Tonight, if a ghost were to appear in his room, Nick's practicality would take over, and far from being frightened, he would confront the entity and demand answers, starting with what the hell was he or she doing here and what do you want and what the fuck do you think you are going to achieve by running around scaring people at night while they are trying to sleep. What the hell is wrong with appearing in the afternoon? I know, you don't receive as great of a response out of people as you do in the dark of the night, am I right? Your damn right I'm right! Wait a minute, I supposedly did see ghosts in the afternoon sitting on the veranda, but why in the fuck didn't they float around and at least try to give me a fright? Oh, well, I guess there's no figuring out a ghost.

Nick was actually looking forward to seeing something unusual in his room and would be disappointed if none should appear.

Entering the Carriage House Inn, first of all, he noticed that there were rocking chairs on the veranda, then he heard voices in the rear courtyard. He decided to investigate, and a tranquil wine-tasting party was in progress. Remembering the episode on the veranda earlier, he joined the party and searched for the person that seemed to be the leader. It turned out to be a well-mannered docent. He introduced himself, and she remembered checking him into room number ten. Upon overhearing this, he heard many of the other guests commenting: "so he was the one that got number 10"and "that's the one we wanted."

Guests wanted to stay in that room because of the well-advertised ghosts that supposedly occupied the room. You would think that it would be a disincentive to spend a night there, but it was not. It seemed that guests were intrigued and invigorated with the thought of coming face-to-face with a bonafide apparition.

Nick was a little flummoxed and said, "A sweet little girl by the name of Scarlett checked me in."

The Docent replied, "Oh, no, I was the one that saw you come up the stairs, cross the veranda and exchange greetings with the other guests. I checked you in."

Nick figured *Jesus Christ, I've got to get the hell out of here; these fuckin' people are all crazy.*

Eventually, after being very alert and jumpy around these Goddamn nuts, he made his way to his room and prepared himself for any possible occurrence.

Nick by this time was feeling extremely combative. He actually was hoping that an apparition would come forth so he could knock the shit out of it, and if he couldn't knock it around, he would have a few choice words for it.

He was experiencing problems getting to sleep, but when he did, it was the sleep of the dead. If something came into his room that night, Nick never knew it. Nick woke the next morning feeling fresh and renewed, packed his suitcase, and was off.

Extremely happy but with some gut reaction that he had just experienced a visceral episode that he will never forget, but at the same time, he knew he could never tell another soul about this occurrence. It would cause the person hearing this to question Nick's sanity. Would you talk of a million dollar deal with a guy that just told you of this incidence? I don't think so.

As he drove north on Route 17, he stopped at another historic town called Georgetown and decided to have a bite to eat.

While having lunch at a restaurant situated on Winyah Bay, he reached for his credit card and inadvertently pulled out the slip of paper that Scarlett had signed. He remembered reading the name "Scarlett Mullins," but it now read Scarlett O'Hara. He was so shocked at this turn of events that the piece of paper seemed to burn his fingers. Instead of making him stumped and stunned, it only served to make him angry. He had watched enough magicians to know that anything was possible, and so he knew a gigantic hoax had been perpetrated. He crumpled up the slip of paper and threw it into Winyah Bay, but for the life of him, he could not figure out what or why these spooky events had taken place.

A sneaky suspicion started to invade his brain. Wasn't it Vinnie that suggested Carriage House Inn? *Could it be that Vinnie and the entire Pittsburgh operation was behind this little vignette, and I was the one that played a cameo role? I bet that at this very moment they are rolling on the floor holding their sides laughing at ol' Nick.*

As soon as he arrived in Myrtle Beach, he called Pittsburgh, and he was right. The hilarity was still on going at his expense.

"Right after you left the Inn this morning, the docent called to tell us what happened, and I can tell you Nick, we haven't laughed so hard since Jesus Christ was a carpenter."

"Yeah, well, when Vinnie gets down here, I think I'm going to kill him, and maybe he could have a good laugh with Jesus, which is highly unlikely because he'll be laughing with the guy in red with horns and hooves for feet—and that's not much of a laughing matter."

The expected call from Vinnie was received.

"We hope you aren't too pissed off Nick; you have to be appreciative of one of the best practical jokes of the year, maybe the best we have ever pulled off."

"To tell you the truth, now I can see the humor, but at the time I was starting to question my sanity. Having said that, you must remember, I will have my revenge."

Chapter Thirty-One
Myrtle Beach and
Golf Course Procurement

The next call he made was the reason he was here in Myrtle Beach. It went to Linda Baker and Joan Lyons, the two real estate agents that had informed him of the golf course that was for sale. They were ecstatic that he was now able to do something on this golf course deal and that he was not just a blow hard.

Linda's eyes got bluer and Joanie's eyes got greener. If they could pull this off, it may well be the biggest commission they had ever earned on any one deal. They informed him "The best way to view the course was to anonymously play the development." Joanie was the golfer of the two, and Linda's only participation as far as golf was concerned was to hold the flag stick for her fiancé.

Joanie arranged a tee time, and the following day, they played a course in North Myrtle Beach called As Eagles Fly.

Nick's game was rusty and a bit off, and Joanie played from the men's tee and gave him a sound thrashing. Nick was taken aback by this attack on his male ego, but then he thought "for Christ's sake, she lives down here and plays all the time—what the hell did you expect?"

He loved the course even though it was a little on the marshy side and needed additional drainage. The course did encompass one hundred eight acres, which gave enough room for additional homes or condos to be built. The price that had been mentioned was well within the ability of the corporation to afford. He informed the agents to arrange a meeting with the guy that made all the decisions for the corporate stockholders and to make sure he was talking to *The Man*. He was insistent that whomever he would be in contact with would be able to give an immediate decision. He was emphatic that he would not be put in a position to waste his time.

Nick did not know it at the time, but these agents were very eager, and they knew how to play hardball. When they got back in touch with *The Man*, he told them that "the course was no longer for sale."

Why not?" Linda asked.

"I just did not think this was the right time," he replied.

"Well, when do you think the right time would be?"

"When I think the time in my estimation is right."

Joanie chimed in, "Listen to me, we called the investor and told him this course was for sale. Based on our recommendation, he proceeded to put a lot of the other things that he had in the fire aside and come down here to spend time with you exploring the possibility of a meeting of the minds. He is here right now waiting to see you."

With a dismissive signal of his hand, The Man said "tell him to go right back to where he came from, because I'm not interested in talking to him."

Linda, getting madder by the minute and wanting to use words that were not generally in her nature to say, and belying her diminutive size said, "How in the hell can you sit there and just dismiss completely out-of-hand a person that traveled a great distance to talk to you?"

313

"Well, I just did. Now, I want both of you out of here."

Linda said, "Before I leave, I just want you to know you are being extremely rude."

Joanie echoed that sentiment.

"What if we turned this situation around, and you were the one that had just traveled one thousand miles to see someone, then they refused to see you? Don't you think this would upset you?"

"Listen, I'm not here to talk, I'm here to make money and not waste time. I decided not to sell, so it would be wasting my time to talk to this guy. Just tell him for me to try to go steal another course and leave me alone. You see, I'm saving him his precious time." He said, laughing as if he had just pulled a huge joke on them.

Joanie could see that Linda's face was getting red and decided to escort her out of the office before any recriminations took place. When they got outside, Linda turned to Joanie. "Thank you, my cork was getting ready to blow. Joanie, how were you able to maintain your cool?"

Joanie looked down and thought about that for a moment. "Linda, I had an abusive marriage for twenty years, and that SOB sounded just like my former husband. During that time, I learned a modicum of self-control."

They went back to the office and immediately started to figure out a way not to lose Nick as a customer. The best way was to find him another golf course to purchase. So, the balance of the day was spent contacting the hierarchy of the multitude of courses in the area and finding that the pickings were pretty slim. Most were not interested, and the ones that were interested quoted figures that they had probably made up in their dreams and were figments of their imagination. Finally, they had to call Nick and give him the sad news.

Upon hearing the news, Nick did not seem unduly upset. He proposed a meeting of the minds at dinner that night. He knew they had worked hard and deserved a little down time.

They eagerly accepted, and Linda said, "I had promised my fiancé dinner with me this evening, and—".

"He is more than welcome to join us this evening," Nick interrupted. "I am sure he will add to the festivities. By the way, can either of you suggest a place to dine?"

"May I suggest a place?" Joanie replied. "It's a high-end restaurant and a little on the expensive side."

"Please do. The way you ladies have worked today, I'm sure you deserve to be pampered."

That evening they had dinner at a restaurant called The Library, where Keith, Linda's fiancé, was introduced to Nick. He was a little apprehensive about meeting Nick, knowing that he was probably, at least in his estimation, connected to the Mafia. He really was worried about Linda getting involved with someone who had the ability to decide if you live or die at his whim.

The evening went in a manner that brought the courtly manners and comportment of Nick to the forefront. As the evening wore on, Keith could not believe that this gentleman could possibly be considered a part of the "underworld," but as they were lingering over the wine, Nick asked exactly what was said between the ladies and *The Man*.

They gave him the sordid details, and Nick's expression changed and became dark and menacing. For a while, all was quiet.

Nick broke the silence with a soft voice just above a whisper. "Ladies, I would greatly appreciate if you would give me what time of day he is likely to be at his office. I will personally guarantee that a sale of that golf course will be at hand, so proceed to get the necessary papers ready, and I will give you a 'heads-up' when he is ready to sign." The ladies and Keith now knew who Nick was, and nothing more had to be said.

That night, Nick called two gentlemen that were in the employ of the CCC (Congress of Concerned Citizens) that were in charge of keeping any wayward members in line. These men were large and ominous looking, and they did their job well. He asked them to hire a private plane and make the journey to the Grand Strand as this area was commonly referred to. He would pick them up at the North Myrtle Beach Airport when they arrived. He expected that they would return to Ohio that same night.

They arrived as expected; now all they had to do was find when *The Man* was at his Office in the clubhouse. This was easy: simply call the course and ask for *The Man*, and if he was there, hang up and head out knowing he was there.

At this point, Nick did not have a plan; he would feel the situation out as it developed.

They calmly stepped into the club and asked the person manning the reception desk where *The Man's* office was located. She pointed it out and said, "I'll ring his office and see if he is busy."

Nick said, "You do that," while he and his escorts continued into the office. The Man looked up, surprised at this interruption, and said "If you gentleman will wait outside of the office, I'll be with you as soon as I can."

The Man was not a small man by any means but was no match for the two behemoths that were accompanying Nick. Nodding to one of his associates, Nick's colleague stepped forward, went behind the desk, grabbed The Man by his neck, slammed him against the wall, smacked him with his free hand, and then held his hand over his mouth in order to stifle any screams. In a calm and soft voice, he said, "screaming and hollering are not allowed at this time." As he went to remove his hand from The Man's mouth, the guy started to say something, and this time he received a blow to the solar plexus and doubled up in pain, unable to say anything.

The associate placed him back in his seat gently and said, "I must request that you speak only when required to do so by this gentleman," indicating Nick.

The Man held his stomach with one hand and the other over his mouth then started to vomit all over his desk. Nick and associates had to step back to avoid being splattered with the nauseating fluid.

Nick expressed dismay and articulated a response. "I am sorry that you are experiencing a problem with fluid in your sinuses."

Viewing the mess that this guy made was upsetting Nick's stomach, so he directed one of his associate's to go to the bathroom and retrieve some towels. When he returned, Nick said to *The Man*, "I hate messy offices, and before we continue, I'm requesting that being you are the one that made this mess, I believe you are the one to clean it up. And don't forget the floor." He did not hesitate and completed the task as requested.

"Now that you are in a more receptive mood to listen to my problem, let me reiterate it for you. Yes, I, too, have a problem. My name is Nick Lasko. Yesterday, two very hard-working ladies that represent me in real estate matters came here to negotiate a transaction with you. They were presented with the problem that you were no longer willing to sell the property at this time. You can just imagine their astonishment when you arbitrarily withdrew your offer. The question is—why did you withdraw your offer to sell this cruddy golf course? You see, you weren't wasting my time; it was their time that was being wasted. These Ladies get paid only when they sell something. Now, how would you feel if you had just lost about $500,000 in commissions? Not only that, but you rudely invited them to leave your office."

At this time, the employee that was handling the desk out front came knocking on the door in response to the scuffling emanating from The Man's office. Nick sent one of his associates to keep her company while he completed his business in the office.

"You know that these real estate agents are acting as my emissaries, and the message they relayed from you to me was

317

that this asshole of a course was for sale. Upon hearing this, I set aside my affairs at my office in Youngstown to come down here to hear your proposal. You can just imagine my consternation when you had no proposal and then treated those fine ladies in the manner that you did."

"Now after having met you and realizing what a truly fine man you are, I'm going to have my ladies meet with you again, and they will have a proposal for you to accept. Please know that my offer will be fair. However, if you do not accept it, you will run the risk of never seeing your loved ones again."

"After I leave, I want you to check with friends you may have in Ohio, and they will be happy to inform you of who I am."

"I want to thank you for your time, and you will be hearing from my representatives. Remember, you should be ready to sign any papers that they put in front of you."

Nick contacted the agents and conveyed to them the information that The Man was ready to deal. He then proceeded to give them the information that they needed to know, including the amount he was willing to pay. He explained that there would be no negotiation.

When Joan and Linda tried to call, they never seemed to get *The Man* on the phone, so they called Nick. He immediately raced to the golf course. On his way, he picked up a baseball bat.

As he entered the clubhouse, he proceeded to smash the glass display cases. Turning to the frightened cashier, he said, "I'm sorry that you are scared, but this is a message for your employer not you. If you are smart, you will not report this to the police because that could involve you in more shit than you can handle. This is not your problem; it's a problem your employer has created. Just inform him the next time he gets a call from me or my representatives to make sure that he answers the phone." Then he walked out.

Nick decided to see where The Man lived and found him in the phone book. Nick drove to his home in an upscale section of North Myrtle Beach and boldly walked to the front door and rang the bell.

When The Man answered the door, upon seeing Nick, his face took on an ashen pallor. Shocked, he said, "What the fuck are you doing here?"

"I came here to remind you that your life up to now has rather idyllic connotations, and I'm sure that you want your life to go on as it has in the past. But I'm here to tell you that if you give me or my representatives any more shit, your life will never be the same again. I hope that you have learned a lesson about how to treat people. Where I grew, up my people took many affronts to their persons. They were shit on by police, by bosses where they worked, not to mention discrimination that occurred in everyday life."

"Look, Mr. Lasko, I, too, had it tough, but do you think it's fair to beat a person around and force him to relinquish something that he worked very hard for?"

"I can tell you these consequences were brought on by yourself when an agreement was made to speak to me and my representatives about the sale of your golf course, and then disdainfully treated us like some kind of lepers and acted as if you played a joke on us. It reminded me of the rich bastards who treated my family like shit when I was a kid."

"I can still remember when my grandmother, during the depression, had to get her ass out every day and go knocking on doors of rich people asking if she could get work from them, hanging wallpaper, painting, cleaning their homes, and she was treated like less than a human being."

"So, you can see how I might have been offended when you took a condescending attitude and coulda cared less that I came a thousand miles to talk to you. Well, what the hell do you care—fuck ol' Nick. Who the fuck does he think he is; that sonofabitch is just another Gombah."

The Man had a rather stupefied look on his face and seemed speechless, so Nick turned and walked away.

After that incident, negotiations seemed to go smoother, and soon the golf course was under the auspices of the Empirical Corporation of America (ECA).

Nick went on to acquire other properties.

Chapter Thirty-Two
The beginning of the end

As time passed, the expenses became overwhelming, and time and again Nick had to go back to the investors for additional capital. This was the catalyst that brought him so much more grief than he had ever expected.

Many unexpected expenses came to light, and Nick was put in a position of tapping out the stockholders. He turned to the banks for additional resources, but no matter how hard he tried, the Corporation continued to bleed assets. This turn of events caused deep divisions in the CCC Board of Directors; they wanted to remove Nick as CEO of not only the ECA but also as a paid consultant to the CCC. Dissatisfaction became virulent, and soon Nick came to the Board and requested a full hearing. This was granted, and a time and place was set.

Nick was caught completely off-guard. Didn't they know who the fuck he was? After the board meeting, they would damn-well know who he was! He called Larry Ditullio, a Capo with the Pittsburgh faction who was an observer when Nick originally organized this group, and informed him of what was going on, then he asked him to attend this meeting of the CCC.

Larry said, "Nick, you bit off more than you could chew, and now you are suffering the consequences. You should have exercised more prudence and responsibility in your discretionary use of other people's money. Your personality has come to the forefront, and your egalitarianism has failed you at this crucial time in your life. Even here in Pittsburgh, they are hollering for your scalp. I hate to say this Nick, but one way or the other, you are on your way out. If I were you, I would resign all posts that you now hold and accept a lower profile. Recast your life in another mode. You and I know you have been living high, wide and handsome, living in a mansion you can't afford, having racehorses you can't afford, trying to run golf courses you don't have time for. The business of accepting wagers on athletic events is over. Those bastards that are running off-shore books put that business on a computer and put us out of business as far as that end of it is concerned."

"Nick, you know what we are doing (i.e., drugs). I don't want to talk about it on the phone, but that's the one way we have to bring in more money than we ever thought possible. You opted out, and we honored that stance."

"Larry, your damn right, I did not want anything to do with the shit you're peddling. Hell, if I get arrested for bookmaking, I get six months max. If I get caught laundering, okay one year. But I get busted for doing your shit, ten, twenty years in the crapper. I may not have that mansion much longer, but at least my retirement years will not be spent in the penitentiary kissing everybody's ass that holds my faith in their hands. Larry, I hope you never get busted, but take my word for this: make it and get out as fast as you can."

"Nick, I don't think that is possible. Once you're in, you will always have the Sword of Damocles hanging over your head, as I'm afraid you are about to find out. Going down the crapper may be the least of your troubles."

"So, based on this conversation, you will not be at the meeting?"

"You got that right."

As Nick cogitated on this discussion, he contemplated calling a Patrone in the Cleveland mob. Maybe he could entice John Black to give him a recommendation. But before that, he decided to call Tony Vilanotti and ask him for advice. He had unusual trust in Tony, and given his natural suspicious personality, he gave Tony a tremendous amount of accolades, which could be dangerous in the climate that Nick operated in. He must remember that Tony was and is Mafia, and Tony's first obligation is to the organization.

Nick went ahead and called Tony. When he reached him on the phone, he explained his problems and asked for his advice on whether or not to call John Black, who was really Tony's boss.

Tony said, "Nick, I'll be straight with you as I have always been. In good conscience, I cannot tell you to contact John Black. First of all, if there was even a hint that I authorized a call to him from you, I would be called up before the Commission, and that's not an event I want to contemplate. Nick, think of this: if you go running to John with hat in hand, begging for help, he's going to treat you like a beggar. You, more than anyone else, should know that you can only negotiate from strength not weakness. When you were on top, the way was open for you to become Cosa Nostra, but you turned away because you wanted to do things you own way. If you would have joined, you could have written your own ticket. Of course, there are things that they would have asked you to do that went against what you consider your high morals, but, Nick, when you belong to something, you have to obey the rules. Look, if you want to live in this country, you have to adhere to all of the fuckin' bullshit that they put you through. If you want to belong to our thing, you have to adhere to all the bullshit they put you through. If you want to do your own thing, then you—and you alone—suffer the consequences of your actions."

"Listen to me. Take some time off, keep a low profile, don't put yourself in a position that somebody may say 'hey, this Goddamn Lasko kid is nothing but trouble. I don't think we need him to be around anymore' and—poof!—no more Nick."

Chapter Thirty-Three
Decline and Decay
A New Beginning

The meeting of the Congress of Concerned Citizens convened and was opened by the president of the organization. His opening remarks:

"We are all facing tough times, and much of our membership has cried out for new leadership. We have been whip-sawed by the computer revolution, and the colossal downturn of the steel mills caused by the greedy unions and racketeering bosses that led those unions. In my view, and in the opinion of the vast majority of our members, we have had incompetent people leading the Empirical Corporation of America that took much of our money and brought it to such a state of insolvency that it is unlikely we will ever see our money again. The man that led this Corporation is here with us tonight."

"Before we vote to oust him from the presidency of the ECA and as a paid consultant of the CCC, we will give him a chance to defend his dismal performance with the ECA."

"Nick, you have the floor."

"You may be able to fault my performance with the ECA, but—if I may be so bold to remind you—you can't denigrate the absolutely superb record of achievement from the time I organized this group and took on two factions of La Cosa Nostra and gave you, the little bookmakers of Ohio, a fighting chance to survive against the guys that would have shaken you down until you were out of business. I then went on to establish healthcare, pensions, and protection from the local police."

"Hassling came to a screeching halt when your local constabulary realized that you were not a one-man operation but, part of a much bigger undertaking that could bring political and other types of pressure to bear."

Nick went on to eulogize the part that he had played in this company, but it all went for naught. The recent pain they felt over the loss of a substantial sum of money and the downturn in the general economy put them in a mood to take their revenge on somebody, and Nick was it.

Nick fought long and hard to retain his positions with the entities he had created, but it was to no avail. Even Pittsburgh had turned in opposition to him.

Several factors were working against him. First was the political machine who wanted no more to do with him; his name was anathema to everyone in political circles. To have Nick Lasko visiting or calling you was a no-no, and to have had an association with Nick would cast aspersions on you. This even filtered down to mob guys in Cleveland and Pittsburgh and to the big boys in New York; the Genovese mob gave the order to tighten-up on him. In other words, Nick was "persona non grata."

He closed his offices in Youngstown but was still on the hook for the lease, and he laid off his secretary.

Holly's request for additional capital went unheeded.

He and she tried to keep the racing operation going, but as time rolled by, the handwriting was on the wall: both he and Holly knew that the end had finally come.

Nick eventually drove to Chardon and faced up to Holly. He found her, as usual, working in one of the barns. As he approached, she could see that his eyes were a little misty. He said "Holly, when we first met, we went to a little restaurant down the road and got a bite to eat. Well, if you don't mind, let's do that again."

Holly whispered, "Don't mind if we do."

Before they left, Nick went to Big Moe's stall, fed him a sugar cube, and in a quiet, low voice, he said, "You truly were the Magnificent One. Well, maybe I'll be seeing you around, and if I don't, you know I'll be betting on one of your colts."

Nick and Holly walked out of the stables arm-in-arm.

The weather turned chilly, and instead of sitting outside at Skeeters 19th Hole, they were forced to sit inside. Neither was hungry, so they decided to have just a drink. She asked Nick,

"What are you going to have?"

"A shot and beer."

"I've never drank that in my life, but Goddamn if that doesn't seem to fit the bill today."

They sat back and nursed their drinks quietly for a while before Nick finally said, "I'm sorry."

"About what?" asked Holly.

"Oh, about this whole thing. Just your devoted, unflinching and committed participation in this dream of mine, has meant a lot to me."

"Nick, until you came along, I had no dreams, and suddenly you appeared and gave me hopes and dreams and expectations far and above what I had ever thought about. You know, when I look back and remember that bullshit soliloquy you gave me about how nice of a guy you were... well you know what? Now I believe it. What's the next step?"

"Holly, I'm signing the whole racing operation over to you. I know that at auction, Big Mo will bring a nice price, and others we have in the string are highly valued and should give you enough compensation to pay some of the bills. Unfortunately, it's not enough to give you your true worth."

"Let me say this, Nick: just knowing you was worth it. It's true that all things must end, even life itself, and one day it will come about that after all the things you've been through and the heights you have reached, you won't even be a footnote in history. But, Nick, if there is anything I can do for you in the future, I'll be at your beck and call."

Tears were flowing from both of them.

Holly suddenly stood up, said good-bye to Nick, and ran out.

Nick sat back, had another drink, and watched her drive away.

All Nick had left was his little bookmaking operation, and that wasn't enough to keep the wolves at bay. He knew his estate was at risk, and he was doing all he could to keep it together.

As the Seventies arrived, other economic realities were starting to act unfavorably on Nick and his business. The backbone of Youngstown was steel, and now Japan was undercutting prices and pressure was on the steel companies, especially Youngstown Sheet and Tube. Nick was born and raised just across the street from the blast furnaces of the Sheet and Tube company.

The animosity between the workers and the Company reached a crescendo in the Seventies, and strikes and hostility created much acrimony between these tough steel workers and the company. In their hearts, they believed that the company was trying to cut them out of what was rightfully theirs. The company, for its part kept trying to tell the unions that the profits they were making had to go into modernizing their mills with new technology, just as the Japanese were doing. That explanation was not good enough for these workers, who had lived through the depression and were used to being lied to by big business and the Robber Barons.

They were not that far removed from the bitter strikes of 1916 when they had to riot against the mills for better working conditions. They won some points but not before they burned East Youngstown to the ground, which when it was rebuilt was renamed Campbell Township. The National Guard had to be called in to quell the uprising.

The Campbell works finally closed permanently in 1977, and the Briarhill works closed in 1979. Now Youngstown was completely on its ass, and so was Nick.

Nobody was calling Nick anymore; he was a pariah. Many times he had called Pittsburgh and Cleveland interests, and they never returned his calls... except for one person: Tony Vilanotti. Tony called and informed Nick that he would see to it that Cleveland would put him on the payroll so he would have a little something when he turned sixty-five, he could collect Social Security. "Nick," he said, "I only wish I could do more. If push comes to shove, I want you to know that I'm on your side, and anytime you want some conversation, a good meal, and vino, just make a little trip up here. It's not that far."

"I want you to know, Tony, you are the only one who called me, and I will never forget that. I don't know what will happen to me in the future, but remember I, too, am on your side."

Nick was many months behind on his payments to the Union pension fund, which was secured by his estate.

He had already gathered together his little family: Liz, Joey, little Marie, John, and the two dogs F. Scott and Zelda, with tremendous sadness in his heart. He informed them, "The sheriff and deputies will be here in the near future to repossess the estate, and all of the furniture will be carried out and put on the auction block."

He was able to give them a small severance, and he asked Joey and Liz if they would keep the dogs because he would be renting a place and not be able to have pets. Besides, those animals belonged more to them; they were really the one's that raised them.

The gloom was pervasive, and Joey and Liz very reluctantly vacated the home. They walked out, leaving a man they loved, who was more like a brother than an employer. They knew he was vilified as a gangster, but they never felt that way at all.

After everyone left, Nick looked around and never felt more alone in his entire life. He now was fully aware that he had not a soul in his life that he was really close to... someone that he could tell of his victories and his failures, his loves and his idiosyncrasies. How the hell can you go through an entire life and not have at least one person you can talk to? No matter how successful you are in all of your endeavors, if you never made a close friend, than you are a failure.

Several days later, the trucks came. They were there to take his beautiful furniture and many things that he highly prized: mementos of times in his life when he had known and participated in great victories; various trophies and paintings, that carried so much enjoyment and memories; gifts that he had received when he was lobbying in the halls of government, things that brought back the memories of the Gulf Stream, Miami, California, Jenny, Bermuda, The Cave, Zany, Palm Beach, the Contessa and dancing in exotic places. So many, many things.

The memories came flooding back, and Nick sank to the floor in the foyer as his personal and precious things were loaded on trucks by men that he did not know and who could care less. In fact, Nick was more of a curiosity than anything else.

Soon, all was quiet, and the mansion was totally empty. There seemed to be an echoing in the home. If you listened very carefully, you could hear children laughing, dogs barking, and the sounds of celebrations that had taken place here—happier times. All of a sudden, those pleasant sounds stopped, and an oppressive silence took its place. Too soon, it was time for Nick to leave this formerly joyful place.

He slowly stood up, brushed himself off, straightened and pulled his shoulders back as much as he could, and with an abrupt change of outlook, thought to himself, *Goddammit, I'm young, I'm smart, I'm charismatic, and I'm **Nick Lasko**. I am inherently a tough bastard, and I'll be back bigger and better than ever. I don't know when, I don't know where, but it will happen,* and with that, he strode out of the mansion and did not look back.

Epilogue

As I considered writing this book, the sheer work that it would involve made me humble in the face of the memories it would evoke. But more than that, it brought a multitude of concerns involving other things that could be brought to the forefront once this is published.

Considering that scenario, I set about changing the names of many of the people that would think they had been denigrated in some way.

I initially considered this work going the way of non-fiction, but the more I wrote, the more I realized that the life of the person I was writing about, and expounding upon, even though connected with the ignoble things of life, was not as exciting as my own varied existence. So, even though this work was originally thought to be the life and times of a racketeer, after all was said and done, it seemed that his life was rather mundane, and my life and my imagination was where the excitement occurred. Consequently this document ended up being excerpts from two lives, or should I say two lives, and the imagination of the author.

Is it fiction or non-fiction? Well, it is both. It leans more to the side of reality rather than fiction. A writer would call it allegorical which is a fancy word meaning; this work is some fiction and some non-fiction.

Each chapter was inspired by a true incident, taken from the author's reverie of years long past.

Whatever it is, I hope you enjoyed it, and I trust this book gave some enjoyable and enlightening moments.

Ron Chicone

All things eventually come to an end, whether it's an endeavor or an era that you once encountered that no longer exists. In our youth, we were full of energy, ideas, plans, hope, and we were out to grab life and shake it and dance on it and make it ours. But alas all of that falls by the wayside, and we are left with our aches, pains, and memories.